BELOW THE SURFACE

Below the Surface

Talking with Teens about Race, Ethnicity, and Identity

Deborah Rivas-Drake

Adriana J. Umaña-Taylor

PRINCETON UNIVERSITY PRESS

PRINCETON AND OXFORD

Published by Princeton University Press
41 William Street, Princeton, New Jersey 08540
6 Oxford Street, Woodstock, Oxfordshire OX20 1TR

press.princeton.edu

Library of Congress Control Number: 2018943161
ISBN: 978-0-691-17517-1
British Library Cataloging-in-Publication Data is available

Editorial: Meagan Levinson and Samantha Nader
Production Editorial: Ellen Foos
Jacket/Cover Design: Lorraine Doneker
Jacket images courtesy of Shutterstock
Production: Jacqueline Poirier
Copy Editor: Cathryn Slovensky

This book has been composed in Adobe Text Pro

Printed on acid-free paper. ∞

Printed in the United States of America

10 9 8 7 6 5 4 3 2 1

CONTENTS

For Tom, Liliana, and Diego, who remind me every day of what is at stake.

To Bianca, Mateo, Tomás, and all children living in culturally diverse societies who need brave adults in their lives to engage in the difficult conversations of race, ethnicity, and social justice.

ACKNOWLEDGMENTS

I (Debbie) would like to thank my dear friends and close colleagues (you know who you are): Thank you for every open and generous conversation about race (and everything else) we've been able to have together. I appreciate you so very much. Thanks, too, for the laughter and "side-eye" when one of us gets it wrong, and for all that I have been able to learn by knowing you. Thank you to my students at the CASA Lab—especially Mike, Abby, Tissyana, Fernanda, Aixa, Kevin, Mercy, Adam, Luis, Bernardette, Stephanie, Delina, Erika, Jess, and Jose—for all your support and encouragement of this work.

Thank you to my parents and my sister. My parents were my first and most important teachers of the value of a strong work ethic ("immigrants get the job done!"). I also feel lucky that I had the opportunity to spend my formative childhood years in Woodside, Queens—a child of immigrants growing up amid other immigrants from all over the world. You didn't do this intentionally, but it has profoundly shaped who I am. Monica: Thank you for reflecting on these experiences with me, challenging me to defend my ideas, and for just being such a supportive person in my life.

Finally, and most importantly, I am incredibly grateful to my partner and children. Tom, thank you for your patience, support, and advice. You are my partner in all things, and I could not have written this book without your unwavering belief in me—thank you. Diego and Liliana: You are my most important inspiration for this book. I wrote with you in mind, hoping that in some way, however modestly, the ideas within may contribute to a more socially just world. I also hope that when you read it one day (soon), you'll challenge me to think even more deeply about these issues.

I (Adriana) would like to recognize many people who made this work possible. First, I want to thank Matt for his constant, unwavering support and for believing in me and in the importance of this topic. His sacrifices along the way, including many stretches of single parenthood while I traveled to Michigan or extended conference trips to write, did not go unnoticed. I also thank Bianca, Mateo, and Tomás, who unknowingly gave up time with me, and who also served as a constant motivating factor for the importance of this book. Their experiences in school and with peers, their random questions or comments that inevitably led to a conversation about social justice, and our specific conversations about their multiethnic heritage were a constant inspiration for me. I am also grateful to friends and colleagues who shared their personal stories with me and helped me think deeply about this book from a parent's, rather than a scholar's, perspective. Finally, I thank the many students and research staff who made this book better by providing feedback and helping with research along the way: Michelle Capriles-Escobedo, Olga Kornienko, Stefanie Martinez-Fuentes, Anne Mulligan, M. Dalal Safa, Danielle Seay, Benjamin Smith, and the students of the CASA Lab at Michigan.

PREFACE

The motivation to write this book was complicated. As researchers, we're accustomed to sharing our ideas in scholarly articles in academic journals, to be read, for the most part, by other researchers. But in writing this book we aspired to reach a broader audience, and doing that somehow makes this endeavor feel more personal. It represents our contribution to a larger conversation, one for which there is no single entry point or exit. We hope readers will see themselves in dialogue with the ideas in this book and that they'll see the relevance to their daily lives and work.

As researchers, we are trained to "stay close" to the findings themselves—that is, we are taught (and teach our graduate students) to not overstate results of our research, because they are meant to be incremental. Indeed, our training leads us to understand that, over time, a body of literature can speak more definitively about an issue relative to any single study. From our perspective, this is, in fact, where we currently find ourselves in the literature on ethnic and racial identity. We felt it was time to share "what we know" from the field of ethnic and racial identity research in youth with people who, for many reasons, might never pick up an academic journal article, much less read an entire body of work spanning multiple decades.

We were particularly motivated to write this book because, when we look around us, what we see are many missed opportunities to use "what the research says" to address everyday race relations among young people in schools and communities across the United States. As parents and educators ourselves, we immediately sensed a need for an introductory book that would help our friends, neighbors, students, and practitioner colleagues make connections from theory and research to their everyday experiences. To do this, we have tried to write in an intuitive way for anyone interested in gaining insight into how youths' identity is linked to race relations and who strives to support positive intergroup relations in the next generations of youth in the United States. We envisioned this book being read by parents, teachers, educators, school administrators, and clergy—essentially, any professional engaged with youth. As college professors who have taught thousands of students over the course of our careers, we also wrote with our past and future college students in mind.

What we offer you is a synthesis of current research that addresses how features of social spaces and situations intersect with youths' identity development to promote better relationships. Throughout the book, we draw from research—including our own—to provide a comprehensive yet concise introduction to psychological research on the development of ethnic and racial identity and intergroup relations among diverse youth in the contemporary United States. We also draw numerous examples from popular films, TV shows, websites, novels, and memoirs, as well as existing programs and curricula, to bring theoretical ideas to life. In doing so, we address different types of ethnic and racial diversity—for instance, being Black in a Latino school, diverse Asian American anecdotes, Multiracial perspectives, and so on—that more accurately reflect the sorts of experiences that are likely to become more prevalent among US youth in the coming decades.

We have thoroughly enjoyed the process of pulling these ideas and this literature together. Our hope is that this serves as an important resource and tool for those who are grappling with how to engage in productive discussions about issues of race and ethnicity, particularly with youth. Furthermore, we hope this book provides useful guidance for scholars interested in advancing research in this area and serves as a guide map, so to speak, regarding the areas in the literature that would benefit most from additional research.

Preparing for the Future: Now Is the Time

Our changing demographic landscape assures that today's kindergartners will be the parents, neighbors, employees, and voters of a place largely unrecognizable to most adults today. Although it is certainly the case that racial and ethnic discord is part and parcel of the history of the United States, persistent racism and xenophobia should engender a sense of urgency to *today's* conversations about race, ethnicity, and difference in the United States. At the same time that Latinos, Black Americans, and Asian Americans increasingly reflect a larger share of the youth population, the inequalities in education, health, and life opportunities threaten to undermine the promise of the country's blossoming diversity. It seems like a headline pops up on our newsfeeds daily to remind us of the precarious nature of race relations in the United States. Youth who have participated in our many research studies are certainly aware of these realities, too. For instance, when we asked them to consider if anything had happened in the past year to make them think about their ethnicity differently, a number of youth noted the hostile rhetoric being used to describe people like them in broader society, brought to the surface throughout the 2016 election season. As one teen put it, "there is much talk about my ethnicity right now with what is going on in the political world." Another respondent wrote, sarcastically, "Nothing really happened to me to make me think differently about my ethnicity. *Except* for Donald Trump calling Mexicans rapists, drug lords, and troublemakers" (emphasis added).

We should listen carefully to what youth have to say about their identities and the many messages they receive about the ethnic and racial (and other social) groups to which they belong. They, better than anyone, can illuminate how they make sense of those messages as they come of age in a diversifying country. What they learn now is certainly the foundation upon which they will navigate their future interactions and relationships with others who are different from them. What are we teaching them?

Deborah Rivas-Drake and Adriana Umaña-Taylor

1

What Does It Mean to Move below the Surface?

"Bias Isn't Just a Police Problem, It's a Preschool Problem"

Ethnic-racial tensions in US society are not new.[1] They bubble up in all types of places, from rural communities in California to the multicultural mecca of New York City's neighborhoods. We can look to historical and current events that not only reflect our society's tense atmosphere concerning ethnic-racial relations at any given point in history but also continue to ignite and exacerbate such tensions. For instance, the US government has passed immigration policies to exclude individuals from certain countries. This was true in 1882 with the Chinese Exclusion Act and in 2017 with Executive Order 13769, also known as the Muslim ban. Our society has also forced ethnic minorities to choose between their culture and their survival. We have seen this with the government-imposed boarding schools for American Indian children and in English-only legislation that persists despite well-documented evidence of the benefits of bilingualism. Moreover, we have consistently witnessed the disproportionate use of force and violation of basic human rights as the default in how law enforcement approaches communities of color. As the headline above illustrates, these issues persist and make their way into the lives of our young people.

To some, these tensions convey that there is a devaluing of members of groups that do not represent the historically dominant group (i.e., White, European descent, Christian, economically advantaged). This devaluation is like salt in a wound for those who are all too acutely aware of social inequalities that have pervaded US society since its founding. Indeed, there are myriad disparities in the life outcomes of members of marginalized groups compared to members of the dominant group. To others, however, these tensions are thought to be blown out of proportion, exaggerated, or of no relevance to their lives. There is a sense that those who are actively voicing their concerns about the racial tensions are being too sensitive.

Although ethnic-racial tensions are typically presented as an "us" and "them" issue, it's important to recognize that mere membership in a particular social group (e.g., being Latino) does not provide enough information with which to predict how committed or engaged individuals are to addressing the ethnic-racial tensions that exist in our society. To really understand what is driving or informing the perspectives that people have on these different topics, we must go beyond surface-level categorizations and assumptions made about individuals based on their age, gender, race, or ethnicity. Instead, we must consider the psychological and subjective meaning-making processes that underlie how people respond to situations or events such as those above. One way to go below the surface, then, is to better understand how people experience these tensions differently based on their personal understanding of themselves and the social groups to which they belong.

Ethnic-racial identity is an important lens through which individuals experience events and situations related to race and ethnicity. On the one hand, for individuals who have not thought about race or believed they were living in a postracial society, the events "shake them up" and may ignite a reexamination of their views and understandings of race and ethnicity. On the other hand, for those who have examined or considered the role of race in their lives more thoroughly, the event or situation may confirm their existing understandings. Moreover, each individual may view the culpability or responsibility of other social groups differently depending on their sense of how their own group relates to other groups. Consider the following remarks in response to the 2016 election by two individuals who both identify as Muslim American:[2]

> How is it possible that here in America in 2016 could a man who has based his campaign on hatred, bigotry and divisiveness win the hearts and minds of so many American people? —Shadin Maali, well-known Chicagoan social activist

> The Republican Muslim Coalition is looking forward to working with [P]resident Trump. —Saba Ahmed, leader of the Republican Muslim Coalition

According to the report from which these quotes were taken, Shadin Maali was "in a state of disbelief," whereas Saba Ahmed was "super-excited that Republican candidate Donald Trump had won the presidency." These individuals are referring to the same event, yet their characterization of the result is radically different. Certainly, at the core of these divergent perspectives are differences in awareness, understanding, and tolerance of xenophobia and racism. It will be impossible to align understandings and awareness, and to decrease tolerance of prejudice and racism, if people do not examine the role of race and ethnicity in society *and* in their daily life.

In the context of the United States, one does not need to go far to encounter situations in which racial and ethnic dynamics are at work. Youth in the United States are bombarded with messages about race and ethnicity in their everyday lives. Such stories, images, situations, and broader conversations often evoke fear, pain, and guilt among even the most socially conscious adults who consider themselves well versed in the complexities of ethnic-racial relations in US society. It's challenging to reconcile the disparate perspectives on these ethnic-racial tensions, much less have open dialogue about them, but our social fabric is weakened by not engaging in meaningful dialogue about these issues.

To be fair, there are a number of barriers to such dialogue. First, as sociologist Eduardo Bonilla-Silva has explained, some people espouse a blatant denial of racism, xenophobia, and other forms of prejudice.[3] But the reality is that in the United States, racism is part of the social fabric, and young people learn it whether they want to or not. Recent findings regarding the dehumanization of Black children in the United States merit consideration in this regard. In one study, Philip Goff and his colleagues asked predominately White college students to rate their perceptions of innocence of Black and White children.[4] When the children who were being rated were nine and younger, there were no differences in how innocently— that is, needing of protection and deserving of care—they were viewed by participants in the study. But when asked to rate children who were ten or older, Black children were rated as significantly less innocent than White children. In another study, Rebecca Dore and her colleagues asked a predominately White sample of five-, seven-, and ten-year-olds to rate their own pain in response to a series of events, and they were then asked to rate the pain of Black and White children in response to those same events.[5] Five-year-olds did not differentiate the pain of Black and White targets, but the ten-year-olds thought Black children's pain would be less than that of White children in response to the same events. Together, these studies indicate that young Black youth may not be afforded the privilege of innocence or the same humanity in terms of pain as their White counterparts. Studies that have focused on evaluations of Black adults show that they are also similarly dehumanized.[6]

Avoiding the topic of racism altogether is arguably justifiable, given that it can be complicated and, for some, emotionally overwhelming to think about. Other people are aware and willing to have the conversations but are unsure about how to begin such a dialogue. They may believe that merely talking about race *is* racist, or they may be overly concerned about political correctness or about engaging in such discussions from an uninformed place and saying something that would inadvertently offend others.[7] And yet others are ambivalent because of the seemingly insurmountable barriers and what appears to be a lack of progress since the civil rights movement.

People respond to the challenges of open dialogue differently. For example, one response might be "don't tell me what to think or try to make me more 'politically correct,'" whereas another person may rightfully be tired of being tasked with teaching others. An illustration of this latter sentiment is evident in a blog post by multicultural education scholar Gloria Ladson-Billings, titled "I'm Through."[8] She writes:

> I am through acting like I don't notice when I'm the only black person in a room of white people with authority and power;

> I am through pretending like I don't notice that college football fields and basketball courts are filled with black players earning enormous sums of money for universities that have stadiums and arenas filled with white fans;

> I am through indulging comments like, "everything is not about race," when most times it is;

> I am through explaining my style—hair, dress, swagger;

> I am through being your teacher when I am not paid to do so.

Yet another response to racial dehumanization is greater resolve and commitment to social justice.[9] This alternative involves conscious engagement with inequality, prejudice, and racism as a step toward combating them. The #BlackLivesMatter movement is an example of such a response.[10] In the words of founder Alicia Garza, Black Lives Matter is "an ideological and political intervention in a world where Black lives are systematically and intentionally targeted for demise. It is an affirmation of Black folks' contributions to this society, our humanity, and our resilience in the face of deadly oppression."[11] And the commitment to raising consciousness and promoting social justice not only emerges from people who belong in the groups most immediately impacted by racial disparities but from others as well. For example, in 2016 a group of Asian American young people were concerned about their family members' lack of understanding and empathy for the dehumanization of Black lives in the United States, so in an effort to communicate their concerns to their elders, they created a template letter to their family that others could modify and share to increase understanding and empathy. Among other things, the letter stated,[12]

> Even as we hear about the dangers Black Americans face, our instinct is sometimes to point at all the ways we are different from them. To shield ourselves from their reality instead of empathizing. When a policeman shoots a Black person, you might think it's the victim's fault because you see so many images of them in the media as thugs and criminals. After all, you might say, we managed to come to America with nothing and build good lives for ourselves despite discrimination, so why can't they?

> It's true that we face discrimination for being Asian in this country. Sometimes people are rude to us about our accents, or withhold promotions because they don't think of us as "leadership material." Some of us are told we're terrorists. But for the most part, nobody thinks "dangerous criminal" when we are walking down the street. The police do not gun down our children and parents for simply existing.

> I support the Black Lives Matter movement. Part of that support means speaking up when I see people in my community—or even my own family—say or do things that diminish the humanity of Black Americans in this country. I am telling you this out of love, because I don't want this issue to divide us. I'm asking that you try to empathize with the anger and grief of the fathers, mothers, and children who have lost their loved ones to police violence. To empathize with my anger and grief, and support me if I choose to be vocal, to protest. To share this letter with your friends, and encourage them to be empathetic, too.[13]

Although this example illustrates how young people can open lines of communication with their older parents, it is also important to consider how parents and others who have regular contact with young people can foster contexts that support open dialogue about these issues with youth. Though many of us already work hard to emphasize the importance of treating everyone equally—respecting the differences that exist and celebrating the diversity around us—this is not enough. These messages are certainly important, but we must also teach children about the injustices that disproportionately affect members of some groups and not others. For nonminority children, this raises awareness and helps create a space for understanding the experiences of marginalized groups. For minority children, this validates their lived experiences, sends a message that the experiences of injustice are real (not imagined, not blown out of proportion), and that those in more powerful positions of authority (parents, teachers, youth leaders, clergy) are not going to sit by and let these injustices go unnoticed or unaddressed. Everyone benefits from this more transparent approach because, as eloquently stated by Dr. Martin Luther King Jr., "No one is free until we are all free."

In this book, we openly discuss many current ethnic-racial disparities and tensions about which conversations are usually stifled. We discuss why these conversations are challenging but also provide ideas for language and approaches to use when engaging in this difficult, yet crucial task with youth. Furthermore, we present information to help readers understand the different developmental capabilities of young people at different ages and what types of conversations and activities can be most effective with children, adolescents, and young adults.

Why Focus on Youth?

From a child development perspective, children have a strong preference for equality and fairness, and they demonstrate an increasing concern for fairness and others' welfare with age.[14] Scholars such as Melanie Killen, Adam Rutland, and their colleagues have shown the prevalence of children's moral concerns regarding equality and justice.[15] Children's moral concerns about fairness and justice are in direct opposition to the realities of various manifestations of inequality in society. As youth become increasingly aware of the disconnect between their moral ideals and the unequal opportunities afforded to non-White Americans, adults have an important choice to make. We can be silent, teach them to blame the victimized groups for the oppression they experience, or choose to have the difficult conversations that expose the imperfections of our society. The last option is likely the most challenging for adults who themselves have not explored these topics in great depth; however, this approach shortchanges youth. To paraphrase noted scholar bell hooks, we cannot empower young people to critically examine the inequalities they perceive in society without personally facing these issues in ways that may make us feel vulnerable, too.

Young people understand this vulnerability all too well. As they mature during the course of adolescence, youth are thrust into a meaning-making process about society's racial and ethnic zeitgeist. They must develop a sense of who they are and who they can be in a deeply conflicted society, and the experiences and knowledge gained during childhood serve as the foundation for this process. Making sense of diversity in a developmentally attentive way involves helping adolescents grapple with the question "Who am I, and how do I fit in this diverse world?" To best foster the development of skills and competencies that will help adolescents make sense of their identities and of the diversity that exists in society in productive ways, adults must engage in the difficult conversations— both among ourselves and with our youth. Indeed, some of the most significant opportunities to engage in these conversations occur during adolescence. During this developmental period, youth gain more freedom to explore the world outside their immediate family and gain the cognitive abilities to think about more complex and abstract social issues, such as racism and societal hierarchies. As one fifteen-year-old Latino male adolescent study participant wrote in response to a survey question asking, "What does your ethnicity mean to you?":

> I am proud to be Mexican even if White people (some, not all) might [not] think we are as smart or as equal to them. I love my ethnicity. I love the foods, culture, people, and many more. Some White people out there want us to go back to our country. (I

guess they haven't tried our food.) I am proud of my ethnicity and I wouldn't change. It is the best.

As noted in the work of Melanie Killen and her colleagues,[16] without knowledge of how social groups function in relation to one another in a given context, youth are at a loss for understanding why differential treatment based on a particular group membership is unfair and unequal.

Events that highlight ethnic-racial tensions and inequality, such as those that are well publicized in the national news—as well as those situations taking place closer to one's community that are less well publicized—strike a chord because we may have uncritically accepted the rhetoric that we live in a color-blind society where individuals are judged by their merits and treated in a just and fair manner. In fact, following the 2016 presidential election, many of us, Democrats and Republicans alike, were shocked to learn that white nationalism is not a relic of the past and, quite to the contrary, is a thriving movement that had enough momentum to shape the discourse during the election. Cabinet appointments, such as the one announced in the following news account, underscore their influence:

> White nationalist leaders are praising Donald Trump's decision to name former Breitbart executive Steve Bannon [prominent leader in the white nationalist movement] as his chief strategist, telling CNN in interviews they view Bannon as an advocate in the White House for policies they favor ... The leaders of the white nationalist and so-called "alt-right" movement—all of whom vehemently oppose multiculturalism and share the belief in the supremacy of the white race and Western civilization—publicly backed Trump during his campaign for his hardline positions on Mexican immigration, Muslims, and refugee resettlement.[17]

Furthermore, news stories following Donald Trump's election suggest that this agenda will continue to gain steam in the coming years:

> [W]hite nationalists inside the Ronald Reagan Building in Washington on Nov. 19 ... threw Nazi salutes and shouted, "Hail

Trump, hail our people, hail victory!" The man they were saluting was the white nationalist who coined the term "alternative right," Richard Spencer, who had just given an anti-Semitic speech in which he quoted Nazi propaganda and called the United States a "white country."[18]

Much of this racist rhetoric, and the election of a candidate who is perceived by many to be overtly racist, galvanized many people to express their opposition to and outrage about the white nationalist perspective, for instance, by making record-setting donations to organizations such as the ACLU.[19] This is a useful way for adults to feel a sense of agency in combatting separatist agendas. Another way for adults to be agentic in this effort is to work with youth to help them develop the skills needed to recognize social injustices, understand their own social identities, and work constructively toward improved intergroup relations. As we discuss in greater depth in chapter 2, this work is critical because such injustices have real implications for the health and the *literal survival* of members of marginalized groups via poorer health, shortened life spans, exposure to stress, and diminished life chances.[20]

Undoubtedly, parents, educators, and others who work with young people want all youth to reach their full potential; the problem, however, is that many of us struggle with how to best help our youth understand the complicated issues that arise as a function of ethnicity and race. The activities of a White, award-winning former English Language Arts teacher in Texas, Emily E. Smith-Buster, provide an excellent example of the potential challenges for educators.[21] In a speech to her colleagues at the time, she explained her evolution from being an excellent teacher who was hesitant to talk about race to one who accepted the challenge of questioning her own views on race and ethnicity; this consequently transformed her pedagogical approach so that it more fruitfully met the needs of her Latino, Black, and White students:

> [T]hings changed for me the day when, during a classroom discussion, one of my kids bluntly told me I couldn't understand because I was a white lady. I had to agree with him. I sat there

and tried to speak openly about how I could never fully understand and went home and cried, because my children knew about
white privilege before I did. The closest I could ever come was
empathy.

My curriculum from then on shifted. We still did all of the
wonderful things that I had already implemented in the classroom, except now the literature, the documents, the videos, the
discussions, the images embodied the issues that my children
wanted to explore. We studied the works of Sandra Cisneros, Pam
Munoz Ryan and Gary Soto, with the intertwined Spanish language and Latino culture—so fluent and deep in the memories
of my kids that I saw light in their eyes I had never seen before.
We analyzed Langston Hughes's "Let America be America Again"
from the lens of both historical and current events and realized
that the United States is *still* the land that has never been . . .

Looking back, I think that my prior hesitation to talk about
race stemmed from a lack of social education in the classroom.
A lack of diversity in my own life that is, by no means, the fault
of my progressive parents, but rather a broken and still segregated school system. Now that I'm an educator in that system,
I've decided to stand unflinching when it comes to the real issues facing our children today, I've decided to be unafraid to
question injustice, unafraid to take risks in the classroom—I am
changed. And so has my role as a teacher.

I can't change the color of my skin or where I come from or
what the teacher workforce looks like at this moment, but I *can*
change the way I teach. So I *am* going to soapbox about something after all. Be the teacher your children of color deserve. In
fact, even if you don't teach children of color, be the teacher
America's children of color deserve, because we, the teachers,
are responsible for instilling empathy and understanding in the
hearts of all kids . . .

So teach the texts that paint *all* the beautiful faces of our children and tell the stories of struggle and victory our nation has
faced. Speak openly and freely about the challenges that are
taking place in our country at this very moment. Talk about the

racial and class stereotypes plaguing our streets, our states, our society. You may agree that black and brown lives matter, but how often do you explore what matters to those lives in your classroom?[22]

As demonstrated by Smith-Buster's comments, understanding others' ethnic-racial experiences can be critical for developing an understanding of one's own ethnic-racial identity. With an informed sense of one's own self, one can begin to align diverse perspectives of ethnic and racial dynamics.

Throughout this book, we present what we know about ethnic-racial identity and how fostering its development in *all* young people can provide building blocks with which they can begin to reconcile the diverse ways in which race and ethnicity matter in US society. We provide this information with the goal of helping to advance conversations not only about widely publicized incidents in which race is acutely salient to youth (for instance, the police brutality inflicted on Black people that is widely circulated on a seemingly daily basis online and in media reports) but also more subtle, everyday instances in which ethnic and racial dynamics bubble to the surface.

This increased understanding is valuable for all youth, regardless of whether they are members of socially dominant or marginalized groups in society. Furthermore, such understanding is absolutely essential for building the foundation for productive relationships between members of different groups. Finally, efforts to foster respect for the ethnic and racial diversity that exists in our society, and to which youth are regularly exposed in their communities and schools and via the media, are critical for developing ethnic and racial empathy.

In addition to developing empathy, we also need to be reflective about the role each of us plays in maintaining or actively resisting the status quo. It is through intergroup dialogue and the development of genuine relationships between people who are members of different social groups that we will be able to engage in this reflection and bridge the gap between our divergent understandings of race, ethnicity, and social injustices. Here, it's instructive to consider a comment made by Derek Black—a former prominent white nationalist who famously disavowed those ideologies—about the need for "honest listening" when interacting with members of other groups. His willingness to reexamine his own identity involved intensive, thoughtful discussions with others who held quite disparate views and identities from his own. When asked to provide advice on how to change others' mind-sets about race, he commented, "That kind of persuasion happens in person-to-person interactions and it requires a lot of *honest listening* on both sides. For me, the conversations that led me to change my views started because I couldn't understand why anyone would fear me" (emphasis added).[23] While reflecting on his journey, Black explained how his identity evolved from white nationalist to social justice activist, and how those honest conversations with diverse peers were critical in this transformation.

> I was born into a prominent white nationalist family—David Duke is my godfather, and my dad started Stormfront, the first major white nationalist website—and I was once considered the bright future of the movement.... Several years ago, I began attending a liberal college where my presence prompted huge controversy. Through many talks with devoted and diverse people there—people who chose to invite me into their dorms and conversations rather than ostracize me—I began to realize the damage I had done. Ever since, I have been trying to make up for it.

Black's experience is an extreme case, but we know from the work of Derald Wing Sue, and Mahzarin Banaji and Anthony Greenwald, respectively, that we all carry implicit biases.[24] Reflection is necessary for individuals of all persuasions, and it is most certainly a lifelong process.

Can Youth Have a Strong Ethnic-Racial Identity and Still Value Other Groups?

At this point, you may be thinking, "Okay, that's great. Everyone needs to feel good and proud about their ethnic-racial group membership. But won't this just lead to more divisions because, by feeling more connected and proud of our own group, don't we have to downgrade the value of other groups?" You are not alone in this logic. For many, the concept of ethnic-racial identity conveys a sense of pride in a particular group, and only that group. Working from this perspective, it may be difficult to imagine how promoting ethnic-racial identity can help promote positive intergroup relations. This may be why public and academic communities alike continue to wrestle, uneasily, with the presumed tension between a desire to support youths' ethnic and racial identity, on the one hand, and promoting positive interracial interactions, on the other hand. At first glance, these two goals seem to be at odds with each other, but they need not be. First, in work conducted by Jean Phinney and her colleagues,[25] adolescents from Latino, Black, Asian, and White backgrounds who had thought more about their ethnic-racial identities actually reported more positive views about engaging with others who were from different ethnic-racial groups, a skill that has been referred to as "ethnic-racial competence," or the ability to behave in ways that invite positive relationships with peers from other ethnic groups.[26] Second, having a positive sense of one's ethnic-racial identity promotes social competence with peers, such as the ability to productively navigate social interactions and form friendships.[27] In Denise Newman's work with American Indian youth, those who were more interested in learning about their culture were more likely to have prosocial relationships, and less aggressive interactions, with their peers. Thus, rather than impeding the ability to interact or engage with others, a stronger ethnic-racial identity actually promotes competencies in youth that help them engage in more positive relationships with their peers.

In addition to adolescents' ethnic-racial identity informing positive social relationships with peers, in our own work, we also find that having more ethnic-racially diverse friendship groups promote increases in ethnic-racial identity exploration among middle school boys and girls six months later.[28] Furthermore, in our focus group discussions with Black, White, Latino, and Asian American high school students, they explained that the process of learning about their own ethnic-racial background was facilitated by learning about others' ethnic-racial backgrounds.[29] Thus, when youth engage in dialogue or share experiences with each other regarding either person's background, this engages both peers in their own ethnic-racial identity development process.

> I have a lot of friends who aren't of the same like ethnicity and stuff, and they're very, they're very into their own faith, but they're very open to other faiths. Like, you say something like out of the blue, like, you're like "oh I have to do this type thing" or you know like, "oh today is this day" and they're like "what is that?" and you're like, you explain it to them, and they're so intrigued by it, and then, that's ... and they're like "oh well, I have something like that in my fest- or in my culture and stuff" and then you learn about their culture, and then it really opens up the spectrum to say "wow" like there's not one single culture.
> —Eighteen-year-old Asian Indian female adolescent

> [I]f you go in a mixed group, like, and you see what other people's culture is like, then you get to see, like the differences between yours and theirs and then like you can think about yours more. —Sixteen-year-old Latino male adolescent

From the adolescents' perspectives, exposure to and increased understanding of groups different from their own increased their curiosity about their own background and motivated them to learn more about themselves. Such curiosity opens up possibilities for youth from different ethnic and racial groups to form bonds based on their shared engagement in the process of developing their identities in ways that are mutually beneficial.

We also know from the work of Patricia Gurin and her colleagues that young people of diverse backgrounds need to engage in intergroup dialogue to develop an understanding of their identities, not only on a personal level but also within a broader context of power and oppression. Doing so comes with many benefits. In their own words:

> IGD [intergroup dialogue] also promotes understanding one's racial-ethnic, gender, and other social identities as well as

understanding those of others ... Furthermore, these identities are located in systems of power and privilege, which are not viewed as static but rather as dynamic and allowing for change ... Thus ... a critical analysis of inequality and commitment to social responsibility and action are tied to identities as central issues in intergroup dialogue.[30]

In their work, Gurin and colleagues emphasize the need to keep social identity at the forefront and intentionally use teaching methods that encourage students from different backgrounds to learn about one another both as individuals and as members of social groups.

In sum, theory, research, and practice suggest that having a secure sense of one's ethnic-racial identity can, under the right conditions, actually help to promote positive intergroup experiences through increased understanding of ethnic-racial injustices and the emergence of ethnic-racial empathy. Furthermore, the extent to which youth have engaged in examining their ethnic-racial identity is, for many, intertwined with their awareness of prejudice, because in the process of learning about themselves, they learn about the status of their group compared to others. Drawing from everything we have learned from our work and that of many others, we conclude that not only can youth have a strong ethnic-racial identity and still view other groups positively, but having a strong ethnic-racial identity actually makes it possible for youth to have a less superficial or more genuine understanding, and therefore value, for other groups. Indeed, the title for this book was inspired by the idea posed by the famous social psychologist Gordon Allport in his seminal work, *The Nature of Prejudice*. Briefly, he commented that for intergroup contact to reduce prejudice, it must be based on experiences that help us get beyond the superficial and toward those that allow us to form meaningful common bonds. We believe that providing opportunities for youth to figure out their ethnic-racial identities together is a kind of meaningful connection that is essential for positive intergroup relations.

In the chapters that follow, we provide tangible language and tools to help parents, teachers, educators, school administrators, and clergy—essentially, anyone who has regular contact with youth—engage productively with young people regarding these issues. We end the book with an overview of existing programs and approaches that show promise for engaging with youth to promote empathy and perspective-taking, positive intergroup relationships, awareness of racism and prejudice, and positive development of ethnic-racial identity. Readers will find many of the resources presented to be useful in their work with youth moving forward.

Organization of the Book

We've organized this book to first present a general introduction of the significance and relevance of race and ethnicity for those living in diverse societies such as the United States. In this chapter, we have introduced the notion that nurturing young people's ethnic and racial identity development will be an important way to promote positive intergroup relations and, ultimately, a better-adjusted society. In addition, we place this topic in the current historical context to help readers understand why this is a timely topic, and one that merits our immediate attention. Chapter 2 provides readers with a detailed demographic portrait of the US population. Beyond presenting basic demographic characteristics, we discuss some of the most pressing concerns involving ethnic-racial disparities that fuel stereotypes and related tensions in our society, which inevitably pose significant risks to youths' positive adjustment in multiple realms. We also introduce the critical need to engage in productive dialogue regarding race and ethnicity and explain that an essential ingredient for engaging in such dialogue is understanding our own biases. In order to understand our own biases, however, we explain that we must first come to understand our own ethnic-racial identities.

Chapter 3 provides readers with an in-depth understanding of ethnic and racial identity. We walk readers through the relevance of this topic for all members of a diverse society—those who are members of socially dominant and marginalized groups alike. This chapter provides readers with basic definitions, but it also provides an in-depth discussion of how individuals develop their ethnic-racial identity, what it consists of, and the consequences that this aspect of the self-concept can have for well-being. We also devote a significant portion of this chapter to distinguishing ethnic-racial *identity* from the labels that are often used to classify individuals according to their race or ethnicity. Chapter 4 is devoted to presenting how the multiple settings in which youths' lives are embedded—such as family, schools, and neighborhoods—are constantly sending messages regarding race and ethnicity, which play a significant role in the identity that youth develop, as well as their dispositions toward having positive relationships with those who are different from them. In this chapter we discuss the many opportunities that authority figures in these various settings have for promoting positive ethnic-racial identity development in young people.

Chapter 5 synthesizes what we know about ethnic-racial identity development and positive intergroup relations to introduce readers to the notion that promoting positive ethnic-racial identity development among youth can ultimately lead to youth engaging in more positive and productive relationships with those who are different from them. Relying largely on decades of research that has been conducted on both intergroup contact and ethnic-racial identity, we walk readers through the evidence that supports the idea that understanding and developing our own ethnic-racial identities can help, rather than hinder, our ability to have more positive relationships with others. In chapter 6, we provide concrete examples of how those who interact regularly with young people can promote ethnic-racial identity development in youth and, in turn, help youth engage in more positive relations across difference. Together, the chapters in this book provide readers with a more profound understanding of what ethnic-racial identity is, how it can help promote positive interactions across difference, why this is a timely and important issue, and how those who work with youth can promote this important developmental competency in young people.

———

As we will outline in chapter 2, the population of youth in the United States is more ethnically and racially diverse than ever before. Ethnic and racial minorities currently comprise more than 45% of the population under the age of eighteen,[31] and these numbers are only expected to increase. According to a December 2012 Census projection, the United States will become a majority-minority nation in 2043 and, by 2060, ethnic and racial minorities will comprise 57% of the US population; non-Latino Whites will remain the largest single group, but no group will make up a majority. Alongside these demographic projections, recent highly publicized and traumatic events taking place across the United States reveal persistent tensions that threaten to perpetuate a deeply divided society in which experiences with ethnic-racial discrimination and marginalization are commonplace and will continue to pose significant threats to our collective health.[32] Furthermore, the prominence of these events increases the likelihood that youth from all ethnic-racial backgrounds are aware of ethnic-racial tensions and thus must develop a sense of who they are and who they can be in a deeply conflicted society. If we leave youth underprepared to navigate well-established racial and ethnic tensions in the United States, we do so at our own peril, as these conditions threaten to undermine the potential for youth of all groups to develop healthy, integrated communities as adults.

2

Coming of Age
in a Changing America

OPPORTUNITIES AND CHALLENGES
OF YOUTH DIVERSITY

The population of the United States has changed dramatically over the last fifty years, and projections of the next fifty years suggest that it is only going to continue to diversify. Indeed, today's youth are growing up in an increasingly diverse America, due in part to burgeoning numbers of people who identify as Latino, Asian American, and Multiracial. This generation of youth will ultimately live in a plurality that looks more and more like them: White, Latino, Black/African American, Asian American, American Indian, and Multiracial/Mixed. On the one hand, this future holds promise and brings opportunities for youth to work together to realize ideals of racial equality; on the other hand, such diversity evokes challenges that emerge from a lack of competence with respect to engaging with members of groups different from one's own. How might we help youth productively navigate this future? To begin to answer this question, it is helpful to consider some key demographic factors that characterize the experiences of various ethnic and racial groups in the United States.

Who Are We and Who Are We Becoming?

The United States is the third most populous country in the world, behind China and India, respectively. A key defining characteristic of the United States, both historically and presently, is the range of ethnic and racial diversity of the population. We have arrived at this diversity via the complex legacies of conquest, slavery, and immigration, which have undoubtedly contributed largely to the contentious nature of issues of race and ethnicity in our society. In addition, although the United States has always been a more heterogeneous population relative to other large countries, there has also always been a significant numerical majority comprised of White individuals of European origins. The changes in ethnic and racial composition that have taken place in the United States in the past fifty years, however, have significantly altered the social landscape in this society.

Currently, White Americans make up 61.3% of the US population, with the next largest group being Latino Americans (17.8%), followed by Black Americans (13.3%), Asian Americans (5.7%), Multiracial/Mixed Americans (2.6%), American Indian/Alaska Native Americans (1.3%), and Native Hawaiian/Pacific Islander Americans (.2%).[1] These figures are vastly different from the statistics that characterized the US population in 1970: White (87.5%), Black (11.1%), and Other (1.4%). And, as can be seen in figure 1, the increasing diversity of the United States with respect to ethnicity and race is projected to continue in the next fifty years. Thus, the national conversation about race and ethnicity is occurring against a background of significant demographic change.

The answer to the question of who we are collectively is continually evolving. One part of the story of the changing demography of the United States is certainly about the decline of the White population, as shown in figure 1. In 2015, almost 62% of the adult population was White, whereas this figure is projected to be less than 50% in 2044.[2] The primary reason for this decline is that White Americans have a significantly lower birth rate than other groups in the United States, as demonstrated in figure 2.[3]

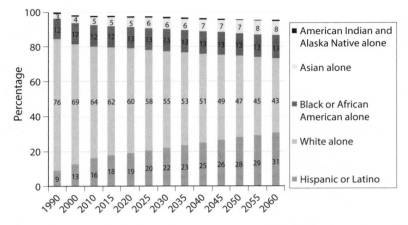

FIGURE 1. Changes in ethnic-racial population distribution (demonstrated in percentages) in the United States from 1990 to 2060. The percentage for American Indian and Alaska Native is less than 1% across all years. Data compiled from the following US Census Data Tables: US Census Table 3 Population by Race and Latino Origin for the United States: 1990 and 2000 (PHC-T-1); Census 2010 Redistricting Data Summary File Tables P1 and P2; and US Census NP2012-T4 for Projections of the US population for 2015 to 2060. Figure originally presented in Umaña-Taylor (2016) and reprinted with permission from Taylor & Francis.

This means that the decline of the White population will continue even if there is no new immigration to the United States by any group. For instance, if we expect immigration trends to persist, the proportion of the White population will decline as noted earlier, but even if immigration were to crawl to a halt, the White population would still be projected to decline to 56% in 2065.[4] This change is largely a function of the aforementioned low birth rate for Whites, coupled with the rapid rate of growth documented for the Latino population, whose growth is currently informed more by high birth rate than immigration.

As noted in the Pew Research Center analyses summarized in figure 3, the population of Latinos will continue to grow irrespective of immigration.[5] Although growth in the Latino population in the 1980s and 1990s was more a function of immigration than of births, this trend reversed in the 2000s, with births having a much greater influence on growth in the Latino population relative to the influence of immigration.

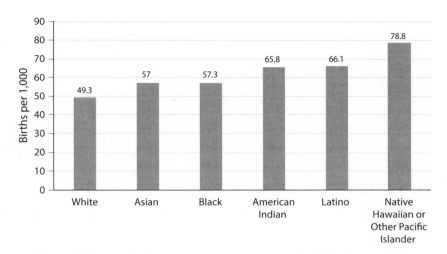

FIGURE 2. Birth rate across ethnic/racial groups in the United States in 2012. *Source:* Table 3. Women Who Had a Birth in the Past 12 Months per 1,000 Women 15 to 50 Years Old by Selected Characteristics: 2012–Con. (Data based on sample. For information on confidentiality protection, sampling error, nonsampling error, and definitions, see www.census.gov/acs/www/).

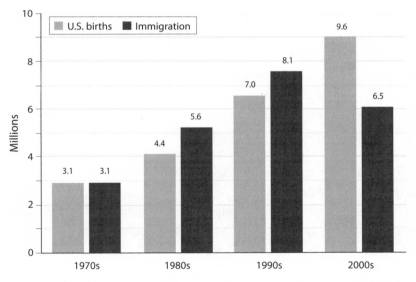

FIGURE 3. Hispanic population growth between the 1970s and 2000s, as reported by the Pew Research Center. *Source:* http://www.pewhispanic.org/2014/04/29/hispanic-nativity-shift/.

So the White decline is only part of the story, as it happens in the context of a relatively stable Black youth population and an increasing representation of Latino and Asian-origin youth. Specifically, the population of White youth under the age of eighteen was 52% in 2014, and it is projected to decrease to 35.6% in 2060. The population of Black youth was 13.8% in 2014 and is projected to decline only slightly to 13.2% by 2060. However, a more drastic change in the opposite direction is occurring among young people of Asian and Latino heritages. For instance, the population of Asian-origin youth will almost double from 4.7% in 2014 to 7.9% in 2060, and those of Latino heritage will increase by a third, from 24.4% in 2014 to 33.5% in 2060. Together, these young people are a large part of the so-called browning of the United States, which has been unfolding since the mid-twentieth century.[6]

The forthcoming changes in the ethnic-racial distribution of the US population are also clearly evident when one considers the decreasing proportion of non-Hispanic Whites among younger age-groups, as illustrated in figure 4. The changes that have been observed on a broader scale are also clearly evident in the shifts that have taken place in the racial composition of our public schools. Data from the National Center for Education Statistics demonstrate that the population of students in public schools in kindergarten through the twelfth grade changed dramatically between 1995 and 2015, and these changes are expected to continue through 2023. For example, as shown in figure 5, schools on the whole are already majority-minority, and by 2023, they will be a plurality—with no single majority group.

These shifts are part of a longer historical trend that has been documented by Gary Orfield and colleagues at the Civil Rights Project,[7] noting that from 1970 to 2013, the racial composition of public schools changed dramatically. Specifically, the population of White students declined from 79.1% to 50%, whereas the population of Latino students during the same period increased from 5.1% to 25.4%, and that of Asian-origin students shifted from 0.5% to 5.2%. It is also important to note that these trends have been evident across all regions of the United States, as demonstrated in

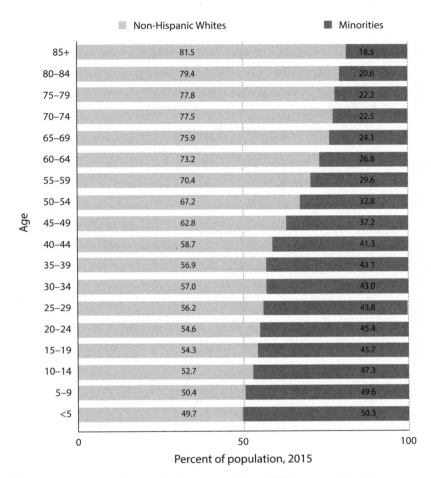

FIGURE 4. Proportion of population that are non-Hispanic White versus minorities across age-groups, as presented by the Pew Research Center. *Source:* http://www.pewresearch .org/fact-tank/2016/06/23/its-official-minority-babies-are-the-majority-among-the -nations-infants-but-only-just/.

figure 6, with the South and West demonstrating the most significant shifts, as shown below.

With these shifting demographic trends, there has been increasing alarm about the resegregation of students in K–12 schools. Recent reports by Orfield and colleagues show that despite all the efforts to integrate schools following the landmark *Brown v. Board* (1954) decision, we have been losing ground, and schools have become increasingly segregated since then. For instance, in 2015 almost

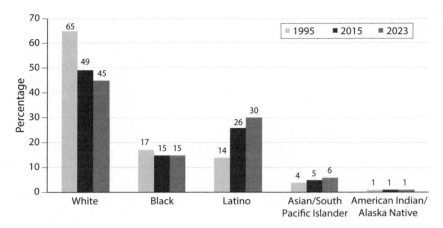

FIGURE 5. Actual and projected K–12 public school enrollment over time by race and ethnicity. *Note:* Graph created by authors based on the following: Table 203.50. Enrollment and Percentage Distribution of Enrollment in Public Elementary and Secondary Schools, by Race/Ethnicity and Region: Selected Years, Fall 1995 through Fall 2023. *Source:* US Department of Education, National Center for Education Statistics, Common Core of Data (CCD), "State Nonfiscal Survey of Public Elementary and Secondary Education," 1995–96 through 2011–12; and National Elementary and Secondary Enrollment Projection Model, 1972 through 2023. (This table was prepared December 2013.)

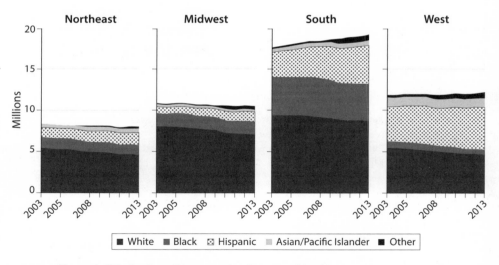

FIGURE 6. Changes in US school enrollment over time by geographic region.

90% of White students attended schools in which 20% or less of the student population was Black. In their report, "*E Pluribus ...* Segregation: Deepening Double Segregation for More Students," Orfield and colleagues note that "80% of Latino students and 74% of black students attend majority nonwhite schools (50–100% minority), and 43% of Latinos and 38% of blacks attend intensely segregated schools (those with only 0–10% of white students) across the nation."[8] These statistics paint a clear picture: White students tend to attend White-segregated schools, and minority students are overrepresented in minority-segregated schools.

Concerns regarding resegregation are well founded for several reasons. Segregated schools (in which ethnic-racial minority youth are the majority population) tend to have higher levels of teacher turnover, inadequate facilities, and less qualified teachers.[9] As succinctly stated by Orfield and colleagues in their report, "it is a simple fact that segregated black and Latino schools have profoundly unequal opportunities and student outcomes."[10] It also is important to note that most majority Black and Latino schools are not only segregated by ethnicity and race but also by poverty. As noted by Orfield and colleagues, such double segregation is linked with even greater teacher turnover. Thus, there are many negative implications for ethnic-racial minority student learners who are isolated in minority-segregated schools.[11]

The poorer-quality schooling in minority-segregated schools is not the only reason to be concerned about resegregation. We know that there are important benefits to having students from diverse ethnic-racial groups learn together in integrated settings. Specifically, researchers in the field of higher education find that exposure to diverse peers confers a number of important social and academic skills.[12] For example, Uma Jayakumar found that White students who were exposed to racially diverse peers in college reported better cross-cultural workforce competencies, such as the "ability to see the world from someone else's perspective, their openness to having views challenged, their tolerance of others with different beliefs, and their ability to discuss and negotiate controversial issues," as well as leadership skills.[13] Studies of school diversity with teens also show that peer relations are more positive in diverse school settings and that such peer relations are linked to positive youth well-being.[14] Therefore, another reason for concern about resegregation is that it deprives students of these benefits.

The good news is that there are many places in the United States that are becoming more diverse. Some of the changes in the school population reflect the dispersion of immigrants to places beyond what are called continuous "gateway" cities, such as New York, Los Angeles, and Miami. The racial and ethnic composition of the United States has been evolving in more places than ever before, and myriad communities around the country are more diverse than they have ever been.[15] In some places, the number of immigrants in areas that had few immigrants prior to 1990, especially the Southeast and Plains states, has increased exponentially. Indeed, the story of Latino immigration and internal migration within the United States has been characterized by dispersion across these so-called new destinations. And, depending on the group in question, a city that has been considered a traditional gateway for decades in regard to one immigrant group may, in fact, be a new destination for another.

In the 1990s and early 2000s, the conversation about new destinations centered on their growth in the Southeast, in places such as North Carolina and Georgia. And while there has been continued growth in this region, since then new destinations have emerged in other areas, such as other parts of the South and the Plains states. As the Pew Research Center notes, from 2000–2012, "the five states with the fastest-growing Hispanic populations were: Tennessee (up 163%), South Carolina (161%), Alabama (157%), Kentucky (135%) and South Dakota (132%)." And the three counties with the fastest-growing Latino populations were all in North Dakota.[16] As an example, it may be useful to consider the Mexican-origin population in 1980, when it was primarily concentrated in the West and Southwest, as compared to 2015 (see maps in fig. 7). By 2015, the proportion of the Mexican-origin population who settled in the Pacific Northwest, East, Southeast, and Plains regions had grown exponentially. As a specific example, take a closer look at the modest or

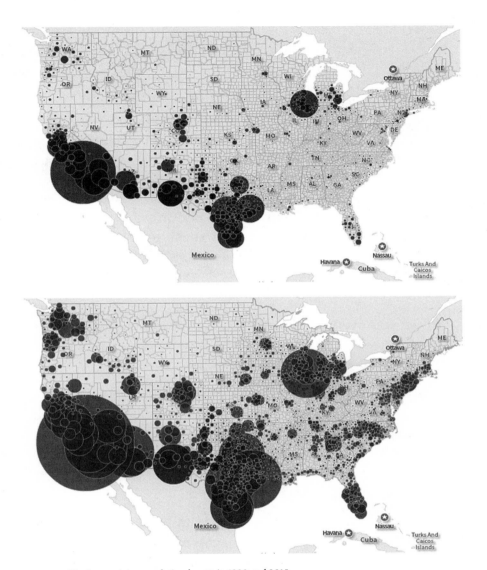

FIGURE 7. Mexican-origin population bursts in 1980 and 2015.
Maps created by authors in Social Explorer.

nonexistent Mexican-origin population in Washington, Kansas, Virginia, and Florida in the 1980 map, and compare their ballooning representation in those same states in the 2015 map.

Similarly, sociologist Amy Stuart Wells notes that the racial composition of communities across the United States has shifted with the increasing number of Black, Latino, and Asian individuals who have moved into the suburbs.[17] A recent *New York Times* article examined one Atlanta suburb as such:

> At first blush, this bedroom city of 83,000 a half-hour north of Atlanta might be mistaken for the perfect example of a white-flight Sun Belt suburb ... But something has been happening in Johns Creek—and, indeed, across much of the vast archipelago of cul-de-sac communities north of Atlanta.... Today, 24 percent of people in Johns Creek are of Asian heritage. Indian-Americans shop for saris at the Medlock Crossing strip mall and flock to the latest Bollywood hits at the multiplex. Chinese-Americans and food lovers of all stripes head to the Sichuan House, near the Target and Home Depot stores, for sliced pork ears in chili sauce and "tearfully spicy" mung bean noodles.[18]

William Frey of the Brookings Institution refers to these diversified communities as "melting pot suburbs," which mirror the composition of the United States more broadly. He notes:

> Minorities represent 35 percent of suburban residents, similar to their share of overall U.S. population. Among the 100 largest metro areas, 36 feature "melting pot" suburbs where at least 35 percent of residents are non-white. The suburbs of Houston, Las Vegas, San Francisco, and Washington, D.C. became majority minority in the 2000s.

> More than half of all minority groups in large metro areas, including blacks, now reside in the suburbs. The share of blacks in large metro areas living in suburbs rose from 37 percent in 1990, to 44 percent in 2000, to 51 percent in 2010. Higher shares of whites (78 percent), Asians (62 percent), and Hispanics (59 percent) in large metro areas live in suburbs.[19]

The changing demographics and greater geographic dispersion of immigrants from Latin America and Asia mean that, over their life course, White Americans' experiences will ultimately be embedded in a plural society, which will make race and ethnicity more salient and relevant for Whites—and continue to be so for all other groups.[20] Thus, we must prepare all youth to engage with the diversity they will inevitably encounter in the future as coworkers and citizens.

The Challenges We Face

To be clear, we are a diverse society but also a divided one in many respects. We will not be able to reap the full benefits of living and working in a diverse society unless we build bridges to people who are different from ourselves. A first step to building such bridges is to recognize that our divisions are rooted in the disparities in how different social groups are treated by our institutions. Perhaps, we might think, such disparities are blown out of proportion. Are they? To help answer this question, let's now turn to some of the information that can help us better understand the state of racial and ethnic inequality in the United States. Here, we focus on two institutions that are most relevant to the experiences of youth in this society: schools and the justice system.

Turning first to our educational system, the success and prosperity of our nation depends ultimately on having a well-educated citizenry. Yet we face challenges to that aspiration right from the start of children's academic paths in schools. Ethnic and racial disparities in educational outcomes begin as early as the preschool years. For example, data from the National Center for Education Statistics from 2005 to 2006 demonstrated that, at about four years of age, 49% of Asian children and 37% of White children were proficient in letter recognition, compared to 28% of Black children, 23% of Latino children, and 19% of American Indian/Alaska Native children. Similarly, whereas 81% of Asian children and 73% of White children were proficient in numbers and shape recognition at age four, these figures were 55%, 51%, and 40% for Black, Latino, and American Indian/Alaska Native children, respectively.[21]

These significant disparities are evident throughout the educational pipeline. For example, consider the following reading achievement levels as assessed by standardized tests among fourth graders, eighth graders, and twelfth graders presented in figure 8. At all grade

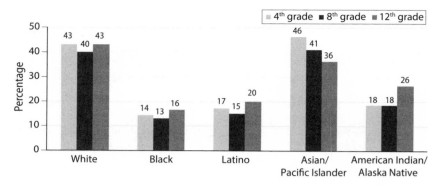

FIGURE 8. 2007 National Assessment of Educational Progress (NAEP) reading test scores by ethnic/racial group. *Source:* Aud, Fox, & KewalRamani (2010).

levels, while 40% or more of White students are proficient in reading, 20% or less of Black and Latino students are reading at this level.

Ultimately, we see the K–12 educational disparities across groups mirrored in their degree attainment as adults. For example, in 2015, among those twenty-five years old or older, 93.3% of the White population, 89.1% of Asian Americans, and 87% of African Americans had completed at least a high school degree, but just 66.7% of Latinos had done so. In addition, whereas 53.9% of Asian Americans and 36.2% of White Americans had obtained at least a bachelor's degree, only 22.5% of African Americans and 15.5% of Latino Americans had done so.[22] The long-term consequences of these disparities in educational attainment are significant because such credentials ultimately set the stage for what jobs individuals can get, what neighborhoods they can afford to live in, their physical health, and, ultimately, how long they will live.

As has been well documented by social scientists, those with higher educational attainment have better health outcomes, and they even live longer. For example, reviewing data from 2008, Black men in the United States who had at least 4 years of college education were expected to live 9.7 years longer than those who had less than a high school degree.[23] The differences in life expectancies for these same comparisons for White men, Hispanic men, Black women, White women, and Hispanic women were 12.9 years, 5.5

years, 6.5 years, 10.4 years, and 2.9 years, respectively. Thus, regardless of which ethnic-racial group was examined, more education led to a longer life expectancy. Scholars explain that these better outcomes that come with higher education are due to a number of factors, such as higher incomes, better access to health insurance, greater opportunity to learn about health risks and lifestyle choices that promote better health, and less exposure to stress related to economic deprivation.[24]

Although all groups are at risk for living shorter lives when their educational attainment is compromised, we can't lose sight of the fact that Black and Latino individuals are the most disadvantaged at all levels of education. In addition to concerns regarding educational attainment, recent disconcerting findings have emerged that reflect both the less-than-ideal conditions in which Black and Latino individuals experience the educational system and their disproportionate exposure to punishment across the span of their lives. For example, data gathered by the US Education Department's Office for Civil Rights indicate that from 2013 to 2014, Black students were 2.2 times more likely than White students to be referred to law enforcement or experience a school-related arrest.[25] The disproportionate rates of disciplinary action against ethnic and racial minorities relative to Whites are shockingly evident as early as the preschool years. This same report cited that Black preschoolers were 3.6 times as likely as White preschoolers to receive out-of-school suspensions. This statistic is not only alarming, but it also underscores how we fail Black children right from the very beginning of their education.

Turning now to another important social institution, it is imperative to consider the profound disparities observed in youths' contact with the justice system as well. According to a 2014 report by the National Center for Juvenile Justice and the Office of Juvenile Justice and Delinquency Prevention, in 2010 Black youth comprised 17% of the youth population but 31% of juvenile arrests.[26] Contrast that with the fact that in that same year, White youth comprised 76% of the youth population but only 66% of the arrests.

Unfortunately, the statistics regarding the disproportionate punishment of ethnic and racial minority youth forecast the more extreme ethnic-racial disparities in incarceration rates among adults. For example, in 2015 Black Americans made up 12.4% of the US population yet 35% of incarcerated prisoners. In contrast, White Americans made up 62% of the US population but only 34% of incarcerated prisoners. Overrepresentation in the justice system is also evident among Latinos, who made up 17.6% of the population in 2015 but 22% of incarcerated prisoners.[27] Another way to interpret these alarming statistics is to consider the statements made by the watchdog organization the Sentencing Project: "Black males have a 32% chance of serving time in prison at some point in their lives; Hispanic males have a 17% chance; white males have a 6% chance."[28] At the same time, according to the same source, "the rate of prison incarceration for black women was 2.5 times higher than the rate for white women [and] the rate for Hispanic women was 1.4 times higher."

Together, the differential treatment of youth by race and ethnicity in the realm of education and in the justice system has implications for the health and literal survival of members of marginalized groups. These social injustices severely limit our nation's capacity to fully realize the potential of its blossoming diversity, as Black and Latino young people must find a way to thrive in a society whose institutions significantly constrain their life chances. It is also important to recognize that these social disparities do not and should not define any particular youth's life. Many ethnic and racial minority youth do thrive in the face of these significant challenges. What's important to keep in mind, however, is that this is the broader context in which all youths are developing their understanding of one another and their understanding of their own identities.

STARTING A DIALOGUE ABOUT RACE AND ETHNICITY

Learning about numerous social disparities can sometimes perpetuate stereotypes about marginalized groups. So how can we productively communicate with youth about these disparities in a way that informs them about the inequalities yet does not reinforce stereotypes? One of the reasons that conversations about educational and other social inequalities do wind up inadvertently reifying negative misconceptions about others is that many of us are not well prepared to explain differential outcomes in ways that do not fall back on group deficiencies.

So it's clear that starting this dialogue with youth is no easy task, but it is absolutely critical in order for them to have an understanding of the root of the many stereotypes to which they are exposed about different groups. All youth today are growing up in a context in which the ethnic-racial White majority will no longer represent the composition of this nation, but they are being raised by parents who can only imagine what it is like for youth to come of age amid this changing US context. Despite our limited experience and understanding of this context, the current generation of adults bears the responsibility of setting youth on a course to productively navigate these spaces as they make their way through adulthood in an increasingly diverse society. We must take on this challenge and accept that we, too, will learn as we go.

Helping youth to think about race and ethnicity more generally involves challenging ourselves to work through our own biases. And make no mistake, we *all* have biases to contend with. In fact, because we have been exposed to many stereotypes that we have not questioned throughout our lives, we may not even be aware of the biases we harbor. Psychologists Mahzarin Banaji and Anthony Greenwald call this "implicit bias," or the views we have about different groups in our society that we are unwilling or unable to express explicitly.[29] They argue that these unconscious biases tend to play out as "blind spots" in our lives, in that they may be unknowingly shaping our relationships with others who are different. So, in order to genuinely help youth grapple with issues of race and ethnicity in their increasingly diverse world, it's clear that we must first willingly grapple with our own racial blind spots. Because, as the Project Implicit website explains, "the difference between being unwilling and unable is the difference between purposely hiding something from someone and unknowingly hiding something from yourself."[30]

DEALING WITH OUR RACIAL BLIND SPOTS

Naming our racial blind spots is paramount to moving a dialogue forward that is genuine and not deterred by fear of what we do not know about ourselves. This means taking on, headfirst, those areas of ignorance and intolerance that may be undermining our best intentions for interacting across difference. And we must work hard to figure out how we came to have those biases. In essence, we need to be clear about our own views and histories in order to be clear about what we're trying to help youth to achieve in their understanding of race, ethnicity, and difference.

One important barrier to having a frank assessment of the significance and meaning of race in the United States is a belief that race is only a matter of physical characteristics and so racism only occurs between individuals, as when one individual uses a racial slur or excludes another due to the color of their skin. But race and ethnicity are dynamics that function in ways that may not be obvious to us. Even if we can agree that, yes, the playing field is not level and some groups have better odds than others of "success," we may not see how those odds are the legacy of a long history of social exclusion in our country *and* contemporary forces that limit the opportunities of some groups and not others.

Some people reading this may wonder, "But how do you explain to youth that contemporary inequalities are not due to group inferiorities but rather to long-standing and ongoing injustices that have been perpetrated upon some groups and not others?" First, it is important to understand that this will be an ongoing conversation with youth, and that youths' understanding of this information must gradually evolve over time. There are multiple forces that work together to systematically limit the life chances of marginalized groups in our society, and expecting anyone to understand this complexity after a conversation or two is unrealistic. One's awareness and understanding of these forces evolve, and continue to evolve, over a lifetime.

Second, adults will benefit from increasing their own awareness of specific manifestations of inequality and the multiple forces that work together to produce (and reproduce) these inequalities across generations. Such examples help youth understand, in a concrete way, the manner in which different expectations, opportunities, privileges, and resources ultimately set groups of people up for success or failure.

Take, for example, the significant social problem of ethnic-racial educational disparities. In helping youth understand why such few Black and Latino Americans have a college education, it can be useful to explain that oftentimes Black and Latino youth have restricted access to the same quality of education as White youth, which ultimately makes it more difficult for them to successfully compete for admission into selective universities and to have the skills necessary to succeed in such settings. In her book, *Institutional Racism*, social work scholar Shirley Better walks through an analysis of how experiences across life contexts work together to lead to unequal outcomes for marginalized youth:

> The educational norm in America is neighborhood schools. Most families of Middle America send their children to a local school, one within two miles or less of their home. Thus, the neighborhood in which you reside becomes crucial in the determination of the quality of your education. The quality of education, like housing, depends on what you are able to afford. Minorities restricted to certain living areas, often regardless to income, have their life chances curtailed by the quality of the schools in their neighborhood. *Life chances* refer to the opportunities available to a person, such as a good education, adequate health care, and a well-paying job.[31]

Better goes on to explain that Black and Latino children who may be above average in intelligence will not receive the same high-quality education as children from the dominant group simply by virtue of their racial background and their social class. As noted earlier in this chapter, Black and Latino children will likely be attending minority-segregated schools.

Furthermore, their schools will have fewer well-trained teachers and insufficient access to important resources such as books, technology, and supplemental activities (e.g., internships). As a result, even if these students are the best in their class, the educational foundation that they receive may leave them ill-prepared to succeed in a higher-education setting. As young adults, their limited educational attainment will inform their employment opportunities, which will inform their income, which will inform where they live—and the cycle continues for the next generation.

Exposing youth to this information can provide them with a clearer perspective on the structural reasons for the disparities that exist in educational achievement when comparing Black and Latino youth to White youth. This information is essential for dispelling stereotypes, suggesting that there is some innate characteristic about Black and Latino youth that makes them inferior to White youth, particularly in the realm of education. Importantly, such information can also help youth understand that reducing and eliminating inequalities in primary and secondary education is an essential goal toward realizing a more just society.

It's also useful when having this discussion to explain to youth that, for decades, ethnic and racial minorities experienced significant discrimination in access to quality housing, and that it is still very much a part of how race and ethnicity shape families' lives today. As sociologists Doug Massey and Nancy Denton laid out in their seminal book *American Apartheid*, the residential isolation of Black people into predominantly Black cities did not happen by chance. It resulted from a long history of policy and individual choices made by Whites during the early part of the twentieth century. They explain:

> [W]hite Americans made a series of deliberate decisions to deny blacks access to urban housing markets and to reinforce their spatial segregation. Through its actions and inactions, white America built and maintained the residential structure of the ghetto. Sometimes the decisions were individual, at other times they were collective, and at still other times the powers and prerogatives of government were harnessed to maintain the residential color line.[32]

At the government level, practices made possible by the National Housing Act of 1934 and discriminatory lending practices by banks worked together to exclude suburban residential markets to people of color.[33] And the legacy of such practices, known as "redlining," still haunts us today. As recently as 2015, the US Department of Housing and Urban Development was able to prove that redlining practices were in active use by Associated Bank, which resulted in a settlement of $200 million—the largest ever reached.[34] Specifically, it was determined that Associated had "engaged in discriminatory lending practices regarding the denial of mortgage loans to African-American and Hispanic applicants and the provision of loan services in neighborhoods with significant African-American or Hispanic populations." In addition to such institutionalized practices continuously carried out by large corporations, residential segregation continues to be perpetuated in contemporary society by individual choices, such as landlords who refuse to rent to African Americans, Latinos, and other minorities.[35] Thus, racial discrimination in housing is not only a story of our distant past, but it unfortunately continues to this day.

Our discussion thus far has only scratched the surface. Our goal is not to provide a definitive analysis of these issues but rather to illustrate that the racial and ethnic patterns we observe today are the product of a complex web of historical forces, institutional practices, and individual choices. So when young people attend a school that is unable to adequately prepare them for their futures, or are denied a job interview or an apartment due to the name on their application, it is not merely an isolated exception but rather part of a larger set of social forces that we grapple with, and must challenge, every day. This complexity is important to recognize and communicate to youth to help them think critically about how this web may be informing the patterns they observe in their environments, so that they can identify and question their own racial blind spots about issues of race, ethnicity, and inequality. There is no question that these conversations will be challenging, but in having them, we break through our individual and collective barriers to engage in genuine interactions across difference. What's more, we model something fundamental: we don't have to be silent about the patterns in our society that are perplexing and blatantly unjust.

As we were in the process of writing this book, in fact, a White mother shared with us a conversation she had with her nine-year-old daughter, Faye. As they were discussing their new Black Lives Matter yard signs and making plans to share extra signs with neighbors, Faye told her mom that she couldn't understand why anyone in their neighborhood *wouldn't* want to put up a sign. The mother reminded Faye of previous conversations they had had regarding the pervasive negative messages about people of color in our society that we are "marinating in," and that are soaking into our minds and our behaviors "even when we are working very hard to learn different messages." With trepidation, Faye then confessed to her that *she* was worried that racism might have been "soaking in" because she had been disappointed at being placed in the fourth grade classroom for English-language learners. Rather than make Faye feel guilty or ashamed, the mother explained that no one is immune from racism, and told her that the best we can do is hope to be "antiracist racists" and constantly work to recognize when racism has soaked in. She also let Faye know that she was really proud of her for recognizing that racism had been soaking in and encouraged her to keep looking for these things and keep working to make sure they didn't soak in. Hearing these stories makes us optimistic that parents and authority figures who regularly work with youth will take on this challenge.

————

We realize that everything we've discussed and presented in this chapter has been in the context of aggregate group labels (for example, Latino, Black, White). This is how information is presented, reported on in the media, and digested. Moreover, it's crucial to report on disparities in this manner in order to rectify them. But relying exclusively on these group labels and their accompanying statistics can mask meaningful diversity within groups. Equally important to the point of this book, relying on broad demographic patterns to make generalizations about particular groups can interfere with young people's ability to develop a healthy identity as it relates to *any* of the aforementioned groups we have discussed in this chapter. When we rely on these broad categories to define "what a group is" for youth, we limit their ability to engage in a task that is critical for the development of adolescents: to define their own identities. Let us turn now to chapter 3, where we move beyond these labels and think through how youth can productively examine their ethnic and racial identities in this increasingly diverse society.

3

More than Labels

THE PSYCHOLOGY OF ETHNIC
AND RACIAL IDENTITY

Who in the world am I? Ah, that's the great puzzle.
—LEWIS CARROLL, *ALICE IN WONDERLAND*

"What are you?" This is a question that many of us who do not look "White," "Caucasian," "European American," or "[fill in your preferred label for those who are considered to be part of the US American majority]" repeatedly encounter throughout our lives. We vividly remember being asked this question during childhood, adolescence, and our college years. As adults, we find that this question still persists, though it seems to come up less often. Nevertheless, we still encounter this question in new social situations, such as when our children start a new school or join a new sports team; encounters with new acquaintances in these situations inevitably involve small talk, and the conversation eventually turns to, "What are you?" or "What is your background?" Sometimes it's in the context of "Oh, I can tell you can sit out here in the sun for hours; you tan so well! Where are you originally from?," and other times it's just plain and simple "What's your background?" (with an unspoken *I can tell you're different*).

Although the question seems open-ended, the person asking the question has a general expectation regarding the response options that will appropriately satisfy the curiosity that led to the question in the first place. And, of course, the "What are you?" question is frequently raised in the context of filling out forms when visiting a doctor, applying for a job, or registering for school. There are many different labels that people use to categorize others (and themselves) with respect to race and ethnicity, and in US society, many people rely on these labels to make assumptions about individuals who are perceived to be members of any given group. In this chapter we move beyond the labels to explain what decades of research have now taught us with respect to how children develop an identity related to their ethnic and racial group membership. We also discuss why developing an informed understanding of one's ethnic-racial identity can be quite beneficial for youth as they progress from childhood through adolescence and into adulthood. But before embarking on a conversation about how children develop an ethnic and racial identity and the positive consequences it can have for youth, we must address our working definitions of race and ethnicity.

Defining Race and Ethnicity

If you think there is a lot of confusion regarding the words "race" and "ethnicity," you are correct! According to social scientists who have devoted their careers to studying these concepts, race is a categorization system that is defined by those who have the most influence in making policy decisions.[1] In practice, the racial category a layperson ascribes to any given individual is often based on his or her physical characteristics, such as skin tone, hair texture, and/or facial features.[2] Ethnicity, on the other hand, is usually based on a person's cultural heritage—language, traditions, values—passed down through generations, which are not necessarily visible based on a person's physical appearance.[3] Individuals who have the same cultural heritage may also look very different *physically* and thus be of different racial categories (for example, a Puerto Rican whose skin is dark brown and looks more African versus a Puerto Rican with light skin who looks more European). Seems pretty clear-cut: race is based on physical characteristics, and ethnicity is based on cultural heritage. Unfortunately, it's not clear-cut at all.

As an example of what we mean, let's walk through how the US government classifies individuals based on race and ethnicity. The current classification system used for ethnic and racial reporting in the US Census recognizes five unique races (Black or African American, White, Asian, American Indian or Alaska Native, and Native Hawaiian or Other Pacific Islander) and one ethnicity (Hispanic/Latino versus not).[4] When identifying their race, individuals can choose one of the five races or a "two or more races" category, providing six options for race. Individuals must also answer a question indicating whether they are Hispanic/Latino or not. Together, these two questions are used to classify the entire US population according to race and ethnicity. Whether we agree with these categories or not, they are used on a regular basis as we fill out forms for employment, health-related visits, education, and so on. The US Department of Education uses the same categories.[5] Dig a little deeper, however, and you will notice that the US Census definitions for racial groups do not focus on physical features at all and, instead, define race according to geographical origin. For example, the definition for the White racial category states: "has origins in any of the original peoples of Europe, the Middle East, or North Africa." Yet, the US Census defines Hispanic/Latino as: "person is of Cuban, Mexican, Puerto Rican, South or Central American, or other Spanish culture or origin."[6]

So geography defines both race *and* ethnicity according to the US Census. Ethnicity appears to refer to people from mostly Spanish-speaking countries, as everyone else must answer "no" to the ethnicity question if they do not have these origins. This begs the question, does no one else have an ethnicity? And what is an ethnicity? If "origins" in one of these geographical areas (e.g., Europe, Middle

East, North Africa) is what defines race, then why is ethnicity (which is also defined by origins in geographical locations such as Cuba, South America, Central America, etc.) different from race? In other words, both race and ethnicity are defined by geographic origin, so why are they separated?

Understanding the difference between race and ethnicity becomes even more complicated when we consider that "race" categories used by the US Census have changed over time. For example, the 1930 US Census included the label "Mexican" as a race (the racial category "Mexican" pertained to anyone born in Mexico, or having parents born in Mexico, and who was "definitely not White, Negro, Chinese, or Japanese").[7] By 1940, the US Census indicated that Mexicans were to be racially classified as "White" unless they "were definitely Indian or some race other than White."[8] Thus, the very definition of race changed, and a group that had been classified in one way in 1930 now became part of the racial majority in 1940. This supports social scientists' conclusions that race is socially constructed, meaning that it is being defined by the views and practices of society.[9] Definitions of race can and do change over time in any given society.

Up to this point, we have provided two largely accepted (albeit inconsistent) definitions of race and ethnicity that prevail in the social scientific literature and in US society. What we have not discussed, and what is *most* important for this conversation, is the day-to-day experiences of people. Although social scientists and government officials have defined these constructs as unique, the lived experiences of many people suggest that individuals' identities cannot be neatly compartmentalized into their sense of self as an *ethnic* being versus a *racial* being.[10] As an example, a Mexican-origin adolescent growing up in Phoenix, Arizona, may define her identity in part by her Mexican heritage, which may include things such as speaking Spanish with her cousins, eating certain meals that are unique to Mexican culture, and engaging in specific Mexican traditions and practices during holidays. But being of Mexican origin also informs other experiences she has had, such as being in the car with her grandfather when he was racially profiled, pulled over by

the police, and detained until he could prove his legal documenta-
tion status. Similarly, her Mexican-origin background may result in
personal experiences with discrimination in which teachers stereotype her as a student who is not academically talented and less inclined toward academic interests because they perceive her to be
a member of a group that does not speak English well, is lazy, and
uneducated. These experiences, though distinctly ethnic and racial,
simultaneously inform this adolescent's self-concept and understanding of who she is with respect to her Mexican-origin background in the context of the United States. Thus, the *ethnic* part of
one's identity (which is informed by unique traditions during the
holidays, music, celebrations, and values that are passed down from
one generation to the next) is tightly intertwined with the *racial*
experiences that result from that same identity (such as profiling,
stereotyping, and unfair treatment). If we were to ask this young
woman to tell us about her Mexican identity, and tell us about all
aspects of her experience, should we classify her responses as "ethnic identity" or as "racial identity"? We believe neither term, alone,
would be sufficient.

As a way to better capture the intertwined nature of identity that
is based on the ethnic aspects of individuals' lives and those based
on the racial aspects, we assembled a working group comprised of
thirteen social scientists—all experts in the areas of ethnic or racial
identity.[11] We met several times to discuss the terminology, theories, and research findings that had emerged over the past several
decades pertaining to ethnic and racial identity. The result of our
deliberations was a consensus statement, so to speak, that proposed
a new term: ethnic-racial identity.[12] We proposed that the use of the
term "ethnic-racial identity" was needed to reflect the complexity
of considering individuals' identities as they are informed *simultaneously* by ethnic-related experiences (traditions, values) and race-
related experiences (e.g., being discriminated against according
to stereotypes or assumptions others make about them because of
factors such as their physical appearance, surname, or accented English).[13] With our colleagues, we concurred that race and ethnicity
are distinct constructs, but that in defining individuals' identities,

they become tangled. When considering the psychological meaning that individuals attach to these aspects of their identity that are difficult to disentangle, considering the broader construct of ethnic-racial identity, which encompasses both, is a more accurate reflection of what individuals are experiencing on a day-to-day basis. Therefore, in this book, we use the term "ethnic-racial identity" to acknowledge individuals' experiences with developing their understanding of their identities that pertains to our societally imposed labels of Black, White, Asian, American Indian, and Hispanic/Latino.

A final note about labels: The definitions and classifications imposed by the US government have a major influence on society's understanding of race and ethnicity because the categories described above are required to be used for federal reporting, such as in the US Census and for record keeping in the Department of Education. These categories are then continually used to label individuals (in the news, for example), and to report on population-level statistics (such as voting patterns, for example) outside the purpose of federal reporting. The continuous use of these categories informs the way that people who are perceived to be members of groups are treated and often perpetuates stereotypes. But tracking disproportionate access to resources in areas such as education, health, and legal systems of this society is essential to mitigating the significant ethnic-racial disparities that exist. So these broader, externally imposed labels are real, and they can have real consequences for individuals' experiences in terms of privileges, rights, and opportunities—or lack thereof.

However, when considering how individuals *define themselves*, labels ascribed by society and powerful actors within any given society are but one aspect of their identities. People have more control over the identity that they develop internally than over any label ascribed to them. To put it differently, we cannot always control how we are labeled by others, or the boxes that are available for us to "check" when we are filling out a form for school or at the doctor's office, but we *can* control the meaning that we make of those labels that are imposed upon us. And, as will be presented later in this chapter, it is not the ethnic-racial labels that matter (in terms of young people's adjustment related to race and ethnicity) but rather the identity that individuals form relative to these labels. Let us begin by considering how such an identity starts to develop early in life.

Developing an Identity in an Ethnically and Racially Diverse Society

[Ethnicity] means to know where you came from and who you are, and it gives you more yourself, more identity, and makes your life more meaningful than, "oh, I'm just another American" ... there's thousands of us.

—SIXTEEN-YEAR-OLD EUROPEAN AMERICAN MALE REFLECTING ON THE MEANINGFULNESS OF KNOWING ONE'S ETHNICITY

Ethnicity means a lot to me. Each time I'm called Mexican or something, I feel proud because that's something that makes me feel proud of. I love my ethnicity because my people are known for being tough, strong, brave people full of pride. I don't care if someone says Mexicans are dumb or they are short, because I know that's just a stereotype. That's why I'm proud that my ethnicity is different, because it makes me feel one of a kind.

—THIRTEEN-YEAR-OLD LATINO MALE REFLECTING ON WHAT HIS ETHNICITY MEANS TO HIM

The development of the ethnic-racial domains of an individual's identity is especially relevant in a place such as the United States, where there is much diversity along these lines, and where these social group categories carry meaning because of the nation's historical and present-day practices of discrimination based on these categories.[14] In understanding the process of identity development, scientists have long argued that adolescence is a critical time for the formation of one's identity.[15] Although this is true, and we will review what changes are taking place in adolescence that make it a critical time for identity formation, it is important to note that there is quite a bit going on during earlier periods of development that provides a foundation for the identity that develops later in life.[16] There are many biological and social changes that take place during the early stages of human development that set the stage for individuals' identity development and, specifically, their understanding of the part of their identity that has to do with their racial and ethnic background. Thus, we begin with a discussion of early childhood and the awareness and experiences that shape individuals' understanding of the social world and how they fit into it.

HOW DO YOUNG CHILDREN MAKE SENSE OF ETHNICITY AND RACE?

As children mature, they gain cognitive abilities that inform their thinking, reasoning, and understanding of the social world. Cognitive abilities gained during childhood include, among other things, the ability to categorize objects, engage in symbolic thought, understand that the physical properties of certain objects will not change despite superficial changes to physical appearance, and classify objects based on a hierarchical structure. With respect to ethnic-racial identity development, these cognitive abilities make it possible for children to categorize groups of people, as well as to understand that superficial changes to a person's appearance, such as putting on a blond wig or painting one's skin, will not change a person's ethnic or racial group membership.[17] Children's cognitive advances also enable them to use more psychological attributes to describe a person rather than exclusively relying on concrete physical characteristics.[18]

A significant body of research has now demonstrated that, as a function of these increasing cognitive abilities, by twelve months of age children can visually distinguish people of different races.[19] By four to five years of age, children demonstrate knowledge of ethnic and racial stereotypes.[20] And by the time they are six to seven years old, children can accurately label ethnic and racial groups according to socially understood norms regarding race and ethnicity that are based on attributes such as skin tone, language, and traditional dress.[21]

Much of the early work in this area was dominated by a focus on children who were racially Black or White, and researchers initially erroneously concluded that Black children's self-concept suffered as a result of the negative stereotypes and racism that existed in society toward Black populations.[22] This conclusion was largely drawn from the famous "doll studies" conducted in the 1940s by Kenneth and Mamie Clark.[23] However, important advances in children's ethnic and racial identity in the early 1980s by scholars such as Margaret Beale Spencer clearly demonstrated that young Black children did not all suffer from a diminished sense of self, and many in fact had very positive self-concepts. Spencer showed that children's increased cognitive abilities enabled them to be aware of race and ethnicity, and knowledgeable of cultural stereotypes, but these stereotypes were not internalized.[24] That is, ethnic and racial minority children were not personally defining themselves according to the stereotypes of which they were well aware.

Although there were some important differences in interpretation of research findings, the indisputable conclusions from the collection of research studies between the 1940s and 1980s specified that, at a very young age, children become aware of different categories of people and the stereotypes associated with these socially determined categories. It is important to note that these findings are not unique to the United States, as scholars studying children in many countries around the globe have documented the salience of group membership and hierarchies with respect to ethnic minority and majority group status. Good examples can be found in the work of Frances Aboud in Canada, Adam Rutland in England, and Drew Nesdale in Australia, to name a few.[25]

Studies around the world demonstrate that children have the cognitive capabilities to recognize distinctions between groups, but how do children become aware of these societal labels and the meaning attached to these labels? Developmental psychologists Rebecca Bigler and Lynn Liben have explained that social stereotyping exists in environments that consistently use specific attributes to categorize people within a given society into groups.[26] At a very young age, children become aware of these categories and the stereotypes associated with them because, on a daily basis, children receive constant cues from their surrounding environments. These social cues include: (a) the use of labels for individuals according to these groups in everyday conversations or media reports (e.g., crime suspects on the news being described using presumed race or ethnicity); (b) the intentional organization of environments based on such groups (e.g., inclusion or exclusion criteria for joining a group, clubs that cater to or focus on specific ethnic-racial groups); and (c) de facto segregation along the lines of these social groups (in the school cafeteria, neighborhoods).[27] Because race and ethnicity are highly salient attributes that are regularly used to categorize individuals in the United States, it is not surprising that US children can classify individuals according to these social groups, and that they are aware of stereotypes associated with specific groups at a young age. But what happens as these children grow older? How does this labeling affect their own self-perceptions and their views of others?

IDENTITY DEVELOPMENT IN ADOLESCENCE

Early in this chapter we introduced the idea that individuals may not have much control over the labels that are imposed upon them by society, but that they do have control over the meaning that is made about their identity with respect to any given label. Although we stand by our statement, it is important to recognize that developing an informed ethnic-racial identity is a complex process.[28] This complexity becomes increasingly prominent in adolescence, a period when youth have the cognitive abilities to form a more nuanced understanding of the *meaning* behind the labels that they learned as children. The constantly changing and illogical definitions of the terms "race" and "ethnicity" described earlier create myriad possibilities for the meaning young people ascribe to their own labels. Adolescents are simultaneously developing their self-concepts and trying to understand the multifaceted meanings of the concepts of ethnicity and race.

Adolescence is also a time when youth begin to recognize that their ethnic-racial group membership can play an important role in their lives—either due to experiences at school, in their communities, in various media outlets (including social media), or a combination of these and other exposures.[29] An example of this increasing awareness appeared in social psychologist Claude Steele's book *Whistling Vivaldi*.[30] In describing his earliest memory of realizing he was Black, he explained that at about age seven or eight, he learned that Black kids were only allowed to swim in the pool at the neighborhood park on Wednesdays and could only go to the roller rink on Thursdays. He also described another experience, at thirteen years old, when he arrived at 6:00 a.m. at a local area golf course to apply for a job as a caddy but was not told until the end of the day that he could not be hired because he was Black. In recounting these experiences, Steele explained that as a younger child, he had a sense that Black kids could be "regular people" and swim at the pool but only in the middle of the week; he was perplexed but didn't consider the broader social ramifications. By adolescence, however, he pieced together that, as a Black male, racism would continue to create contingencies in his life due to the central role that race played in organizing society.

Psychologist Bill Cross refers to these experiences of social exclusion as *encounters*—events that cause an individual to become aware of, or to redefine, how they think about race.[31] What happens during adolescence that makes the interpretation and understanding of racial encounters particularly important for a person's self-concept? First, during adolescence the human brain advances in a manner such that new cognitive capabilities enable individuals to understand concepts such as race and ethnicity that are abstract and not directly observable.[32] Simultaneously, there is increased social exposure that comes with adolescence, when youth are given more freedom to explore the environments outside the home.[33] Considering these two factors in tandem, it is not a coincidence that encounters that make ethnicity and race more salient become more probable as youth progress through adolescence. And it is this greater exposure to nonfamilial environments coupled with the cognitive changes in the brain that make the ethnic-racial identity development process during adolescence particularly active.[34]

Specifically, the increased ability of the brain to think about and understand concepts that are abstract is what enables adolescents to more profoundly consider the implications of race and ethnicity for their self-concept, and to consider the contingencies that exist in their life as a function of this aspect of their identity. Although this sounds relatively straightforward, the ambiguities surrounding race and ethnicity, and the unjust and illogical social norms that defy children's quest for fairness and equity,[35] can complicate the identity development process. The process of developing an identity can be fraught with confusion and unrest for young people as they grapple with issues of identity that involve these elusive concepts. And, as explained by the well-known psychologist Erik Erikson, identity confusion can be quite harmful for a person's overall development and adjustment.[36]

ETHNIC-RACIAL IDENTITY AS A PROCESS

I think it gives me a feeling of like how I know how I got where I am, like how my ancestors got to this country, and why, and how exactly I'm here right now.

—SIXTEEN-YEAR-OLD WHITE MALE REFLECTING ON WHY KNOWING ABOUT HIS ANCESTRY IS MEANINGFUL TO HIM

Where did I belong? ... if I had come to understand myself as a black American, and was understood as such, that understanding remained unanchored to place. What I needed was a community, I realized, a community that cut deeper than the common despair that black friends and I shared when reading the latest crime statistics, or the high fives I might exchange on a basketball court. A place where I could put down stakes and test my commitments.[37]

—BARACK OBAMA, *DREAMS FROM MY FATHER: A STORY OF RACE AND INHERITANCE*

Erik Erikson introduced his theory of psychosocial development in the 1950s to explain the psychological struggles and negotiations that individuals go through at different stages of their lives as they progress from infancy through adulthood.[38] Erikson identified eight stages during this developmental span (determined by the individuals' cognitive capabilities and the social experiences that were expected to be common during a given age), and each major stage had a psychological developmental task that was considered critically important for optimal development during that stage. Erikson explained that in order to have a better chance at success in a subsequent stage of development, individuals had to successfully deal with the tasks in the previous stages of development.

In Erikson's theory, the developmental task of the fifth stage of ego, "identity versus role confusion," was assigned to the period of adolescence (from ages twelve to eighteen).[39] He explained that, during this stage, a personal identity emerges as youth begin to pull together the information they have gathered from all of the significant social actors around them, such as parents and peers. They take this information and weave it together with their own ideas about their values, their beliefs, and their future goals. Erikson noted that the reason adolescence is so important for this process is because it is not until this time that youth have *both* the social exposure and the cognitive abilities to understand the perspective of others. Adolescents have the ability to think about their identities based on their own perspectives, apart from what their parents may be thinking or feeling. Erikson further suggested that individuals were innately driven to have a clearer sense of who they were and who they would become, and this drive became heightened during adolescence because of the social and cognitive changes that were taking place.

Considering Erikson's theory in relation to ethnic-racial identity, it is understandable why the "What are you?" question can play a major role in youths' identity formation during adolescence. Youth are deeply entrenched in the process of defining themselves with respect to the many different identities that make up who they are and who they believe they can become. Furthermore, at this age youth are preoccupied with others' perceptions of them. Questions such as "What are you?" can make youth particularly aware of this aspect of their identity, especially because it signifies that others perceive them *in this way* to be different. This increased awareness of an identity domain at a given point in time is what social psychologist Robert Sellers and his colleagues refer to as *salience*,[40] which we discuss in greater detail later in this chapter.

Returning to Erikson, he also explained that the inability to satisfy the internal drive to have a clearer sense of who one is and who one could become would result in identity confusion, which could have negative consequences for an individual, such as the inability to establish close relationships with others because of the uncertainty present within the self.[41] In contrast, individuals who actively explored their identity, considered many of the different possibilities for their future, and came to a clear sense of who they were and who they would become were considered to have achieved a firm sense of inner identity. Applying these ideas to ethnic-racial identity development, adolescent *exploration* involves seeking information about their group, talking to others about their background, trying to understand the history of their group, and participating in activities that help them learn more about their background.[42] The many different ways people explore their ethnic-racial identity can be seen in the themes of popular memoirs and novels: *The Brief Wondrous Life of Oscar Wao*, *Dreams from My Father*, *Waking Up White*, *When I Was Puerto Rican*, *The Namesake*, and *Americanah*, to name a few.[43] Even more examples abound in film (e.g., ranging from *Moana* to *Real Women Have Curves*) and television (e.g., *Fresh Off the Boat*).[44]

The process of identity exploration is important for helping youth to develop an *informed* understanding of their background rather than merely passively internalizing ideas presented to them. By actively engaging in identity exploration, adolescents gain a sense of ownership and confidence in this aspect of their identity. Youth can be confident about their identity if it is based on information they were instrumental in securing. The ideal goal is to obtain a sense of clarity, or what is referred to as *resolution*, about the identity.[45]

Several researchers who have investigated ethnic-racial identity formation with adolescents have found support for Erikson's ideas. In some of the earliest work in this area, psychologist Jean Phinney showed that younger adolescents were less likely to have explored their ethnic-racial identity, or have a sense of commitment and belonging to their ethnic-racial group, than older adolescents.[46] Phinney's work, conducted in the late 1980s and early 1990s, was limited to youth in California, and her conclusions were based on research comparing youth who were of different ages. However, building on Phinney's early work, several additional studies, including our own, with more stringent methods in which the same youth were followed for multiple years, have been carried out in the Northeast, Midwest, Pacific Northwest, and Southwest.[47]

In their work with students in the Northeast in the United States, for example, Sabine French and her colleagues found that African American, Latino, and European American adolescents significantly increased how much they talked to others about their ethnic-racial background and how much time they spent thinking about their ethnic-racial background from eighth grade to tenth grade. With younger adolescents in the Pacific Northwest, Cindy Huang and Elizabeth Stormshak found similar results for their sample of ethnic-racial minority sixth graders, whom they followed into the ninth grade—the most common type of change that they witnessed in the youth they were studying was one in which adolescents significantly increased how much they had explored their ethnic-racial background and felt connected to their background.[48] In our own studies, which focused exclusively on Latino youth, we found that girls tended to engage in more exploration about their ethnic-racial background and to develop a greater sense of clarity about this part of their identity as they progressed from their freshman and sophomore years of high school through the next four years.[49] Boys, on average, did not have a pattern of increase during this same time;[50] however, boys whose parents were engaged in socializing them about their background did show a pattern in which their sense of clarity about their ethnic-racial identity increased significantly from the first year of the study to the fourth.[51] Generally, findings from these studies show that it is reasonable to expect a pattern of increase in adolescents' exploration and understanding of their ethnic-racial identity from early to late adolescence, and that individuals' understanding of who they are in this regard will continue to unfold in young adulthood.[52] Particularly for ethnic and racial minorities in the United States, youth tend to explore their ethnicity and race, and also feel more confident and secure regarding this aspect of their identity as they progress from their "tween" to teen to young adult years.

The qualification of "particularly for ethnic and racial minorities" is an important one to address here. Experiences of ethnic-racial identity development will be different based on whether youth are members of a minority or majority group in any given society.[53] As explained by psychologist Beverly Tatum in her book, *Why Are All the Black Kids Sitting Together in the Cafeteria?*, everyone goes through a search for a personal identity, and youth will explore different domains of their identity at different times.[54] But we should not be surprised that adolescents of color are more likely to be actively engaged in exploring their ethnic-racial identity than White adolescents. Simply stated, ethnic and racial minority youth (e.g., Hispanic/Latino, African American/Black, Asian American, and American Indian) are more likely to think of themselves in terms of race and ethnicity than Whites because that is how the rest of society thinks of them.

Because White youth are not regularly (if ever) asked the "What are you?" question, issues of ethnicity or race are not typically raised for them in relation to their personal identity. When issues of ethnicity or race *are* raised, White youth are incorrectly guided into thinking that a racial or ethnic identity is not a relevant topic for them because the majority group is always assumed to be "normal"—the standard against which to compare all other groups. In fact, we have heard many White students state that they don't have an ethnic or racial identity. Debby Irving's introduction to her book, *Waking Up White*, provides an excellent reflection on this:

I didn't think I had a race, so I never thought to look within myself for answers. The way I understood it, race was for other people, brown- and black-skinned people. Don't get me wrong—if you put a census form in my hand, I would know to check "white"

or "Caucasian." It's more that I thought all those other categories, like Asian, African American, American Indian, and Latino,
were the real races. I thought white was the raceless race—just
plain, normal, and one against which all others were measured.[55]

Youth who are members of the ethnic and racial majority *do* indeed have an ethnic-racial identity. As explained by counseling psychologist Janet Helms in her seminal book, *Black and White Racial
Identity*, the process of identity development does not differ between majority and minority youth. Rather, what differs is the *content* of what is being explored and defined. As psychologists Moin
Syed and Margarita Azmitia have demonstrated in their work, White
and ethnic and racial minority college students increased their exploration, sense of clarity, and positive feelings about their ethnic-
racial identities at similar rates from their freshman through senior
year in college.[56] Syed and Azmitia surveyed college students in
California during their first semester on campus and followed them
for thirty-six months.[57] Although they expected that White students
may not show as much change in their ethnic-racial identity as
Black, Latino, and Asian American students, their findings did not
confirm this expectation. Although the ethnic-racial minority students did report higher average levels of exploration and a greater
sense of clarity and positive feelings about their background than
the White college students at the beginning of the study, as the study
progressed, Black, Latino, Asian American, and White students
alike increased in all of these areas at the same rate. In other words,
by their senior year of college, students from all of the ethnic-racial
groups had significantly increased their understanding of their
ethnic-racial identity, and no group had changed faster than any
other. These findings are important for showing that the process of
ethnic-racial identity development does indeed continue to unfold
beyond adolescence, and that these normative changes are expected
for both ethnic-racial minority and majority youth.

Thus far, we have focused exclusively on work that emphasizes
the age-based developmental aspects of ethnic-racial identity
development—and why the period of adolescence is particularly

important for these processes to unfold. These aspects are referred to by many scholars as part of the developmental *process* of ethnic-racial identity.[58] However, other theoretical work and empirical studies provide complementary information about ethnic-racial identity *content*—the significance and meaning people ascribe to their identity. Both the process and content of ethnic-racial identity are critical for youth development.[59]

THE CONTENT OF ETHNIC-RACIAL IDENTITY IN YOUTH

As young people develop their ethnic-racial identities, they also have the capacity to construct a sense of what that identity means to them, or what we call its *content*. The content that makes up an individual's ethnic-racial identity is multifaceted. This means that content can refer to many different aspects of how individuals evaluate their identity in terms of how they feel about it, what they think it means for their social experiences, and whether it is a factor in the way others view them and in their life opportunities.

One of the most studied aspects of content is how positively or negatively people feel about their ethnicity or race—alternatively referred to as *pride, affirmation,* or *private regard*.[60] These feelings are what immediately come to mind for many people when they think of a person's ethnic-racial identity—is the person *proud* to be a member of their group? Do they feel *connected* in a positive way to their group membership? Studies with ethnic-racial minority youth have found that youth tend to feel more and more positively about their ethnic-racial identity as they progress from early to middle adolescence, and from middle adolescence to late adolescence. Based on theories advanced by social psychologists, focused on how people form a sense of self in relation to their group membership more generally, feeling positively about one's ethnic-racial identity is linked to one's overall general self-concept.[61] Individuals must feel positively about the social groups to which they belong in order to maintain a positive self-concept, because one's identity is believed to be heavily informed by social group memberships. And, in fact, many studies have found support for this idea.

Most studies gather data on this aspect of adolescents' ethnic-racial identity by asking youth to rate the extent to which: they are proud to be a member of their ethnic-racial group, they feel good about their culture and heritage, and their feelings about their group are positive. Adolescents also respond to questions that help researchers gauge their self-esteem, their academic success (e.g., grades, attitudes toward school), whether or not they are having depressive symptoms, and the extent to which they are engaging in risky behaviors—for example, substance use, stealing, and risky sexual activity. We attempted to summarize the literature in this area by conducting a meta-analysis, in which we essentially pooled together the findings from forty-six studies on this topic that were conducted across multiple regions of the United States and with samples that represented all ethnic-racial minority groups. We found strong support for the benefits of adolescents' positive feelings about their ethnic-racial background. It was clear from our findings that adolescents who felt more positively about their ethnic-racial identity also tended to have better academic adjustment, higher self-esteem, lower depressive symptoms, and lower engagement in risk behaviors. The benefit of this meta-analysis was that it took into account the findings from all studies conducted on this topic—not just those that had found positive effects—and when all findings were considered together, the result pointed to positive outcomes for youth when they feel positively about their ethnic-racial identity.

Another way that people make sense of the role of ethnicity or race in their lives is through what Robert Sellers and his colleagues write about as *public regard*. Public regard refers to one's perceptions of how others generally view one's group.[62] Youth are developing their identities based, in part, on how they think the world around them perceives them. It will come as no surprise that researchers have found that as adolescents report experiencing more ethnic or racial discrimination, over time, they tend to develop the perception that their ethnic-racial group is not valued or viewed positively by society. Messages that youth receive from peers, media, teachers, and other individuals in their lives have significant consequences for the ethnic-racial identity that youth are developing.

And our work with Black, Latino, and White teenagers finds that youths' sense of public regard is linked to important school and mental health outcomes.[63] In one study, we surveyed 1,378 Black, White, and Latino thirteen- to nineteen-year-olds who were attending a high school in the Southwest.[64] First, we were interested in seeing how adolescents' perceptions of how others viewed their group varied across ethnic-racial groups. As expected, White students reported significantly higher public regard than Black and Latino students, indicating that they believed their ethnic-racial group was perceived more positively than did Black and Latino adolescents. We then examined whether experiences with discrimination would impact adolescents' reports of how others perceived their group—we tested adolescents' perceptions of discrimination from both peers and adults in the school setting. An interesting finding was that experiences with discrimination from adults were *not* associated with more negative public regard when adolescents had engaged in high levels of exploration and had greater clarity regarding the meaning of their ethnic-racial identity. Unfortunately, this same protection did not exist with respect to experiencing discrimination from peers. When adolescents experienced peer ethnic-racial discrimination, they were more likely to perceive that their group was viewed negatively in society, regardless of whether or not they had engaged in ethnic-racial identity development processes. These findings likely reflect the important role that peers play during adolescence, with respect to how youth define themselves and the groups to which they belong. When youth experience ethnic-racial discrimination from peers, this information can shape how they define their ethnic-racial group, even if they have a strong ethnic-racial identity. On the other hand, a strong ethnic-racial identity can help to limit the influence that discrimination from adults has on adolescents' perceptions of their group.

Finally, *salience* and *centrality* are two additional dimensions of ethnic-racial identity that have been studied in relation to youth adjustment. The concept of salience was introduced by Robert Sellers and captures the extent to which a person is aware of his or her ethnic-racial group membership at a given moment in time, given the situation.[65] Sellers and his colleagues explain that salience is an important consideration when trying to understand the extent to which one's racial identity will inform how one reacts or is influenced by any given situation.[66] If race is highly salient, then particular features of one's racial identity (such as positive affect) may play a big role in how one reacts to a racially charged situation; however, if race is not salient in the particular situation, then the way one reacts may have nothing to do with how positively one feels about one's ethnic-racial group membership.

In contrast, centrality refers to how much a person typically defines herself or himself with respect to race or ethnicity.[67] As an example, in one of our studies we asked Latino youth to answer the question, "What does your ethnicity mean to you?" One fourteen-year-old Latina girl noted that it wasn't important at all. She stated, "Nothing really. It doesn't describe who I am as a person. It's simply just something that is supposed to make us different from each other." Sellers explains that, unlike salience, centrality does not vary much across situations. If race is a central part of one's identity when one is in an all-White peer group, it will still be a central part of one's identity when one is in an all-Black peer group. Likewise, someone for whom ethnicity or race is *not* central, as illustrated in the quote above, will feel the same across situations.

The way these two concepts work together, for example, is that in a situation that makes race highly salient, a person who has high racial centrality could be more strongly affected by the experience (whether it is a positive or a negative experience) because the person considers race an important part of her self-concept. The person who does not consider race an important part of her self-concept (in other words, has low centrality) may be less impacted by the racially salient experience. In cases where the experience is negative, such as being exposed to derogatory remarks about one's racial group, people with lower centrality may also lack appropriate coping resources. We think one reason for this is that they have not adequately explored this aspect of their identity or come to terms with how to deal with experiences of racial discrimination. A person whose race is a central part of her identity may have engaged in the process of understanding the meaning of race in her life and learned how to cope with potential threats against her group.

Consequences of Ethnic-Racial Identity: How It Matters for Youth Development

Adolescence is a time when youth devote a fair amount of attention to thinking about their identity, defining and redefining themselves, considering all of the different aspects of their lives that make them who they are, and considering who they will be in the future. And everything we have presented thus far helps to explain *theoretically* how youth are developing an ethnic and racial identity, and why this tends to be a major focus during adolescence. But what do we know about the implications of ethnic-racial identity for youth? Are there *particular aspects* of youths' ethnic-racial identity that are important for their development more generally? *Why* and *when* will an ethnic-racial identity matter for youth?

First, it's important to note that several decades ago, researchers incorrectly assumed that the ethnic-racial labels that were ascribed to individuals (such as Latino, African American) were synonymous with individuals' ethnic-racial identity, particularly if the individuals were choosing those labels to identify themselves. After decades of research, however, it is clear that a label is simply a label, and a person's use of any given label tells little about the psychological meaning the person attaches to this label or about the process by which they have formed an identity connected to the label. Labels do not communicate the significance attached to group membership, the extent to which the person has explored this background or achieved a sense of clarity regarding this identity, nor the importance that the person places on this particular aspect of his or her identity in defining the self.

From our perspective, the influence of an ethnic-racial identity, in terms of determining how youth will feel about themselves or how well-adjusted they will be in school, goes well beyond any labels that youth choose for themselves or that are ascribed to them by others. This may be disappointing to learn, given the fascination with labels in our society. For instance, when golfing legend Tiger Woods came up with his own label, "Cablinasian," to acknowledge that he was Caucasian, Asian, Indian, and Black, many opinions surfaced about his self-imposed label. Some people were disappointed that he did not identify as African American, given that this is how he would be perceived based on US practices of hypo-descent (the "one drop rule," in which anyone with one drop of African blood in their heritage is considered Black). Others supported his choice and appreciated his attempt to communicate the message that he did not fit neatly into the illogical US racial classification system. Although Tiger Woods's label does communicate that he has a general awareness that his background is comprised of multiple heritages, his preferred label gives little information about the process by which he has developed his identity in this regard, nor does it help us understand how important this part of his identity is to his overall sense of self. The other realization that has emerged as a result of the abundance of research on this topic is that it is imperative that youth develop an informed and clear understanding of their ethnic-racial identity—especially ethnic and racial minority youth. In the United States, race and ethnicity are social constructs that are constantly used consciously and unconsciously, and this reality makes it very likely that this identity domain will be salient for youth who are members of minority groups. As we and numerous other researchers have found, when group membership is salient, youth will have better mental health, better academic adjustment, and demonstrate better well-being in general, if they have explored their background, have a clear understanding of who they are with respect to this aspect of their identity, feel positively about their group, feel a sense of belonging to their group, and consider this group to be an important part of their general self-concept.[68] This conclusion is based on almost thirty years of research from many different research studies conducted in different regions of the United States, and with samples of youth who are members of myriad ethnic and racial groups.[69] Furthermore, adolescents' own reflections on the meaning of their ethnicity and the value of a more developed identity echo these scientific results—consider the following excerpt from a thirteen-year-old Latina female:

> My ethnicity makes me feel different from other people in a good way. I know a little more than them about my ethnicity and it makes me feel a little confident. It means to me that my living may be different from others but it makes me feel happy. It means that I know two languages and eat different foods and believe in different things and celebrate different ways.

As this thirteen-year-old nicely articulates, there are benefits to knowing you are different, knowing what makes you different, and valuing such difference.

In recent years, developmental scientists have responded to the need for a comprehensive yet concise summary, or bird's-eye view, of what these decades of research tell us about the role of ethnic-racial identity in the education, health, and mental health of diverse populations. Not one but four such reviews of the research have recently been completed.[70] Rather than rely on a single study to elaborate on the state of the evidence, then, we refer to these comprehensive reviews to explain what is known in this field. From these reviews we learn that across Black, Latino, Asian American, and other ethnic-racial minority youth, having a positive view of and feeling connected to their ethnic or racial group is linked to things like better self-esteem, less depression, better mood, more prosocial tendencies, greater acceptance from peers, more positive views of school, greater feelings of competence to do academic work, and less drug use and exposure.[71] One of these reviews finds benefits for White youth in diverse settings.[72] When we consider other aspects of ethnic-racial identity, such as exploration, resolution, and public regard, the list of benefits for youths' positive development is even longer.[73]

Why does developing an informed and positive ethnic-racial identity carry benefits for youth? One answer to this question is found in Erikson's theory about human development. He argued that when individuals feel confident and secure about themselves with respect to who they are and who they expect to become, this confidence and self-assuredness prepares them to deal with uncertainties and challenges they will encounter that could threaten their sense of self. Youth who have explored their ethnic or racial background and have a clear sense of the meaning of this part of their identity are able to draw on this information when trying to make sense of an unfair experience such as ethnic-racial discrimination.[74] Consider the following comment from a fourteen-year-old Latino male: "My ethnicity is my pride of where I come from and one of my identities. That means that I should protect it from anyone who insults it. It is also being part of a group and feeling belonged [*sic*]." This adolescent's knowledge and understanding of how race and ethnicity play out in society can serve as a tool, so to speak, to help him cope with the experience of discrimination. Youth who do not have such tools may be more negatively affected by such experiences because of limited coping abilities or harmful coping strategies, such as turning to substance use or acting out in other ways.

Considering that youth are exposed daily to rhetoric that disparages groups of people based on their ethnic and racial group memberships, it is essential that they are equipped with tools that will help them navigate this inevitable social milieu. For example, during the 2016 US presidential election, Republican Party nominee Donald Trump stated on national television that most Mexican immigrants in the United States were criminals, drug dealers, and rapists, though he assumed some were good people. Another event that made national news in 2016 involved six female high school seniors in Arizona who posed in a picture wearing T-shirts that collectively spelled "NI**ER."[75] This picture was posted on the social media site Snapchat, and the events that unfolded created a hostile environment for all students in the school, whose student body was comprised of 63% White, 14% Latino, 9% Asian, 7% Black, 4% Multiracial, and 1% American Indian students. A small numerical minority of the school population was Black, yet the entire school and the surrounding community was shaken. Many people who appeared on the local news could not believe that such hatred still existed in their community, yet others were outraged that the students had been suspended from school for something so "minor."

Making sense of these experiences (and diverse perspectives) requires youth to have a general understanding of race relations, but also an understanding of stereotypes that exist toward their (and others') groups, and the ability to recognize that acts of discrimination and unfair treatment are a function of stereotypes based on group membership rather than on something specific to the individual victim(s) of discrimination. Such an understanding can help youth better navigate these harmful experiences. Many studies have demonstrated the deleterious effects that ethnic-racial discrimination can have on youths' mental health and academic adjustment; however, a number of studies have also demonstrated that adolescents who have a clearer sense of their ethnic-racial identity, and those who feel more positively about their ethnic-racial group membership, are protected against the negative effects of discrimination on their mental health and their self-esteem.[76]

MOVING BEYOND LABELS

> [P]eople say that, "Oh, like, like, oh, you don't look Indian" or "You don't act Indian," like when people first meet me they're always like, "I thought you were Mexican" ... "Oh, I thought you were mixed" ... and I was like, "No guys, I'm just Indian," so it 'cause sometimes I kinda feel like, well, like what does that mean? Like, I don't look Indian? Like, is there a way that someone's supposed to look? Or a way that someone's supposed to act? And I'm like, "well, *sorry!*"
> **—SIXTEEN-YEAR-OLD ASIAN INDIAN FEMALE**

The labels that others choose for youth or the labels that youth choose for themselves matter less—in terms of their well-being, their adjustment, or their feelings about themselves—than the identities youth develop for themselves.[77] The development of ethnic-racial identity involves engaging in universal processes of exploring the identity, gaining a sense of clarity about this part of the self, and ascribing meaning to one's group membership. Today's youth are growing up in a society where blatant acts of racism and discrimination are still commonplace,[78] and technological advances have only increased direct and vicarious exposure to these negative experiences. Consider that although some may argue that racism is not as prevalent as it was in decades past, today's youth may actually be confronted with the trauma of racism and discrimination on a more regular basis because of constant access to social media.[79] For instance, news of traumatic events is not only reported on twenty-four hours a day on cable television news channels but appears on people's newsfeeds and social media platforms all day long. Thus, youth are continuously reliving the potentially traumatic events. This also means that regardless of whether derogatory comments or incidents are directed toward the group in which one is a member, such toxic rhetoric affects everyone who is exposed to it. Individuals who are members of the target group, however, have the potential to internalize the negative messages conveyed by a discriminatory event. For this reason, developing an informed ethnic-racial identity is particularly important for youth who are members of ethnic-racial minority groups. Such youth are simply more likely to be the targets of ethnic-racial discrimination and are thus at higher risk for threats to their sense of self.

A final comment we'd like to make about the use of labels is that the words "race" and "ethnicity" are not necessarily used by youth on a daily basis, yet they represent constructs that shape youths' everyday experiences. Anecdotally, we have observed in our work with teenagers that many students often ask us to define or clarify the meaning of the word "ethnicity" when they are asked to record their ethnicity on surveys. When we explain that the word refers to a person's heritage, cultural background, or countries where their ancestors are from, they immediately understand, and most of them quickly respond with a label that is reflective of ethnic groups in US society. What is perplexing about this is that adolescents are well aware of the labels assigned to ethnic groups, are aware of stereotypes associated with different groups, and engage with this concept in their lives on an almost daily basis—yet they do not necessarily know what to call it. What does this mean? Perhaps it means that many adolescents are not having conversations with adults in their lives who would be able to help them name the phenomenon of which they are clearly aware. Such conversations could help youth develop a more informed understanding of this concept and the way it shapes people's experiences in the current social and historical context. This type of discussion is necessary to combat erroneous perceptions that the reason labels exist is because there are *innate* differences between groups of people that accurately predict behavior and, in turn, that the constant use of these labels is justified.

———

We talk to our kids about the dangers of smoking, doing drugs, drinking. We teach them—through words and actions—not to hit, not to steal. We tell them over and over again what's right and what's wrong, to eat their vegetables, to say please and thank you, to not lie. But on the subjects of race and racism, many White parents are simply mute. We avoid the specifics of the topic and hope the broader message somehow gets through. But there are numerous experts who say that if we DO NOT have conversations—direct, honest, open dialogue with our children about bigotry, privilege, injustice and violence—we could be teaching them the very thing we are trying to avoid. I would say that pretty much everyone I know would be horrified if that was their child marching in Charlottesville. But before you say, "My kid would NEVER do that," think about this: What message might you be sending them by simply being uncomfortable talking about race?[80]

—GINGER ROUGH, NEWS DIRECTOR/STRATEGIST

There is no question that adolescents' day-to-day experiences involving race and ethnicity will play a role in shaping their understanding and beliefs about race and ethnicity, and how these abstract concepts play a role in their lives, but significant adult figures in youths' lives can intercept the meaning-making process by engaging in meaningful conversations with them, to help them make sense of these experiences. The realization and raw understanding of injustices based on race and ethnicity, without the words to express it and without the freedom to discuss it with adults who might help a teen understand why it is the way it is, contributes to a continued burying of the issue and active discomfort with openly discussing race and ethnicity. Our silence communicates to youth that this topic is something to be accepted (this is just the way it is) and not discussed (we do not talk about it). As presented in this chapter, the lack of attention to this aspect of the self, and the avoidance of directly addressing issues of race and ethnicity, can have significant negative consequences for youths' development and general well-being. As we will discuss in the following chapters, having these sometimes-difficult conversations will be critical for youths' positive development. Furthermore, *without* these conversations, adolescents still develop an understanding of race and ethnicity, but this understanding is limited to the sensationalized accounts of racial tensions and xenophobia they see portrayed in media, or through interactions with peers or other significant individuals in their lives in which stereotypes are often unintentionally perpetuated.

4

How Do Youth Form Their Ideas about Ethnicity and Race?

> Learning race is like learning a language. First we try mouthing all sounds. Then we learn which are not words and which have meaning to the people around us.
>
> —DALTON CONLEY, *HONKY*

Having established that identity is multifaceted and that adolescence is an important time for its development, we now turn to a consideration of the multiple contexts in which adolescents make sense of ethnicity and race in daily life. Although the family remains an immediate influence on ethnic-racial identity during adolescence, as we discuss, school, peers, the broader community, and the media gain significant traction at this time of life, as youth are able to, and desire to, venture beyond the familiar. New experiences displace previously established understandings of race and ethnicity to ultimately help youth more fully flesh out their ethnic-racial identities. What's more, although adolescents are implicitly and explicitly taught about ethnicity and race in myriad contexts, family, school, peer, community, and media influences are not simply unidirectional. Young people's own thinking about ethnicity and race shapes their understanding of interactions and experiences as well. The process of ethnic-racial identity formation is therefore a cyclical one, as new experiences continually reveal avenues to reconsider one's identity. By the end of this chapter, we hope readers will better understand when we say that the question is not "Where do young people 'learn race'?" but rather "Where *don't* they?"

Family

I don't know how to read and write in my language so my dad bought like reading and writing books for me to like learn how to write, 'cause I never learned it at school. So, he like brings books there, but I mean, I try, I don't get the time 'cause of like other school work and stuff. So he tries to make me watch the news and stuff, and so like while I'm watching the news, I have to watch it in my language like 'cause we have the television that's like broadcasted here.

—SIXTEEN-YEAR-OLD ASIAN INDIAN FEMALE

I'm Vietnamese, and I can speak Vietnamese, because my family is all Vietnamese. So, it's like, hard to just like, forget my culture, 'cause it's like, there at home, like they're not gonna like convert to English just for me.

—SEVENTEEN-YEAR-OLD VIETNAMESE FEMALE

Being Mexican means a lot to me. My family regularly visits Mexico and follow[s] all Mexican traditions. We eat lots of authentic Mexican food and celebrate Mexican holidays. We have piñatas on our birthdays and eat tortillas for lunch. Mostly, we embrace traditions and everything about being Mexican. My mom lived in Mexico, so this is normal to her, and it regularly happens in our house, so it is normal to me.

—THIRTEEN-YEAR-OLD LATINA GIRL

In the United States, child-rearing often involves navigating issues of race and ethnicity. Because parents are primarily responsible for where children live and go to school, and by extension who they can most easily befriend, they set the stage for how youth will be exposed to race and ethnicity in their everyday environments. Families, more generally, also model what race, ethnicity, and culture mean in one's life. What youth hear, observe, and notice to be the case in their family context, not surprisingly, provides the first fodder for identity development. Unlike with young children, parents of adolescents are typically not able to shield their kids from the realities of racial and ethnic relations. As they get older, adolescents unquestionably have more access—by virtue of the Internet, peers, and popular culture—to how race and ethnicity are lived beyond one's family. One issue to consider is whether parents' efforts to address or avoid racial issues align with youths' own experiences and understandings of such matters. In some cases, misalignment between what parents say and what youth perceive can be turning points for youths' ethnic-racial identity development. But whether or not parents' and children's experiences concerning race and ethnicity are discrepant, what youth learn in the family context lays the foundation upon which they make their assessments of the meaning of race and ethnicity in the broader social world: Is it something to celebrate, grapple with, actively avoid, or simply ignore?

One way that youth learn race is in the lesson that it should go unnoticed, be avoided, and not talked about (or done so euphemistically). The most basic opportunity to begin a dialogue about race might occur when a young child asks for the first time, "What color am I?" (literally), after noticing the "colors" of other people. In adolescence, however, the questions become more complex, and the issues young people may be wondering about with regard to race, or the worries they may have, require less simple answers. Youth likely won't directly ask a question about race in a context where they have learned they could be reprimanded for even noticing it in some way. For many, in a society that is fraught with racial tensions—and was, until recently, paradoxically referred to as "postracial"[1]—the desire to downplay differences among groups makes intuitive sense.

It is understandable that some parents would like to emphasize our sameness, or to adopt what's known as a color-blind approach to race and ethnicity. It somehow feels as though the "right" or "just" thing to do is to tell children to adopt a color-blind stance. Often, the color-blind approach goes hand in hand with messages about egalitarianism, so that parents might say, "We're all the same *and* we should treat everyone equally." Who could argue with that? But where does that leave us when kids notice that we are not "all the same," which they do at a very young age, as introduced in chapter 3? And what about when youth get older and realize that members of different racial and ethnic groups are *not* treated equally in this society? It's unrealistic to expect youth to make sense of the realities they may personally experience as a result of their ethnic-racial background, or make sense of what they see playing out in the news or social media, when they have been told that "we are all the same." The ethnic-racial injustices they witness at school, in their neighborhood, and in the broader society send a very different message. Thus, we cannot expect adolescents to be prepared to grapple with the consequences and meaning of race and ethnicity in our society if we have not provided the building blocks of understanding during childhood and, instead, have emphasized messages suggesting that differences do not exist.

The need to answer youths' questions meaningfully means that the color-blind approach is *not* the way forward for parents who wish to promote positive identity and race relations among youth in the United States. As one parent states:

> White parents need to be talking to our children about racism. As I've written before, more than once, not talking about racial differences doesn't tell children that we don't notice that people have different colored skin and differently textured hair. It tells them that *we don't talk about things like that*.[2]

As we see it, there are two key problems with the strategy of negating difference. First, minimizing the noticing of difference at home means that youth cannot count on their family to help them understand, negotiate, and effectively engage with race and racial issues when they do notice them *outside* the home, such as at school, among peers, and in the media. Color blindness leaves youth at a loss to engage with parents and other caregivers regarding what they notice in the world around them. These same parents would not want to shut the door to conversations about sex or drugs, so why do it with race and ethnicity?

Second, the color-blind approach at home more or less erases some of the stories that might make up individuals' identities more generally. Knowing that a family recipe has been handed down from an Italian or Mexican great-grandparent might form an important part of an individual's understanding of their family, their heritage, and, by extension, themselves. The legacy of slavery and ongoing racism in the United States also means that sharing stories of survival and self-preservation—as in Ta-Nehisi Coates's letter to his son *Between the World and Me*—are necessary expressions of both an individual's humanity and obligation as a parent:

> I write you in your fifteenth year. I am writing you because this was the year you saw Eric Garner choked to death for selling cigarettes; because you know now that Renisha McBride was shot for seeking help; that John Crawford was shot down for browsing in a department store. And you have seen men in the same uniform drive by and murder Tamir Rice, a twelve-year-old child.[3]

The color-blind approach interferes with our ability to fully know the complex ways race and ethnicity are lived by our friends, neighbors, classmates, and even other family members. But equally as important, by not allowing others to tell their stories, share the histories, process their grief, or celebrate the joys that emanate from that complexity, we constrain their humanity.

One reason why some White parents adopt a color-blind approach is the belief that downplaying difference is a good strategy for mitigating any potential expression of superiority by their children. They might think that if they say we are all the same, then their child will not develop a sense of superiority over others based on their race. As psychologist Phyllis Katz has reported in her work with parents of young children,[4] some White parents are concerned that talking about race will make their children aware of racial differences that they may otherwise not have noticed and perhaps make them more prejudiced. On the contrary, what Katz and her colleagues have found is that children who were least biased at age six were those whose parents had talked to them about race at an early age. An alternative way of framing this is the belief that talking about race implies that one is racist. Yet telling a child that everyone is the same does not prepare her to actively work against perpetrating or perpetuating racial prejudice and discrimination, especially when it manifests in subtle ways. In fact, experimental research by Julie Hughes, Rebecca Bigler, and colleagues has demonstrated that teaching White children about historical racism actually improved their attitudes toward African Americans, in part because these youth valued racial fairness more than they had previously.[5]

Parents need to avoid the pitfalls of the color-blind approach in order to disrupt social exclusion based on other stated nonracial characteristics that may inadvertently result in racial exclusion.[6] Psychologist Melanie Killen has shown that White and ethnic-racial minority youth both recognize social exclusion due explicitly to race as morally wrong. Minority youth, who have presumably been exposed to more subtle forms of discrimination, also recognized that excluding peers due to reasons that were not explicitly race-based, such as lack of familiarity or shared interests (e.g., not liking the same activities), was wrong. If interrupting racism is the end goal, then talking about race and racism in its overt *and* covert forms, rather than denying that it exists, is essential.[7] At the very least, such acknowledgment can help us be aware of how our biases— ones we may not be fully aware of or openly admit—may be undermining our stated values for diversity and equity.

WHEN PARENTS DO TALK ABOUT RACE AND ETHNICITY, WHAT DO THEY TALK ABOUT?

> I think more than anything instilling in them the pride of being ... of being Hispanic, of being Mexican ... the respect, the family, to feel proud of, of being ... of being Mexican. Because unfortunately racism exists here and, well, like to prepare them a little.
> —MEXICAN IMMIGRANT MOTHER[8]

We know from research that parents can serve as an invaluable resource for questions about race and ethnicity, and doing so is important for adolescents' positive development. When families do more to expose their youth to their ethnic-racial background and to help them gain an understanding of their heritage, adolescents demonstrate better psychological well-being, success in school, and a greater sense of social competence. The less youth are confused or at a loss to understand themselves and the world around them—and this includes being grounded in the racial and ethnic aspects of their experiences—the more likely they are to thrive in important ways. Diane Hughes and her colleagues have shown that one of the most common ways families engage with race and ethnicity at home is by inculcating an understanding of cultural values, traditions, and their heritage, known as *cultural socialization*.[9] Cultural socialization is practiced not only by parents but also by extended family members such as grandparents, aunts, uncles, and others who may not be related by blood or marriage but are considered family. Involvement with extended family is seen as integral for reinforcing desired cultural values.[10] In some families, cultural socialization can also take the form of speaking and being exposed to media in the heritage language and traveling back to one's heritage country.

Studies with multiple groups—Black, Latino, Asian American, and White, among others—have shown that cultural socialization is consistently linked to young people's ethnic-racial identity. For instance, cultural socialization in families is associated with stronger and more positive ethnic identity beliefs among youth in those families—a finding echoed in numerous studies of diverse Latino, African American, and Asian American adolescents.[11] In our work, we have found that families' efforts to instill and maintain a connection to one's ethnic group is linked to adolescents' greater exploration of this aspect of their identity, and having a greater clarity about their identity. The few studies of cultural socialization with young adults, which include individuals of diverse ethnic heritages ages eighteen to thirty, suggest that exposure to parents' such efforts also influences young people's exploration of their identity, how important they feel it is in defining who they are as a person, and how positively they feel about their group.[12]

What's more, Black, Latino, Asian American, and White youth have all been shown to benefit socially and academically from cultural socialization at home.[13] Hughes and her colleagues studied Black and White youth in fourth through sixth grade in a racially balanced Northeastern suburban school district to see if cultural socialization would be more beneficial for African American youth as compared to their White peers attending the same schools. They found that in this context, where neither group was in the ethnic-racial majority, both Black and White youth whose parents had emphasized a positive sense of their racial heritage also tended to believe they could master the material they were learning in school and be generally more interested in and like school. In addition, these youth tended to report having engaged in fewer antisocial behaviors, such as having taken money without asking from their mom's purse. Our work in the Southwest region of the United States shows similar positive benefits of cultural socialization for Mexican-heritage youth. In one study, Mexican-origin youth who received more cultural socialization from their mothers as fifth graders went on to develop more positive ethnic identities and, in turn, a more positive sense of mastery about learning in school and greater feelings of social competence, as well as less depression and fewer acting out behaviors as seventh graders.[14]

In addition to providing information and cultivating a sense of one's cultural heritage, some families also address issues of prejudice and discrimination with their adolescent children, a phenomenon referred to by Hughes and her colleagues as *preparation for bias*. Preparation for bias among ethnic-racial minority families is thought to be protective for adolescents and young adults who find they must construct a sense of the importance and meaning of their ethnicity or race in the face of negative messages about their group. There is good evidence from numerous studies, not to mention myriad examples highlighted in the media, that ethnic-racial minority young people encounter discrimination from adults and peers in everyday contexts.[15] As psychologists Howard Stevenson and Diane Hughes and colleagues, respectively, note,[16] a number of parents attempt to prepare their children for such experiences proactively by talking about or telling stories related to discrimination. Parents who engage in this type of activity often believe that having been proactively taught about racism means their children will not be caught by surprise if they should encounter discrimination, and also that they will have had time to develop effective coping strategies should they have such encounters. Indeed, studies by Stevenson and his colleagues show that preparing kids for derogation and devaluation, when coupled with strategies and tools for how to negotiate these experiences, yields positive benefits in school for African American youth.

Many studies also demonstrate that families' ability to prepare their adolescents for discrimination is important for youth of immigrant origins.[17] Asian American and Latino youth who were born in the United States but have immigrant parents can sometimes feel they are neither fully "American" nor fully of their parents' home country. The national debates about race can tend to emphasize a Black-White dynamic. But as they grow up in the United States, Latinos and Asian Americans may come to conclude that their everyday encounters add up to something other than full inclusion.

One seemingly innocuous example of this is when a person who appears to be Latino or Asian American is asked, "Where are you from?" and the response, "from the United States," leads to the follow-up question, "But where are you *really* from?" As one recent Asian American respondent in the *New York Times* video series, *A Conversation on Race*, poignantly notes, "You can ask me where I'm from, but just believe my answer."[18] Empirical studies by Brian Armenta, Rich Lee, and colleagues, for example, show how Latino and Asian Americans are vulnerable to social stereotypes and exclusion due to others' perceptions of their proficiency in English or citizenship status.[19] With regard to the role of parents in youths' awareness of these biases, our own work with Latino students at an elite university found that the more youth had received more preparation for bias from their parents, the more likely they were to believe their instructors held low expectations for them, and the more barriers they perceived to educational and economic opportunity for nonnative English speakers.[20]

Latino and Asian American youth also report blatant experiences of discrimination, as evidenced in a study of Mexican-origin

youth conducted by psychologist Stephen Quintana and his colleagues.[21] Quintana and his colleagues found that youth reported
discrimination in the form of being treated differently at restau-
rants because of their Mexican heritage, and they also perceived
that White students received preferential treatment by teachers,
such that teachers would help them more and treat them more positively. Similarly, in our work with Chinese American and African
American youth in New York City, we found that Chinese American youth actually reported higher levels of discrimination by peers
than did African American youth.[22] Thus, experiences of ethnic-
racial discrimination are a significant reality, and families' efforts
to prepare youth for these experiences can play an important role
in youths' eventual adjustment.

It's worth noting that, regardless of which group particular youth
belong to, exposure to more preparation for bias at home might engender a sense of conflict about their ethnic-racial identities. Simply
put, it might be harder to muster a willingness to interact with individuals from other ethnic and racial groups if you are more attuned
to how those people might exclude, avoid, or generally think less of
you because of your group membership. Those less attuned are less
prepared for it, but they are also less conscious of stereotyping and
prejudice targeted at them. This does not mean that the stereotyping and prejudice actually occur less frequently, objectively speaking, just that youth do not have to expend energy worrying about it.
But to be clear: While "not worrying about it" may seem like a benefit of not directly addressing issues of race and ethnicity with youth,
the negative consequences of this are that unaware youth will not
be prepared for how to cope with these experiences or, possibly
worse, interpret the exclusion they are experiencing to be a reflection of some internal personal characteristic. Rationalizing social
exclusion as being due to some immutable internal characteristic
can more *negatively* impact youths' self-concepts and may instead
attribute the negative experience to external bias against a group
and the negative experience to bias against something inherently
negative about themselves.[23]

Parents often deliberate about when and how to teach youth about potential prejudice and discrimination, often considering ways to scaffold pertinent information based on how "ready" youth are for particular kinds of conversations, stories, books, excursions, and the like. It is not something to engage with casually or carelessly. We know from Hughes's and our own studies that young people are not just vessels into which parents pour cultural and racial knowledge, but rather parents are responsive to the age of those youth and the questions they themselves raise about these issues as they try to make sense of their social worlds.[24]

Perhaps the most important point we wish to make, then, is that parents and caregivers should be ready and willing to engage youths' questions about racism or xenophobia in ways that make sense, given what they know about their children. Adolescents also more easily recognize hypocrisy than younger children, so it is important to be frank and know that sometimes the most honest response is, simply, "I don't know." And then try to find out. Finally, an important thing to keep in mind is that the more difficult conversations about race and ethnicity that will inevitably arise in adolescence and involve discussions of racism, discrimination, power, privilege, and social injustices will be relatively easier to have if basic discussions, such as acknowledging difference and teaching youth to recognize the value in celebrating and valuing all backgrounds, have not been avoided in early childhood when children first become aware of differences.

Schools

[I]n one of my classes, I have like five friends who are all Filipino and then like some of them can speak Tagalog and so like in class, we would just speak in Tagalog and then like no one else would know what we were talking about, it would be *so* funny … and it's like, it's like your own little club, it's like you have that connection, and um, when you have that, if you have friends who understand like your culture, your um little bubble of life. You like, like you can share things. Like one of my other friends, like he brings in food from the Philippines all the time and he would like feed me. And it would be amazing 'cause like, "How did you get this?" it's like, "I don't know where you got this." He's like, "Oh, I get shipments like once in a while from back home," and I'm like, "Oh my gosh, I haven't eaten this in like forever."

—SIXTEEN-YEAR-OLD FILIPINO FEMALE

My ethnicity means a lot to me, because I feel like when I'm in school or in other places, I look for people with the same ethnicity. It's like a sense of belonging as well.

—FOURTEEN-YEAR-OLD LATINA GIRL

Graduates often find ways to stick out in the sea of robes and mortarboards, and recent ceremonies have seen students draped in flower leis (Asian students) maile and/or orchid leis (students of Pacific Islander heritage), or stoles that indicate their ethnicity or affiliation with their major or Greek organization. In Montana they're going one better: Gov. Steve Bullock just signed a bill that allows Native American students to decorate their robes with culturally traditional touches (eagle feathers, beads, etc.) to mark the occasion. There had been objections from some school administrators and acceptance by others. Now this removes that resistance.[25]

—K. G. BATES, EXCERPT FROM NPR'S *CODE SWITCH*

LEARNING TOGETHER

Putting aside what youth learn at home, we concur with social scientists Adriana Aldana and Christy Byrd, that a great deal of ethnic-racial socialization occurs in school halls, cafeterias, and classrooms in adolescence, and on college campuses in later years.[26] Everywhere one turns, it seems there is evidence of how race and ethnicity shape the daily experience of youth in school: who they learn with, who they sit with at lunch, and who they hang out with. It makes a lot of sense that youth turn to each other to pick up signals about what is expected when it comes to racial and ethnic identity. And though we focus on the US context here, this process is not unique to the United States, as scholars examine how school experiences shape youths' ethnic and racial identities in various places around the world, such as Germany, Greece, the Netherlands, Italy, the United Kingdom, and essentially any countries that have undergone, or are undergoing, dramatic shifts in their youth populations due to immigration. Thus, it turns out that the question posed by Beverly Tatum almost twenty years ago—"Why are all the Black kids sitting together in the cafeteria?"—is one that can be and has been asked more broadly, for instance, in Ananthi Al Ramiah and colleagues' recent work mapping out social divisions among White and South Asian students in a UK high school.[27] From studies in the US context, we are learning that if youths' ethnicity or race is important to their sense of self and they are in schools in which they are not the majority, having peers around from their own group can help them feel more comfortable with their identity, as Sara Douglass, Sheena Mirpuri, and Tiffany Yip have found in their research with Asian American youth in New York City.[28]

One reason the kids sit together literally and figuratively, then, is to figure out who they are and where they belong, and it is the case that friends tend to be alike in their ethnic-racial identities. In a study of college students, Moin Syed and M.J.D. Juan found that pairs of friends were similar in the extent to which they explored and felt strongly connected to their ethnic-racial groups.[29] The similarity of pairs in which both students were ethnic minorities was explained in part by how much students said they typically rely on friends as a sounding board for thinking through ethnic and racial issues. This suggests that, for young people, friendships are important contexts for the evolution of their views regarding ethnicity and race. Syed's work suggests that not only are friends similar in their ethnic and racial identities, but that they may shape each other's thinking about those identities over time.

Indeed, this is just what we have found in our studies of middle school students in US communities in the Midwest and Southwest.[30] In these studies of ethnically and racially diverse students attending diverse schools, we found that students become even more similar in their ethnic-racial identities over the course of one year.[31] Although many adolescents indeed flocked together along ethnic-racial lines, as is typical, members of each "flock" significantly influenced each other's subjective, psychological sense of identity, too. In other words, youths' views *evolved* as a function of their friendship. This opens up possibilities for youth from different ethnic-racial groups to form bonds based on a shared process of developing their identities (e.g., talking through ethnic-racial issues) rather than demographic categories that are relatively more superficial. Consistent with this idea, we also found in the same study that boys and girls who had more diverse friends at the beginning of the academic year also reported engaging in more questioning and information-seeking about their own ethnicity and race at the end of the academic year.

Friends, simply put, matter a great deal in the ethnic-racial identity process among adolescents, just as they do for myriad issues during this period of life. This is not surprising, given their increasingly greater reliance on peers, more generally, as harbingers of what is good, acceptable, and desirable in a particular social and cultural context, such as school. Studies by Prudence Carter, Stacey Lee, Susan Rosenbloom and Niobe Way, and Natasha Warikoo, among others, have shown how young people pick up and negotiate information about language, style, and dress from peers in school in ways that help them to construct their own ethnic and racial identities.[32] Yet peers not only serve as models of what particular ethnic-racial identities can look and sound like in school, but they also regulate each other to maintain conformity to particular identity ideals and social hierarchies.

The social cues to which youth are exposed range from ones that are relatively innocuous (what's cool) to ones that can inflict psychological harm. Consider the following exchange that a sixteen-year-old Asian Indian female adolescent recalled having with a peer during the eighth grade:

> So one time, it was in the eighth grade, um, this guy thought I was Arabic or something and then he like brought up, he just like brought up the 911 or something, and then he was like "Oh,

do you have a bomb with you?" and I was like "That is *so mean*," and I was like, how does that like, that doesn't even make any sense like, why would you just like associate that with *me*, just because I look Middle Eastern or whatever, and then he was just like "Oh, well I jus—, like, I was just joking."

Peer interactions regarding racial and ethnic issues such as the one described here can leave youth feeling ambivalent at best. Studies by education researcher Mica Pollock and psychologist Sara Douglass and colleagues, respectively, show that kids in school use humor to convey their expectations to one another regarding norms concerning race-based behaviors.[33] As documented in recent work by Douglass and her colleagues, adolescents will say things like, "Yeah, I play around with them, like 'Stop being a lazy Mexican and get on the drums.' It's just like that."[34] Seemingly innocuous hallway humor and teasing is often seen as a way to communicate suggestively racist messages while minimizing the extent to which one is accused of being racist, because perpetrating youth can safely claim that they were "just making jokes" or "JK" and, worse, that those expressing offense or discomfort "can't take a joke."

Meanwhile, target and bystander youth must decide what to do in such situations, leading to a host of questions: What does it mean that they laughed—or didn't? Will challenging the joke incur a social penalty, such as ostracism? What do they do with the feelings brought on by racist jokes and the circumstances surrounding them? Indeed, there are several blogs about how to navigate the often hurtful minefield of racialized humor among targets and bystanders (some examples are provided at the end of this chapter).[35] An important note here is that Douglass and her colleagues found that, in general, these experiences of ethnic-racial teasing are *not* harmless and do have negative consequences for adolescents' mental health.

Another way for youth to regulate each other's identities is to accuse each other of wanting or trying to be of a different ethnic or racial group. Much has been written about the accusation of "acting White," a notion initially put forward by Signithia Fordham and

John Ogbu, based on their observations of Black youth in a predominantly Black school,[36] but there are other variations of this
idea. As Prudence Carter clarifies, being accused of acting White
is a way for youth to reject not Whiteness per se but rather those
peers who are perceived to repudiate Blackness. Considered in this
light, an accusation of inauthenticity serves the same purpose when
it is levied by any group and references any other: Puerto Rican
youth trying to be Asian, White youth wanting to be Black, and
so on. Eddie Huang writes in his memoir *Fresh Off the Boat* about
the dilemma of growing up as a Chinese American who identifies
strongly with hip-hop culture:

> All my life people would call me a [ch-nk] or a [ch-gger]. I
> couldn't listen to hip-hop and be myself without people ques-
> tioning my authenticity. Chinese people questioned my yellow-
> ness because I was born in America. Then white people ques-
> tioned my identity as an American because I was yellow ... We
> can't fucking win. If I follow the rules and play the model mi-
> nority, I'm a lapdog under a bamboo ceiling. If I like hip-hop
> because I see solidarity, I'm aping.[37]

Being taunted for behaviors and styles considered "fresh off the
boat," or, conversely, accused of being "too Americanized," similarly signal what is considered more and less acceptable among
groups that can be subdivided into US-born and foreign-born. As
Stacey Lee has shown,[38] even youth who *others* might consider to
be part of the same group (e.g., Asians, Koreans) can make important social distinctions among themselves by accusing each other
of belonging to a presumably less desirable category, namely, being
an immigrant or behaving, dressing, or talking like an immigrant.
Conversely, as Angela Valenzuela and others have observed, from
the immigrant youths' perspective, adopting undesirable American dispositions and tastes also justifies admonitions for being "too
Americanized"—for example, straying too far from the presumed
ideals of their homelands or not speaking the native language.[39]

The point is that adolescents are vigilant about one another's dispositions and behaviors, and they construct mutually negotiated

boundaries of authentic group membership. They reject their peers' presumed repudiation of what, in their particular school context, is understood to be Black, White, Mexican, Korean, and so on. Never mind that there is no single way to "be" part of a group. What matters is that, in their accusations, it is understood that youth have the authority to regulate one another and stigmatize those who deviate from arguably arbitrary, and often locally defined, norms for particular social identities. And they are well versed in the discursive practices (e.g., making jokes, hurling accusations) that establish and maintain norms. The central role of peer norms is not surprising, given their importance for a number of other activities, such as substance use, sex, and academic achievement, during this time of life.

THE ADULTS IN THE BUILDING

Adolescents are not just watching their peers, and issues of race and ethnicity do not just bubble up in peer interactions and culture in school. How race and ethnicity are negotiated among youth in school should be understood within a broader framework of schooling, the conditions for which adults are ultimately responsible. Are peer interactions about race couched in a conflicted, alienating, and inequitable space or one that is harmonious, emotionally supportive, and equitable? School staff—the adults in the building, which include teachers but also administrators and other staff—make the rules and set the widest-reaching ethnic and racial norms.[40] Accordingly, the adults are the ones who set the scene for some of the ways in which students engage with racial and ethnic issues in schools and, importantly, for whether youths' identities will be compatible with the aims of education. Often, as Angela Valenzuela poignantly wrote in her seminal ethnography of Latino high schoolers, "schooling is a *subtractive* process. It divests these youth of important social and cultural resources."[41] As explained by Valenzuela, the school does not provide a context where relationships can be based on authentic caring between teachers and students, students' names and identities get altered in the process of schooling, and

students' ability to speak a language other than English is devalued
and considered a barrier to overcome.

As they do with parents and peers, youth are observing and
making sense of what adults at school do (or ignore) and say (or are
silent about) with regard to race. When White youth attend an all-
White school where race is never addressed explicitly, they too are
learning about race: they are learning how to not notice and talk
about it, perhaps how to avoid it altogether. Mica Pollock has written eloquently about how adults struggle to talk about race, coining
the term *colormute* to describe the anxious ways in which adults in
schools simultaneously engage with issues of race while also avoiding explicitly naming them as such.[42] In her ethnography, for example, she finds that in attempting to address racial inequalities,
educators often used the term "all" or referred to "all students" due
to concerns about appearing racist. She writes:

> There is a word that pervades contemporary educational dis-
> course, revolutionary to some and evasive to others. It functions
> as both a strikingly precise and strikingly vague call for educa-
> tional equity. The word is "all" ... Race is nowhere explicit in talk
> of education for "all" ... race is deeply buried in the word—and
> as a policy word that is colormute and race-loaded simultane-
> ously, "all" can be both a useful and a dangerous word for equal-
> ity efforts.[43]

Such colormuteness is paradoxical and potentially confusing to
youth, of course, given that race manifests in many ways, regardless
of whether it is explicitly acknowledged by the adults. So what are
some of the things youth might notice?

One is the sorting of different groups of students across courses
with different academic and (occupational) expectations, such as
honors, advanced placement, and general education. Youth notice
who surrounds them in class, especially if they are the only, or one
of a few, members of their ethnic-racial group. Because academic
tracking is by definition hierarchical, the (lack of) representation
of groups at each level also sends a signal about more general societal expectations for each group's future, for instance, who is and

can be college-bound. This socialization occurs even in a school that has a predominantly racial minority population, as we see in a study conducted by Gilberto Conchas of three academies within one high school.[44] He showed that academically achieving, college-aspiring Latino students can have vastly different understandings of whether their identities are compatible with school success depending on the academy in which they were enrolled—one group felt they needed to shed their ethnic ties to move up in the world, while the other felt their academic success was a way to positively represent their ethnic community.

Numerous studies of disproportionality in the administration of discipline in school, such as work by Jeremy Finn, Russell Skiba, Pedro Noguera, and their respective colleagues,[45] have also highlighted racialized patterns in who gets punished, suspended, and expelled. In one seminal study of an elementary school, Ann Ferguson explained how adults' attitudes toward African American boys and about their possible futures (or lack thereof) were implicated in their surveillance of such youth.[46] This ultimately resulted in the overuse of a place she referred to as "the Punishing Room" and another place the boys themselves called "the Jailhouse." We know from national studies that Black and Latino youth are more likely to be suspended and expelled than White youth for the same misbehaviors,[47] and recent reports out of the US Department of Education Office for Civil Rights demonstrate that these disparities shockingly begin in the preschool years: Black preschool children are 3.6 times more likely to be suspended than White preschool children.[48] What message do these practices send to youth about what it means to be Black or Latino in this society?

Against the backdrop of more general ethnic-racial patterns and placement, youth must also navigate their own individual interactions with adults at school. Adolescents notice the dynamics, positive and negative, of such interactions. With regard to race, these dynamics signal how adults view the youth, not only as individuals but also as members of ethnic-racial groups.

Negative interactions with adults at school due to race or ethnicity are well documented in studies by Celia Fisher, Aprile Benner,

Niobe Way, Diane Hughes, and in our own work in the Northeast, Southwest, and Midwest regions of the United States.[49] For example, in one study we asked Black, Puerto Rican, Dominican, Chinese American, and White sixth graders in New York City how often they felt adults at school treated them negatively—such as presuming they were troublemakers, perceiving them as threatening, or according them less respect—because of their race or ethnicity.[50] Black youth reported more instances of discrimination by adults at school than all others. Lest we leave the impression that this is solely a problem for Black youth, however, it is worth noting that Dominican and Chinese American youth also reported more instances of adult discrimination at school than White youth. Furthermore, research by Selcuk Sirin and Michelle Fine documents the discrimination that Muslim youth encounter.[51] One recent illustration is the notorious clock incident in Texas, which is widely regarded as a particularly egregious example of Islamophobia in school. As one outlet described:

> A 14-year-old boy says he was just trying to show off his engineering skill when he brought a digital clock he had made to his new high school in Irving, Texas. But Ahmed Mohamed was detained and reportedly suspended from school, after a teacher thought that his clock looked like a bomb.
>
> The aspiring engineer repeatedly said that it was not, in fact, a bomb. But the teacher and the principal of MacArthur High School were alarmed, and they called police, who questioned Mohamed, handcuffed him and led him out of school. He was then fingerprinted before being released to his family, who say he received a three-day suspension from school.
>
> Ahmed Mohamed also gave the newspaper his account of the day in a video in which he says, "It made me feel like I wasn't human. It made me feel like I was a criminal."[52]

Youth might ask themselves, then, why do teachers treat the kids who speak, look, act, or dress like me in a hostile, uncaring, or disrespectful way? Youth may further wonder, rightfully, why being a member of a particular ethnic or racial group automatically implicates them as troublemakers, or worse, potential criminals.

Meanwhile, Asian American youth contend with the particular burden of the model minority stereotype, or the idea that they are smart, industrious, hardworking "good kids." These are all seemingly positive traits, so why do we refer to them as a burden? To answer this question, it is helpful to consider Stacey Lee's ethnographic work, recent studies by psychologists Desiree Qin and colleagues, and research by Taylor Thompson, Lisa Kiang, and Melissa Witkow.[53] As Thompson, Kiang, and Witkow explain:

> The well-known, "positive" Model Minority Stereotype (MMS) may seem benign or less worthy of urgent scrutiny compared with the negative characterizations encompassed by ethnic discrimination. However, simply because a stereotype involves conceivably favorable characteristics does not guarantee its association with favorable outcomes or that it will be received as a compliment by the stereotyped community.[54]

With regard to ethnic-racial identity development, studies addressing this stereotype essentially tell us that, understandably, exposure to these expectations in school is conflicting for youth. Thompson, Kiang, and Witkow's study shows that youth tend to feel negatively about the model minority stereotype, but hearing these comments also potentially sparks a desire to understand how race operates in their lives. Indeed, the more youth report encountering such stereotypic attitudes about Asian Americans, the more they explored their identities over time.

Yet youths' experiences regarding race in school are not all antagonistic. They can be *additive* as well. The good news is that youth also recognize when teachers, administrators, and other adults at school value their ethnic-racial identities and when adults try to engage these identities as potential assets to the learning process. That is, youth also take note of when an adult "really cares about me and other students like me." This caring can manifest in several ways.

Angela Valenzuela has written about *authentic caring*,[55] in which adults enact respect and a profound sense of relatedness with and investment in their students, which, of course, includes valuing their cultural backgrounds. She argues that adults' sense of value for youths' identities can be felt in their consistently respectful interactions with youth "like them," high expectations that are met with resources and support, and deployment of the cultural and linguistic resources that youth bring to school. In short, it means that adults challenge themselves to combat implicit biases or stereotypes ("positive" and negative) they might have to ultimately convey that youth are worth their care.

Other important ways youth get the message that their identities are valued are when adults support multiculturalism at school, such as when they facilitate the availability of cultural clubs or unions or use multicultural or antiracist curricula. In a recent study of African American, Latino, and White adolescents, we found that those who perceived greater support for multiculturalism at their school reported having engaged in more ethnic-racial identity exploration and had greater clarity about their identities sixth months later—this was true for *all* three groups.[56] Similarly, students who felt that teachers at school were supportive of students, generally speaking, proceeded to engage in more ethnic-racial identity exploration as well, and, as before, this was true for African American, Latino, and White youth alike.

Communities

Less studied, though no less important, are the everyday messages about race and ethnicity that young people receive in their neighborhoods. Certainly, given persistent patterns of segregation, neighborhoods are important contexts in which youth learn about race—and their identities—in the United States. The ethnic-racial composition of youths' neighborhoods serves a potentially critical function in the formation and development of ethnic-racial identity.[57] In a study of Latino adolescents in California, Andrew Supple and his colleagues found that youth who had more Latino neighbors tended to feel more positively about their ethnicity. Recent research by Rebecca White and her colleagues shows that Latino youth in neighborhoods with more Latinos are more likely to internalize ethnic values and dispositions. This makes sense, and it also highlights the potential role of ethnic enclaves in youths' ethnic-racial identity development. Our own work and that of Niobe Way's corroborates that having neighbors who share youths' cultural heritage and values, as well as community cultural infrastructure such as parades, social clubs, ethnic-owned businesses, and the like, can facilitate the development of a sense of ethnic pride.[58] By contrast, youth in new or emerging destinations, places in which their ethnic group has not historically resided, must either build such cultural infrastructure or make do without it.[59]

The quality of youths' daily experiences and interactions in their neighborhoods also matter. For instance, how safe do youth feel where they live? What is the nature of the interactions youth have with their neighbors—antagonistic, friendly, or ambivalent? Some neighborhoods are characterized by their shared values among neighbors, for being places where "we look out for each other." Others are socially alienated. These qualities are layered onto the demographic diversity (or lack thereof). Sometimes, these more personal experiences are more important than the composition of the neighborhood itself. For instance, developmental scientists Dawn Witherspoon and her colleagues found that children's positive views of their neighborhood perceptions were associated with a stronger sense of belonging and more positive views toward their ethnic-racial group.[60] In another study involving Witherspoon, we examined the role of neighborhood racial composition alongside other indicators of the quality of interactions among neighbors in shaping racial identity among African American adolescents in a mid-Atlantic county.[61] We found that what mattered more than composition was the extent to which youth encountered positive and negative neighbor social dynamics. Youth who resided in neighborhoods in which adults were less willing to intervene or respond to problematic situations tended to be more pessimistic about how other groups viewed African Americans. Specifically, these youth believed that society viewed African Americans less positively. In addition, those adolescents who resided in neighborhoods characterized by positive community dynamics consistently reported feeling happy and proud to be African American in adolescence and young adulthood.

Numerous news accounts in recent years underscore that the disproportionately greater surveillance that African American and Latino youth, in particular, encounter at school follows them into their neighborhoods as well. Walking to the store to buy candy can become a hassle, or worse, a matter of life and death for these boys and girls, as was the case for Trayvon Martin, a seventeen-year-old African American teen who was killed by a neighborhood watch volunteer when he was walking back home from the store in his father's gated community in Florida. Furthermore, antagonistic interactions with police erode young people's sense that their ethnic-racial group receives fair treatment in the United States, and, over time, their ethnic-racial identity can become implicated in their understanding and expectations of procedural fairness from these authority figures. Indeed, in a study of African American juvenile offenders, Joanna Lee Williams and her colleagues found that the stronger the youths' identity, the more they perceived that police engaged in unfair and inequitable treatment.[62] Yet they also discovered that youth were somewhat conflicted about their views of the police, as more strongly identified youth reported a greater sense of respect and deference to the police.

Media

Like, in all movies it's only the Blacks like that's doing bad, like selling weed and doing all that stuff, but you'll never see like Whites like robbin' and drugs ... or something, so like when we look back and you guys ask us, what do we think about our race, it can't be nothing positive because it's been trained in every movie, like the songs when people is cussing and stuff it's mostly Blacks, it's just like everything we do is bad and especially on TV, it's like nothing good, like you'll never see a like strong Black person who's doing something good for once, it's always robbin' a bank or something like that.

—SIXTEEN-YEAR-OLD AFRICAN AMERICAN FEMALE

Intersecting all the messages youth receive from family, school, and community settings are those they encounter in the media. Youth draw on media to learn more about their identities or to express their identities with a broader social world. Indeed, researchers' inquiries, including our own, about how youth explore their identities, often include some reference to listening to music or consuming movies or other materials on the Internet related to their ethnicity or race.

For some youth, this may also involve media consumption in their family's heritage language. Yet, media has multifaceted roles in youths' identity development. Not only does it provide opportunities to explore and connect with other like-minded individuals in positive ways, it also exposes youth to widespread ethnic-racial tensions and injustice. Certain media—especially the Internet—can serve as an echo chamber in which traumatic events in one place become apparent to youth everywhere. The prominence of the most publicized events in the national media make it likely that youth from all ethnic-racial backgrounds are aware of group tensions and, consequently, that they are forming a sense of who they are and who they can be in a deeply conflicted society.

Unfortunately, popular media—television, film, and the Internet, in particular—are incomparably efficient purveyors of stereotypic information.[63] Experts on the racial aspects of adolescent media consumption, such as Brendesha Tynes and colleagues,[64] lament the fact that media expose youth to information that at best promotes ambivalence about race relations and at worst exacerbates intergroup conflict. Marginal, negative, and caricatured representations of ethnic minorities on TV and in film are pervasive; one need not endorse stereotypes to recognize their presence in these forms of media. Consider one study by Srividya Ramasubramanian that surveyed White college students regarding how the "typical"

Black, Latino, and White person is portrayed on TV; the students reported substantially more depictions of criminality and laziness for Black and Latino than White characters.[65] Valerie Adams-Bass, Keisha Bentley-Edwards, and Howard Stevenson conducted focus groups with African American adolescents, who identified four prevalent stereotypical portrayals of Black women on TV: unusually sexualized, caretakers, strong, and angry.[66] Indeed, TV shows whose characters do *not* conform to stereotypes—or challenge them, even subtly—become fodder for a broader conversation about race in the media, as has been the case with *Black-ish*, *Fresh Off the Boat*, *Master of None*, and *Jane the Virgin*, to name a few.[67] With notable exceptions, then, the media is a minefield of social stereotypes.[68]

A current quandary in making sense of the role of media in ethnic-racial identity development is whether media impacts identity or if youths' identities motivate them to seek out certain content. There is evidence for both. In a series of studies, researchers Max Weisbuch, Kristin Pauker, and Nalini Ambady showed that when participants were exposed to video clips that depicted Black characters positively, they reported liking those characters more than did participants in a control condition in which the characters were depicted in a neutral manner, suggesting that viewers' racial attitudes can be molded by what they see on TV.[69] Given that the majority of depictions of ethnic and racial minority characters on television are based on negative stereotypes,[70] the study underscores that such exposure can undermine positive racial attitudes across different groups. Having to navigate myriad stereotypes across multiple mediums likely harms not only those who belong to groups who are particularly vilified in the news and popular media but also youth whose opinions of such groups are being unconsciously formed by stereotypic content.

Considering the media's influence on identity, as eloquently stated by psychologist Peter Leavitt and his colleagues,[71] mass media offers varied characterizations of groups that provide individuals with different possibilities for how to be a person in society. For White middle-class individuals, there is an abundance of positive and varied representations; however, for working-class and ethnic-racial minority individuals, there is a more limited number of representations, and representations are predominantly negative. Furthermore, as Leavitt and colleagues point out, for Native Americans there are extremely limited representations in the media, such that Native Americans are depicted either as historical figures (eighteenth- and nineteenth-century representations) or stereotypical figures (poor, uneducated, prone to addiction). The lack of contemporary and counterstereotypical representations of Native Americans limits identity options for youth. As Leavitt and colleagues argue, having a limited reflection of oneself in the media can constrain individual potential, as youth from these groups see very restricted options for who and what they can be in society.

As they do offline, youth also seek out peers like themselves online, including those who share their ethnic-racial identities. Early research on the role of race in teens' online settings by Tynes and her colleagues documented how youth "announced" their race through their choice of screen names and seeking out similar others in chat rooms; however, some also used the chat room space to perpetuate stereotypes and denigrate out-group members.[72] Tynes's more recent studies uncover how youth are victimized and traumatized by racial discrimination online,[73] such as when they inadvertently open a hate group's page, encounter racist jokes or images on Facebook, or view videos of racially motivated violence on YouTube. According to Tynes's recent studies, almost one-third of African American youth had encountered online racial discrimination themselves, and almost two-thirds had witnessed it vicariously; one in five White youth had experienced vicarious racial discrimination online.[74]

Youths' ethnic-racial identity also provides them with a lens through which they consume media content. For example, Adams-Bass and colleagues have discovered that Black fourteen- to twenty-year-olds with high private regard (more positive views of their racial group) are more likely to agree with positive messages and to disagree with negative messages about Black people in TV and print media.[75] Our own work has provided evidence that ethnic-racial identity helps to counteract negative interactions, such as online racial discrimination, among ethnic minority youth.[76] We found that the more Latino adolescents had explored their ethnic-racial identity, the less likely they were to act out aggressively and break rules if they had experienced greater online racial discrimination. In addition, among African American adolescents, having explored and resolved their ethnic-racial identity was associated with less anxiety in the face of online racial discrimination.[77] Given what we know about the amount of time youth spend engaging with various media and the concomitant implications of negative racial interactions for youths' psychological health, the presence of trusted adults to whom youth can turn to process these experiences seems paramount.

———

As youth receive multiple, sometimes conflicting messages within and across each of their everyday contexts, they necessarily make choices about what to internalize as they craft their own individual identities. Taking all the information together, it is hard to know what to conclude for oneself. It is overwhelming, no doubt, and young people need adults in their lives to help them to unpack, interpret, and process all of these messages. Avoiding the process of sorting out all the ethnic-racial knowledge that youth are internalizing as part of their identity development leaves them in an uninformed, insecure place. Attempting to pursue interactions with others who are from different ethnic-racial groups from such a place makes youth vulnerable to emotional states that often take over, such as fear and anxiety. These feelings might then translate to indifference, or worse, defensiveness. For individuals who would like nothing more than to build bridges across different ethnic-racial experiences, it is critical to plunge into potentially socially and politically tense situations, and to have so-called brave conversations from *steady*, not shaky, ground. Actively exploring and making meaning of one's ethnic-racial identity is one way to establish a little bit of steady ground around oneself.

5

Breaking Down
Ethnic-Racial Boundaries

CAN WE HELP YOUTH HAVE BETTER RELATIONSHIPS WITH DIVERSE PEERS BY HELPING THEM LEARN ABOUT THEIR OWN IDENTITIES?

> You wouldn't do one night of algebra homework and expect to know all of algebra. It's the same with race. Practice, practice, practice.
>
> —DR. HOWARD STEVENSON, *RACE/RELATED, NEW YORK TIMES*

Starting at the Beginning

Let's go back in time to the first time you can remember thinking about your own ethnic-racial identity. For some, this may have been when you started reading chapter 1 of this book; for others, this may be a memory from a month ago, which prompted the reading of this book; and yet for others, this memory may be from grade school. Try to recall: Who was there? Where were you? What prompted you to think about it? For those of us whose memory stems from experiences that occurred when we were much younger, this identity has likely been a salient lens through which we make sense of our interactions with people from our own ethnic-racial group, as well as from other backgrounds. For those of us who really have not thought about our ethnic-racial identity until more recently, it has also informed our decisions, but we just haven't been aware of it. In either case, our identities have shaped the choices we have made with respect to our friends and whom to include in our most intimate social spheres. As we talk about identity throughout this chapter, the choices young people make in this regard have important implications for their well-being during adolescence and young adulthood, and the adults in their lives can influence such choices.

Categories Help Us Organize Our Social World

For most people, an awareness of their race and ethnicity occurs in the context of realizing that they are different from others around them. If this has happened to you, this experience of noticing difference likely really stood out and was notably significant in the moment. Have you ever walked into a room and realized you're the only person there from your particular social group? Consider the experience of Christopher Fong, who writes:

> Back in the Bay Area, my high school lacked the diverse student body large universities tend to have. Being Asian meant I was a part of the majority. Ever since I came [to] UC Merced, that has no longer been the case. In my experience this first semester, I've often been one of the only few Asians in my classes.[1]

Interestingly, Fong's experience of noticing himself as racially different did not come until college, because he had grown up in the San Francisco Bay area, which had a large Asian American population. However, his move to the University of California-Merced, which is a Hispanic Serving Institution—meaning that at least 25% of the student body is comprised of Latinos—resulted in an experience in which he was no longer surrounded by peers who shared his ethnic-racial background. Hence, the salience of this part of his identity was heightened.

Once you had the initial realization of being "one of a few," or more generally that race or ethnicity was an important feature that distinguished you from others, it was likely something that stuck with you and that you've thought about since then if you were regularly in contexts where you were different from others. What's more, people for whom ethnicity-race is more central to how they define themselves are more likely to notice racial characteristics of a situation, even when there are other social categories—such as gender—that could be relevant in the moment. For instance, Nicole Shelton and Robert Sellers conducted a laboratory experiment in which African American women college students were exposed to three conditions.[2] In the racially salient condition, students were in a room with three White men, and together they watched a video of a White man physically assaulting a Black man. In the racially ambiguous conditions, the students watched a video of a White man assaulting a White man, and they watched the video with three other Black women or with three White men. In the racially ambiguous condition, either race or gender (or potentially neither in the room with all Black women) could be salient—race was not the only category that could be relevant in that situation. The participants were asked about their racial identity at the end of the video session. Even in the race-ambiguous, video-watching session, when asked to describe themselves by selecting words from a list, those who reported that race was a more central part of how they defined themselves selected more race-related words to describe themselves than those whose race was a less central identity.

What findings from studies such as the one above signal is that the relevance of race in daily situations varies for people. It's not a uniform experience, so people for whom ethnic-racial aspects of their identity are more central to their sense of self are likely to think about race in both explicitly and more subtly or ambiguously racial situations. Likewise, having a lot of salience-raising experiences, such as constantly being "the only one," can lead to ethnicity and race being more central to their sense of self. Because people are regularly in situations in which racial or ethnic distinctions are being made, race is likely to be salient at one point or another for most individuals living in US society. Further, because we continuously use the concepts of race and ethnicity in our society to categorize people, these social group identities tend to become *chronically* significant across society.[3]

It should not be surprising that we have a tendency to group people based on race, ethnicity, or other social categories, because it is a basic human need to categorize. In fact, cognitive and developmental psychologists have demonstrated that categorization is evident as early as infancy. One reason for this is that it is necessary in order to help us understand our environment in a more efficient way.[4] Furthermore, as explained by Gordon Allport, the human mind must form categories to be able to judge and predict our social world. Hence, it's a basic human process to categorize, but how is it that people jump from noticing difference to *fearing* it? One part of the answer to this question is that negative attitudes about out-groups likely evolved as part of a survival mechanism that alerted humans to respond appropriately with behaviors that would ensure our safety, such as preparing for a fight or running for your life.[5] In other words, we fear what is different because it may hurt us.

Another part of the answer is that our innate tendencies for social categorization also lead us to prefer the familiar. Just as we have somewhat automatic tendencies to categorize people in our social world, we also have a tendency to favor those who we perceive to be similar to us or, as social psychologists put it, those who we perceive as "in-group members." Psychologists have demonstrated this in numerous studies. As one example, Yarrow Dunham, Andrew Baron, and Susan Carey's study with five-year-old White children found that simply being assigned into a group in which the object of categorization was neutral (for instance, being a member of the red or blue T-shirt group) was sufficient to cause in-group preference behaviors.[6] For instance, in one experiment, when children were given the option to distribute coins to one group over the other or to distribute them equally, they chose to allocate more coins to children in their same T-shirt color group. In a second experiment within this same study, children were more likely to assign positive actions and events to members of their in-group relative to out-group members.

In another experimental study conducted in London with children ages six to seven and nine to ten, children were randomly assigned to a control or experimental group.[7] Within both groups, children were assigned a colored cloth tile to wear on their shirts for a two-week period. In the experimental condition, teachers repeatedly referred to the children's color assignment to organize classroom activities (for example, "orange team line up first"). After the two-week experiment, Virginia Lam and Jodi-Ann Seaton found that children in the experimental condition demonstrated a clear bias toward those in their classroom who were part of the same color group—they assigned more positive traits to their in-group members compared to children in the other group. Thus, simply assigning children to a color group and referring to that group membership for a two-week period was sufficient to create an in-group bias along the lines of an arbitrary category such as cloth color.

As explained by social psychologists Henry Tajfel and John Turner, an important part of learning to feel positively about oneself involves feeling positively about the groups in which we are members; furthermore, our evaluation of our in-group inevitably involves considering how our group compares to out-groups.[8] Social psychologist Marilyn Brewer has found that people have a basic need for connection to others, which they achieve via their affiliation with an in-group.[9] And, as illustrated by the excerpt below by a seventeen-year-old Asian American female, some adolescents are aware of this preference and can explain why they view it as beneficial:

[W]hen you have friends of your own like ethnicity, it's more of like a closure, 'cause you can like tell them like all those [*sic*] weird stuff that you do and like your culture, whereas you can't do that and live with like more like … your American friends. 'Cause that would be really weird 'cause like they don't share the same things and it becomes really uncomfortable and they're like, "Oh, you eat that, that's gross" and whereas like if you eat the same thing, as you know, your friends like the same ethnicity, it becomes like it, you're more comfortable.

This adolescent's comment illustrates one of the many ways that youth can meet their need for connection by affiliating with others who share their ethnic-racial background.

Yet Brewer notes that we also have a need to feel unique and distinctive—we often achieve this by comparing our in-group with an out-group. So, in a sense, we are prewired to categorize ourselves into different groups, and our human need for validation and positive self-concept may inevitably result in viewing members of out-groups relatively more negatively when compared to our in-groups. In fact, in Lam and Seaton's study discussed above, children in the experimental condition rated their peers who had different-colored cloths in their classroom with more negative traits than did the children in the control condition.

These tendencies, unfortunately, can make our interactions with others who are different from us rather complicated. This can be seen throughout the United States in communities that were traditionally dominated by one ethnic-racial group but—due to demographic change, for instance—are now experiencing an influx of a new ethnic-racial population. This is illustrated in a *New York Times* article, published in 2014, that documented the changes that a community in Kansas was experiencing.[10] What are particularly relevant are the tensions that longtime residents of this small, rural town experienced as they attempted to integrate the immigrant Latinos who were so desperately needed in this town in order for it to thrive. Unfortunately, these new residents were not necessarily welcome due to their cultural differences, and the community tensions were particularly evident in incidents such as when "the students at a neighboring high school showed up to a basketball game in sombreros and tossed tortillas onto the court." This is also evident in comments from the town's historian, who explained to the

New York Times' reporter that she was so unnerved by the demographic change "that she recently started locking her door" because of her perception of the immigrants bringing a criminal element into the community. She further stated in her interview that "this wave of new people coming into the Midwest is not always a good thing . . . if you talk to the average working person, a lot of them are sort of fed up. Our town isn't what it was." This woman's experience epitomizes how a preference for the familiar can also incite fear that constrains positive intergroup relations.

In fact, some researchers have demonstrated that people have a tendency to expect the worst from intergroup interactions, even though these interactions oftentimes end up being more positive than expected.[11] This is referred to as the *intergroup forecasting error*, and it is true for members of both majority and minority groups. Researchers have found this intergroup forecasting error to exist when it comes to many different kinds of social categories, such as race, age, gender, and sexual orientation. Social psychologists explain that the reason we fall into this trap is because we rely on stereotypes to help us understand and predict how someone from a different social group will think, feel, and behave.[12] These stereotypes then shape how we expect to agree or disagree with those who we are approaching.

But given that intergroup interactions are often actually more positive than expected, we would do well to seek out such opportunities. As Robyn Mallet and her colleagues note, if we were to simply increase our experiences with intergroup contact, over time we would ultimately reduce our tendency for this intergroup forecasting error.[13] So when we consider our basic need to categorize, how we rely on stereotypes to inform our understanding of those who are different from us, and our tendencies to favor those who we perceive to be similar to us, it is easy to understand why we see children separating themselves by ethnicity and race in the school cafeteria, as we discussed in chapter 4. But an important question remains: Can and should we intervene in these tendencies for birds of a feather to flock together?

Intergroup Contact in Youth

Let's first consider the question of whether we can encourage more intergroup connections among youth by providing opportunities for in-groups and out-groups to interact with each other. Unfortunately, it's simply not enough for different groups to be around each other. Decades ago, Gordon Allport introduced his theory of intergroup contact.[14] Beyond the basic opportunity to have the interaction, he highlighted optimal conditions that should be met in order for people of different social groups to interact with each other in positive ways. In the time since Allport originally shared his ideas, social psychologists have emphasized four optimal conditions for positive intergroup contact, and research in this area has generally shown that opportunities to interact directly across difference are linked to less prejudice toward out-groups.[15]

Many psychologists have tested Allport's ideas—namely, the four optimal conditions—with youth. A classic study by Samuel Gaertner and his colleagues provides an example.[16] They assessed high school students' perceptions of equal status, degree of association and interaction, cooperative interdependence, and supportive norms for cross-group friendship conveyed by school administrators. Using a score that combined students' ratings on all four dimensions, they found that students who were exposed to more favorable contact conditions more strongly endorsed the idea that "although there are different groups of students at this school, it feels as though we

---

Intergroup Contact Theory: Four Optimal Conditions

1. *Equal Status:* The groups ideally enter the interaction on equal footing.
2. *Common Goal:* Group members work together toward attaining a shared goal.
3. *Cooperation:* Group members work together cooperatively rather than competitively.
4. *Authority Sanction:* Authority figures in the environment—such as parents, teachers, or other adults—establish and routinely reinforce norms in which group members are expected to be cooperative and to display good-natured behavior toward each other.

are playing on the same team" and reported less bias toward their own group.[17]

In another example, Tabbye Chavous used the intergroup contact framework to investigate African American and White college students' views of race relations on their campus by asking them to rate how much these two groups shared equal status, engaged in meaningful associations, worked interdependently, and enjoyed supportive university norms for cross-group contact.[18] Although African American students reported lower scores than their White counterparts on all four dimensions, African American students who believed that White and African American students were interdependent and that the university supported positive cross-group interactions among these groups tended to feel more socially integrated on campus and be more interested in personally forming cross-group friendships. For both African American and White students, believing that these groups shared equal status was linked to feeling more socially integrated on campus.

Although meeting all four conditions is ideal, because it is associated with the most reductions in prejudice, it turns out that these conditions don't all have to be simultaneously met in order for a setting to be conducive to positive intergroup contact.[19] Given that many of the readers of this book are (or will be) authority figures in youths' lives, it's worth pointing out that the final condition noted above, which concerns authority figures setting norms, is particularly important for the choices that kids make in their daily lives. For example, in a study conducted in the United Kingdom that explicitly investigated the cafeteria integration problem, British and Southeast Asian students were presented with a hypothetical scenario in which they could opt to sit next to out-group students.[20] Youth whose friends and family had encouraged them to have more intergroup contact were more likely to choose to sit with out-group students. Similarly, Thomas Pettigrew and Linda Tropp found that kids who believed that their school's principal and teachers valued and approved of cross-group friendships continued to be interested in befriending cross-ethnic kids six months later.[21] Interestingly, peer norms are also important, as demonstrated in a second study by Pettigrew and Tropp.[22] They showed that when kids' same-ethnic friends valued and approved of having friends from the other ethnic group that they had been exposed to, they felt more comfortable, were more interested in, and had better experiences with cross-group interactions. These studies show that the behaviors of both adults and peers can play a significant role in the choices youth make when given opportunities to bridge across racial and ethnic differences. So there *are* ways to intervene and, as we explain below, there are many reasons we should want to.

The Special Role of Cross-Group Friendships

What we know now from decades of research is that children miss out on important psychological, social, and academic benefits when they don't have cross-group friendships.[23] In one study, Latino youth who reported having more cross-ethnic friendships also reported a greater sense of social and emotional safety at school. Importantly, Sandra Graham and her colleagues recently showed that exposure to diversity is beneficial to youth, but only to the extent that students take up opportunities to make friendships across ethnic groups.[24] Teens in ethnically diverse schools had greater opportunities to engage in cross-ethnic friendships in their classrooms, but it was youth who reported actually *having* cross-ethnic friendships who then reported significantly fewer feelings of vulnerability: they felt safer, less victimized, and less lonely. So being in a diverse environment is a critical first step, but it is certainly not sufficient for kids to be able to reap the full benefits of this environment. They have to take advantage of those opportunities to build bridges to kids who are different from them.

We also know that children who have cross-group friendships are less likely to display intergroup biases.[25] In fact, social psychologists have shown that cross-group friendship is essentially the gold standard for prejudice reduction.[26] Elizabeth Page-Gould and her colleagues conducted an experiment in which cross-group friendships were fostered between Latino and White college students.[27]

They found that the newly formed cross-group friendship was linked to feeling less anxious and to initiating more intergroup interactions following the experiment. Recently, Roberto González and his colleagues found that nonindigenous Chilean children who "felt equal, close, safe, cooperated with, and had a lot in common" with indigenous Mapuche students at their school had more positive views of Mapuche culture and believed it was important for Mapuche people to maintain their cultural way of life.[28]

Finally, it is interesting to note, as well, that there may be significant long-term positive effects of intergroup relationships that carry into the workforce. For example, in her study of White adults, Uma Jayakumar demonstrated that individuals who had more intergroup interactions during the college years tended to have greater competencies in their work settings in areas such as leadership skills and cross-cultural competence.[29] Given the many potential benefits to youth of having cross-group friends, we have a critical responsibility to help youth cross these boundaries.

To begin engaging with young people regarding ethnicity and race in their everyday choices, however, it is important to let go of two commonly held myths regarding youth and ethnic-racial prejudice.

As discussed in chapter 3, children become aware of racial differences early in life, and this awareness emerges regardless of their parents' exposure.[30] Therefore, although it is common for parents to think that not discussing issues of race or ethnicity will lead to children not noticing differences and remaining unbiased, the reality is that children notice difference and form attitudes at an early age.[31] In fact, some research, such as that by Debra Van Ausdale and Joe Feagin, Brigitte Vittrup, and Phyllis Katz, respectively, has

---

Two Commonly Held Myths regarding Youth and Ethnic-Racial Prejudice:

1. Young children do not notice racial differences unless they are pointed out.
2. Children do not develop racial bias unless they are explicitly taught so by their parents.

documented parents' disbelief that children not only recognize differences but hold prejudiced attitudes about other ethnic-racial groups.[32] Thus, regardless of whether or not difference is pointed out, young children will notice differences and form opinions about such difference.

In terms of the role that parents play in children's racial bias, the story is also a bit more complicated than we might think. Yes, parents play a nontrivial role in their kids' attitudes about other ethnic and racial groups, but it's not necessarily the parents' own attitudes that are most important here. Rather, there is consistent research noting that children become aware of racial differences early in life, independent of their parents' exposure, and though children's racial attitudes are somewhat consistent with those of their parents, they are also influenced by their peers and media.[33] In short, they "pick up" knowledge about intergroup relations outside the home, and together with what parents convey, draw their own conclusions. It's our job, in a sense, to put our own attitudes aside in order to meet our children where they are in this process. Consider the following exchange between a White mother and her White seven-year-old daughter:

> CHILD: Mom, I think I'm going to have to adopt a baby when I get older.
> MOTHER: Okay; that's fine. Is there any particular reason why?
> CHILD: Well, I really want my child to have almond-color skin.
> MOTHER: Okay. You do realize that you can have a child with almond-color skin if you choose a partner who has almond-color skin, right? So you don't necessarily have to adopt. When people with lighter and darker skin have babies, the babies often have darker skin than ours. So it is perfectly possible for you to have a baby with almond-color skin.
> CHILD: Well, Mom, I'm going to tell you something, but I think you're going to get mad.
> MOTHER: *[Thinking, "Oh dear ... do I really want to hear what my daughter is about to tell me?"]* I'm not going to get mad, you can tell me.

CHILD: Well, Mom, I'm not sure if you've noticed this. I have noticed this, but maybe you don't know this. People with light-color skin, like mine, tend to marry people with light-color skin, and people with almond-color skin tend to marry people with almond-color skin. So I know it is possible, but I don't know if it will happen. I'm probably going to have to adopt.[34]

So children are aware of difference, and if the adults in their lives do not actively engage in discussions with them in a manner that helps youth navigate the differences they encounter in their schools, neighborhoods, and other social spaces, our society will inevitably continue to be as polarized as it has been. The divisions that adults believe to be intractable actually begin in childhood. If we don't tackle these issues with them, children will "do as we do" and pursue friendships almost exclusively with peers who are in-group members. Cross-ethnic friendships will continue to be rare, and intergroup relationships will continue to be strained.

So you may be wondering, "How can we do this?" An excellent first step is to find ways to promote and foster the four optimal conditions for positive intergroup contact introduced by Allport. As illustrated by the research we reviewed earlier, youths' perceptions of family members', teachers', and school administrators' opinions about the *positive value* of cross-group friendships are believed to affect youths' behaviors, for instance, choosing to sit with a member of the out-group, as well as their attitudes, such as being interested in befriending someone from an out-group. Thus, the views and beliefs that we communicate—verbally and nonverbally—to youth regarding our openness and positive orientation toward cross-group friendships will play an important role in their own attitudes and behaviors. Furthermore, we will have more success at fostering positive intergroup relations among youth to the extent that we (a) create more opportunities for cross-group interactions; (b) structure the environment so that in-group and out-group members must work together toward a common goal; and (c) provide youth in cross-group settings with multiple opportunities to work cooperatively rather than competitively.

Linking Identity and Intergroup Relations

> My ethnicity means to me that even if you are not the same ethnicity
> as other people, you should still be proud no matter what. My
> ethnicity is important to me and I always try and show it whenever
> I can. It is also a pleasure to be Mexican because most people where
> I grew up are not, and I like sharing some of my culture with them.
> —THIRTEEN-YEAR-OLD FEMALE LATINA

Let's turn back now to considering how it is that emphasizing our own identities can facilitate, rather than hinder, positive intergroup relations. At first glance, it seems counterintuitive to think that having a secure and positive ethnic-racial identity can help us navigate difference more effectively. But Allport himself noted more than sixty years ago that identifying with an in-group does not require hostility toward out-groups:

> One's own family is an in-group; and by definition all other families on the street are out-groups; but seldom do they clash. A hundred ethnic groups compose America, and while serious conflict occasionally occurs, the majority rub along in peace. One knows that one's lodge has distinctive characteristics that mark it off from all others, but one does not necessarily despise the others.[35]

Contemporary studies actually help support the idea reflected in Allport's comment as well. Jean Phinney, for instance, found that adolescents from Latino, Black, Asian, and White ethnic groups who had developed a stronger and more positive sense of ethnic-racial identity tended to also say they were more interested in learning about and befriending people of groups other than their own.[36] In our own work, we found that African American, White, Latino, Asian American, and Multiracial middle school boys who were more secure in their sense of ethnic-racial identity at the end of the school year were more likely to befriend more diverse kids the following school year.[37] Having more diverse friendships, in turn, helped boys and girls gather more information in their exploration of their own identities at the end of the following school year. Dina Maramba and Samuel Museus similarly found that Filipino American college students who had a stronger sense of connection and attachment to their ethnic group also tended to enjoy meeting, spending time with, befriending, and being around people from other ethnicities.[38] Finally, Kevin Whitehead and his colleagues found strong evidence that Asian American, Latino, and White ninth grade students who had done more to learn about their ethnic-racial background and felt a stronger sense of belonging to their respective ethnic-racial group tended to have more positive attitudes toward out-group members compared to youth who had less developed ethnic-racial identities.[39]

So there is evidence that having a secure and positive ethnic-racial identity is linked to one's openness to diversity. Nevertheless, some may wonder whether feeling a positive orientation toward your own group is compatible with inviting out-group members into spaces traditionally reserved for the in-group. This potential concern for incompatibility is reconciled by some, in that they view learning about other groups as a way to actually help them learn more about their own group. Consider the following exchange among Latino high school students:[40]

INTERVIEWER: Anything we haven't talked about that you guys think is important for us to keep in mind when we're developing programs and thinking about ways to work with teenagers to basically learn more about your heritage?

ANNA: I'm in this program with [university name;] it's called the Hispanic Mother-Daughter program ... and there was a point ... where they wanted to expand it to like where Americans, African Americans, can do the program with us. But then a lot of us were like, we didn't want that because there's not a lot of programs for our ethnic—, oh I can't say that word, *Hispanics*, and we kind of got mad because that's like our own thing and we just didn't wanna expand it. So they then decided they're not going to.

INTERVIEWER: So do you think that if you do ... if we have like programs to have different activities for high school students to learn about their heritage, do you think that it needs to be specific to groups? Or do you think we can develop programs that, you know, include *multiple* groups and don't have to be specific to one group?

MONICA: I think it would be like a mixture of all, so we can all learn about other like heritages as well, not just our own.

INTERVIEWER: Mhm. Sure.

MIKE: Yeah, because like if you do groups of the same ethnicities like you guys will be used to everything, like you guys do, like similar things, but if you go in a mixed group, like, and you see what other people's culture is like, then you get to see, like the differences between yours and theirs and then like you can think about yours more.

As noted by the last comment, Mike believed that by learning about other people's identity experiences, he would learn more about himself. In this manner, it is possible for youth to form bonds about the experiences that are common to navigating one's respective group membership. Indeed, some work conducted by Lindsey Cameron and her colleagues in the United Kingdom found that the most effective intervention to improve White British students' attitudes toward refugees involved a *dual identity* approach.[41] This meant emphasizing both a shared identity as members of the same school and distinctive ethnic heritages. In doing this, the researchers also found that the students in the study felt less social distance from refugee children. A dual identity approach was also integral to the development of the widely used Intergroup Dialogues program by Patricia Gurin and her colleagues for college students. They argue that asking students to talk about their common experiences, as well as their own identities and unique social and cultural experiences, helps promote awareness and understanding of the experiences of other groups, especially those perspectives that are traditionally marginalized or silenced.[42]

Emphasizing rather than denying ethnic-racial identity can be part of how people start to break down barriers to navigating difference. Indeed, experiences that leverage, rather than mute, knowledge of one's ethnic-racial identities may foster productive intergroup relations by supporting conditions for positive contact. According to Allport's classic theory, these include experiences that help us get beyond the superficial and toward those that allow us to form meaningful common bonds.[43] This is precisely what programs such as the Intergroup Dialogues program seek to achieve, and providing opportunities for youth to figure out their ethnic-racial identities together is a kind of meaningful connection that is essential for positive intergroup relations. Ultimately, students who are exposed to this approach may be able to reconcile a desire to promote a positive sense of individual ethnic-racial identity with a desire to bridge differences across diverse ethnic-racial groups.

Bridging "Us" and "Them": A Few Pathways to Consider

So why might youth who have a clearer sense of their own ethnic-racial background and identity be more interested and open to diversity? And why might they be better prepared to engage productively with people who are different from them, compared to youth who are less informed about their ethnic-racial background?

GREATER SELF-CONFIDENCE AND SELF-ASSUREDNESS

According to Erik Erikson, exploring and understanding one's identity is essential for developing a strong sense of self, feeling more confident in making decisions, and having a generally strong sense of self-assurance.[44] When youth have this sense of self-assuredness with respect to their ethnic-racial background and identity, they are better able to manage challenging situations that involve their ethnic-racial background, such as ethnic-racial discrimination.[45] The greater self-confidence enables youth to feel comfortable enough to let themselves be vulnerable in relationships with others, which, according to Erikson, is essential in forming intimate relationships with others. It's useful here to consider a commentary by developmental psychologist Diane Hughes during a webinar on "Teaching Race to Children and Adolescents," in which she explained her personal experiences growing up:

> As a child at *our* dinner table, my father told story after story about what it meant to grow up Black in the South. And I *always*

knew that even though his father was a surgeon, he and his friends had to enter the Carolina Theatre in Raleigh through the back door service entrance and climb a steep stairway to the upper upper balcony, the only place where Coloreds were allowed ... And the lessons in there were very clear. When my two sisters and I would yawn and start to tune out, he'd say, "I just don't want you to ever forget who you are and where you come from." My dad was very intentional about what he wanted us to learn. So I had a strong foundation, a strong sense of being Black and what it meant and what it should mean. It enabled me to feel more than comfortable in my skin anywhere I went—at the Quaker high school I attended or the elite, predominantly White college I went to in the northern corner of Massachusetts. And it enabled me to know I could be or do anything I wanted to be or do.[46]

So, to put it simply, the more comfortable individuals are in their own skin, the more capacity they will have to engage in a productive manner with others. They will not have as many hang-ups or insecurities about ethnic-racial issues, because they will have explored these topics and understand where they stand on these issues. This lets them approach relationships with out-group members with a strong personal foundation, one that's more conducive to developing genuine friendships across difference because they are open and interested in exploring each other's differences. Linda Strauss and William Cross refer to this process as identity *bridging*. They describe bridging as "the identity activity that makes possible ... [an] intimate and deeply felt friendship with a person from another group."[47]

Ethnic-Racial Identity *Bridging* Involves:

- Feeling comfortable with own ethnic-racial identity.
- Being able to interact in a reciprocal manner with other people who have different ethnic-racial identities.
- Having the ability to be open about the differences that exist between one's group and another person's group.
- Being respectful and curious about each other's "difference."
- Recognizing that differences are part of how the friendship itself is defined.

A MORE FLEXIBLE UNDERSTANDING OF IDENTITY

Another reason that individuals with a more developed ethnic-racial identity may be more comfortable with cross-group interactions is that they may have a more flexible understanding of their ethnic-racial identity as one component of the person they are. For instance, they may consider their ethnic-racial identity as an important part of their self-concept while also understanding that they belong to multiple social groups. This more complex definition of themselves as members of multiple social spheres enables them to navigate diverse environments more easily. For instance, in a study of seventh graders in California that didn't look specifically at ethnic-racial identity, Casey Knifsend and Jaana Juvonen found that adolescents who were involved in multiple social circles in school that didn't overlap were less apprehensive about, and perceived more benefits from, associating with other students from different ethnic-racial groups.[48] By engaging in peer groups that were comprised of different types of people, these students were likely gaining practical skills in how to navigate across difference.

A perspective presented by Daphna Oyserman and Mesmin Destin provides yet another potential pathway between one's own ethnic-racial identity and a positive orientation toward intergroup contact.[49] They explain how, for some, definitions of their ethnic-racial identity can help to motivate them to engage with people from other groups. If individuals perceive their in-group to be welcoming and inclusive of out-groups, then they will be more open to having relationships with out-group members because this behavior is compatible with their in-group identity. However, if their in-group identity content has come to be defined by being closed off to groups other than their own, then it will be harder for them to have positive cross-group relationships. Essentially, people are motivated to act in ways that are congruent with their social identities. Using this perspective, Oyserman found that having an ethnic-racial identity that incorporates a sense of connection to other groups in the broader society promotes better social interactions in spaces such as schools, where youth must encounter out-group members.[50]

Therefore, it's useful for those of us involved in socializing youth about the meaning or characteristics of our ethnic-racial group memberships to define our groups as being inclusive of friendships with people from other groups. This research would suggest that the extent to which we do this will help to shape how motivated our young people are toward forming cross-group friendships.

AN ORIENTATION TOWARD SOCIAL JUSTICE

> To me ethnicity means that I have an amazing history and that the family members, traditions, music, and other people that surround me have something to show me about my culture. Being Latina also means that during these controversial times, I must pay close attention to what is occurring politically, as it will affect both me and others of different cultures.
>
> —FIFTEEN-YEAR-OLD FEMALE LATINA

As part of the process of ethnic-racial identity formation, people can develop an identity that is enmeshed with their beliefs about social injustice. Some scholars refer to this as one's *sociopolitical orientation*. This orientation can sometimes spontaneously emerge as youth are engaging in the identity exploration process. That is, for some, development of one's ethnic-racial identity can also entail a parallel increase in awareness of ethnic-racial injustice, or as Roderick Watts and his colleagues state, people may embark on "a journey from a place of relative uninformed in-action on the social forces that affect our lives to one of sustained, informed, and strategic action" to challenge injustices.[51] For youth from ethnic-racial minority groups, in particular, increased awareness of ethnic and racial injustice is thought to be a beneficial component of their understanding of race and ethnicity and its role in who they are and can become in a sociopolitical context that often limits their life chances.[52]

In addition, this general understanding of ethnic and racial injustice can be particularly helpful if it includes an understanding that they happen for multiple groups. For example, Fantasy Lozada and her colleagues found that Black adolescent boys with a strong and positive racial identity who also believed that multiple ethnic-racial groups experienced social injustices were more inclined to help others in need.[53] These boys also made friends more easily, showed more empathy, and were better able to control their emotions than boys without this orientation. Although this particular study focused on Black youth, we argue that a similar link between concern regarding ethnic-racial injustice and prosocial dispositions toward others could emerge among youth from other groups and that having such prosocial dispositions could also facilitate cross-group interactions.

Concern for racial justice is also essential for unpacking how ethnic-racial identity development for members of the majority group can facilitate, rather than hinder, positive contact with groups who are socially and politically marginalized. For members of the majority group, the development of a sociopolitical orientation must involve an understanding of the social injustices that members of minority groups experience. Recent work by Hema Selvanathan, Pirathat Techakesari, Linda Tropp, and Fiona Barlow provides a good illustration of this process. They found that Whites who felt angry about the racial injustices that Black people face were more willing to "attend demonstrations, protests, or rallies against racial injustice; attend meetings or workshops on racial issues; write letters to public officials or other people of influence to protest against racial injustice; vote for political candidates who support racial equality; [and] sign a petition to support racial justice."[54]

Another study, by Loreto Martínez and her colleagues in Chile, may be informative as well. They investigated the experiences that led six Chilean adolescents and young adults to become advocates for out-group communities. They found that, as the youth were exposed to different communities' experiences, they began to incorporate these encounters into their personal identity exploration processes. Martínez and her colleagues argue that "experiences discrepant to personal realities challenged participants' preconceived ideas and motivated their reflection on the causes of social problems," including social exclusion and bias.[55] For one youth, this new awareness of discrepant realities between her group (non-Mapuche) and those of the Mapuche emerged in the context of discussions with peers. In her interview, one youth noted the interrelationship between the experience of the majority and minority Chilean groups:

> [It] was so obvious that I started connecting my ideas to the reality of the [M]apuche people. I became more interested in the relationship between the [M]apuche and my culture in political terms. I now advocate for their [Mapuche] rights and fight for the cause of our people ... That is how I was able to connect everything.[56]

Thus, for some, the bridge between their own ethnic-racial identity and positive intergroup experiences can be built not only by recognizing and resisting their own biases but also by learning about and working to challenge the racial injustices that affect people of ethnic and racial groups other than their own.

One's sociopolitical orientations are a potentially important part of explaining how individuals from multiple ethnic-racial minority groups can use their ethnic-racial identities to form cross-group collaborations and coalitions. For example, Patricia Gurin and her colleagues note that one reason the Intergroup Dialogues approach "works" to support positive cross-group interactions is that students of diverse backgrounds are asked to link their own ethnic-racial identities with issues of social inequality and oppression. They have found that by doing so, the program results in greater intergroup empathy, collaboration, and action.

Why Should We Focus on Youth rather than on Adults?

Some of you may be wondering why we have focused this book on intervening with youth rather than adults. Intervening during adolescence is promising and may actually be an ideal time to help youth make sense of larger ethnic-racial tensions/events due to individuals' growth in cognitive and social maturity during this time.[57] First, due to greater social exposure relative to childhood, adolescents are more likely to be aware of such tensions or events. In addition, because of the changes in their thought processes during this time, which enable them to understand abstract ideas such as ethnic-racial inequality, adolescents are increasingly aware of and concerned with issues of inequality. In one study, for example, Laura Elenbaas and her colleagues found that youth at the cusp of adolescence (ten- to twelve-year-olds) showed more concern for fairness and the well-being of others than did five- to six-year-old children in their study.[58] Therefore, adolescence may be the perfect time to discuss these topics with youth, because in a sense, they may be ripe for taking it all in.

Although adolescence can be an ideal time for these conversations because of the changes children experience during this time in their social and cognitive maturity—which help them have a better grasp of things such as race, ethnicity, and unequal treatment— it is useful to also keep in mind that peer ethnic-racial exclusion happens at all ages. Although rates of ethnic-racial discrimination for members of ethnic-racial minority groups in the United States are high during the developmental period of adolescence, researchers have demonstrated that children report experiencing discrimination based on their ethnic-racial background during the elementary school years.[59] Therefore, initiating conversations about race and ethnicity in a way that children can understand can and should happen much earlier in development. Ultimately, the most important thing to consider is that the adults in children's lives should be sending messages that encourage discussions about these topics rather than sending messages that suggest to children that the topic is taboo and should be whispered about or, worse, avoided.

What's more, because there is evidence that these attitudes are forming early in youths' lives, it's important to help guide intergroup contact experiences in youth. For example, youths' attitudes about whether it's wrong or right to exclude others based on race are shaped by these early experiences and may ultimately crystallize in adulthood, which is why it's critical to intervene in the younger years. The way in which this process unfolds is illustrated nicely in an experimental study conducted with children and adolescents by David Crystal, Melanie Killen, and Martin Ruck. They found that youth who had more contact with out-group members were more likely to view race-based peer exclusion as wrong.[60] Crystal and his colleagues have found that more contact with out-group members tends to cultivate stronger views toward equality, fairness, and justice with respect to out-group members; these attitudes are then what lead children who have greater intergroup contact to be less likely to support race-based exclusion, essentially because they see those acts as morally wrong. The more children view peer race-based exclusion as wrong earlier in life, the more likely they will be to make choices that promote intergroup inclusion.

Throughout this book, we've been hinting at our collective responsibility to reduce ethnic-racial tensions in our society, and we believe that supporting ethnic-racial identity exploration in youth is one important way that we may work toward this goal. For many youth, engaging actively with their own ethnic-racial identities is linked to a desire to interact with and befriend kids of other groups, and there is good evidence of this in the studies we discussed in the previous sections. In addition, from research conducted by Linda Tropp and Thomas Pettigrew, we also know that by increasing intergroup contact, we can increase empathy and decrease anxieties that often accompany cross-ethnic interactions.[61] In turn, by reducing anxiety and increasing empathy, researchers find that people demonstrate lower levels of prejudice toward out-group members. The potentially important role that *empathy*, in particular, can play in this process can be seen in the findings from a study conducted with children in the Netherlands. Jellie Sierksma, Jochem Thijs, and Maykel Verkuyten found that those who were asked to consider the feelings of another child were more likely to help children who were not their friends than children who were not asked to consider those feelings.[62] Therefore, making empathy a part of their decision-making process led to more equitable treatment of the two groups of kids. In the same way, we argue that making empathic cross-group interactions as part of the ethnic-racial identity development process can promote, rather than hinder, continued contact across difference.

Most of us don't know how talking about and processing our ethnic-racial identities can help, rather than hinder, our comfort level with difference. This is understandable. As we explained at the beginning of this chapter, categories such as race and ethnicity are regularly used to help us organize the world—as social beings we have an innate tendency to use these strategies, which are believed to enable our survival and cognitive efficiency. The meaning we ascribe to these social categories, however, ultimately spills over into our interactions with people from groups that are different from our own. Yet, the extent to which ethnicity-race is salient and central to each of us—and more generally, the meaning of our ethnic-racial group membership in our own lives—is bound to be different. In other words, people (including youth) will be in different places of their awareness, their interest, and their understanding of ethnic-racial identity. Our job as authority figures in youths' lives is to equip them with competencies that help them navigate their respective social milieus. In this book, we have argued that through the process of identity development, we can help youth become aware of their tendencies to categorize along the lines of race and ethnicity, recognize the biases (oftentimes unintended) that bleed into their day-to-day interactions and friendship choices, and help them develop empathy for others. By doing so we help reduce youths' potential anxieties about interacting across difference. And, as eloquently stated by Samuel Gaertner and his colleagues, "with reduced feelings of anxiety, the perceptual field becomes broader and impressions of outgroup members can become more accurate, less polarized, and more favorable."[63] In chapter 6 of this book, we provide several examples of different approaches for capitalizing on the normative process of identity development to improve intergroup relations by promoting empathy and reducing anxieties about difference.

6

A Way Forward

Early in this book we introduced the different ways that readers can approach addressing issues of diversity with youth. One that seems intuitive, appears more egalitarian, and feels possibly less stressful is to avoid explicit engagement with ethnicity or race. In our view, this color-blind tactic is not an effective way forward. Rather, considering the many research findings we have presented in this book, an alternative approach that we encourage is *conscious engagement* with ethnic-racial issues, identities, and interactions. This includes directly talking with youth about issues of inequality, prejudice, and racism, as well as cultivating relationships in which youth feel comfortable and safe raising these issues with us. We've divided this chapter into two parts, and in the first part of the chapter we describe programs and practices that provide concrete examples of how this important work can be achieved in schools, communities, and in the home. In doing so, we note ways in which these approaches have been applied to diverse communities of people. But as scholars, we also recognize there is more to be learned about conscious engagement. The second part of this chapter focuses on how future research can move forward in a way that will improve our understanding of the programs and practices that may be most effective for the increasingly diverse population of youth in our society. There is no doubt that this work is challenging, but by walking through these examples and directions for future research, we hope to make the impossible feel more possible.

Part 1—Strategies for "Doing" Conscious Engagement
In chapter 5, we described three different pathways through which youths' greater sense of their own ethnic-racial background can ultimately support their interest in and openness to diversity and better prepare them to engage productively with people who are different from them. First, youth who have a clearer sense of who they are and how their ethnic-racial background plays a role in their lives may generally have a greater sense of self-confidence and self-assuredness, which helps them engage more productively with those who are different from them. A second pathway involves being able to define their ethnic-racial identity flexibly, that is, in a way that reflects a capacity to befriend members of other groups. The final pathway reflects a sociopolitical orientation that makes it possible for youth to understand, actively resist, and challenge the social injustices that other groups face. In the following sections, we walk through various programs and practices that have been proven effective in developing the skills necessary for these multiple and often overlapping pathways—helping youth learn about themselves, form meaningful bonds with others, and increase their awareness of social injustices. Although these programs often have different objectives, they all seek to increase young people's ethnic-racial awareness and help them develop the skills to promote more positive ethnic-racial relations in our society.

Anti-Bias Approaches: Learning about Oneself, Forming Meaningful Bonds, and Challenging Injustices

One approach that practitioners use is aimed at increasing students' knowledge of diversity and social injustices with the explicit purpose of reducing bias among different ethnic-racial groups. Anti-bias education approaches are particularly important to consider regarding academic curricula.[1] Below, we discuss two examples of academic curricula designed to help youth navigate their social identity development in ways that are conducive to positive inter-group relations—both were developed to be integrated in schools. The examples below underscore that an antibias curriculum can be infused in subject-specific content, in this case, literacy and history.

CURRICULUM INFUSION

Perspectives for a Diverse America. *Perspectives for a Diverse America* is a literacy curriculum that was developed by Teaching Tolerance, sponsored by the Southern Poverty Law Center and grounded in an antibias framework they developed.[2] Interestingly, the *Perspectives* curriculum draws from social-psychological litera-ture on intergroup prejudice reduction, such as the work discussed in chapter 5 in this book. This approach emphasizes using texts as tools for "explicit and guided discussions of identities and bias ... to increase empathy with marginalized and stigmatized groups" in particular. Fostering empathy and promoting antibias dispositions across groups are significant goals of the *Perspectives* approach.[3] The idea is that youth can think about their own identities and ex-periences, and those of people from other ethnic-racial groups, for instance, through their engagement with materials and lessons pre-pared by their teachers. The curriculum authors also developed clear

> standards [to] provide a common language and organizational structure: Teachers can use them to guide curriculum develop-ment, and administrators can use them to make schools more just, equitable and safe. The [antibias framework] is leveled for every stage of K–12 education and includes school-based sce-narios to show what anti-bias attitudes and behavior may look like in the classroom.[4]

As described in a preliminary evaluation of this approach:[5]

> *Perspectives for a Diverse America* ... provides a free online an-thology of hundreds of diverse texts that are meaningful to stu-dents, [and that] promote anti-bias education.

Perspectives' design is oriented around an original set of 20 antibias anchor standards, grouped by domain [including:]

Identity: Each child will demonstrate self-awareness, confidence, family pride, and positive social identities.

Diversity: Each child will express comfort and joy with human diversity, accurate language for human differences, and deep, caring human connections.

Justice: Each child will increasingly recognize unfairness, have language to describe unfairness, and understand that unfairness hurts.

Action: Each child will demonstrate empowerment and the skills to act, with others or alone, against prejudice and/or discriminatory actions.

Antibias standards in each of these four areas are separated by age-group, so that standards are written in an age-appropriate way across the K–12 range. Two examples help to illustrate the standards that drive this approach. One is Standard 4, which states, "Students will express pride, confidence, and healthy self-esteem without denying the value and dignity of other people" (Identity domain). Another is Standard 7: "Students will develop language and knowledge to accurately and respectfully describe how people (including themselves) are both similar to and different from each other and others in their identity groups" (Diversity domain). In the curriculum materials, the outcome associated with each of these standards for a seventh grader, for instance, is written as "I feel good about my many identities and know they don't make me better than people with other identities" (Identity, Standard 4) and "I can accurately and respectfully describe ways that people (including myself) are similar to and different from each other and others in their identity groups" (Diversity, Standard 7).

The authors of the curriculum rely heavily on a repository of texts that were selected for themes that would be relevant across disciplines, such as:

individual and society, membership and solidarity, power and privilege, freedom and choice, rights and responsibilities, struggle and progress. They looked for different text types, considering literature, informational, visual and multimedia texts. Finally, they looked at voice and issue, including topics such as race and ethnicity, gender, sexual orientation, class, immigration, religion, disability and bullying.[6]

The repository is freely available to educators online through a searchable database of literature, poems, personal narratives, interviews, speeches, essays, memoir excerpts, video clips with transcripts, and images. It is a virtual treasure trove of material for educators to use in classrooms and for youth workers to use in and out of school settings, and one is able to filter texts to those specifically related to identity, race/ethnicity, and adolescents (grades six through twelve).

What's more, the online tool was developed to help educators intuitively develop or tailor an Integrated Learning Plan within each of the four areas of the antibias framework, so they are able to select an "essential question" to guide a lesson plan. For instance, one option that is particularly relevant to the points raised in this book is, "How do we express pride in the groups we belong to without denying the value of other groups?" After selecting a question around which to orient students' learning, educators then select a central text from material that has been tagged as pertaining to that question. They then follow a lesson-building tool that provides options for inclusion of writing tasks, an opportunity for students to "do something" ("to demonstrate their awareness and learning from earlier phases through performance tasks that build civic engagement and critical literacy skills"), and engage in deeper literacy skill-building around the text, including other writing and discussion activities.[7]

Facing History and Ourselves. Another approach designed to be integrated into subject-specific courses in schools—namely, history courses—is the Facing History and Ourselves curriculum.[8] This approach foregrounds the work of social identity reflection and development. Through a sequenced process, students engage in learning activities guided by essential questions. For example, the first step is to engage with the theme of "Individual and Society." In doing so, students wrestle with three questions: Who am I? Who are you? Who are we? How we answer these questions shapes how we think about, and how we behave toward, ourselves and others. And our answers to those questions are influenced by the society in which we live.[9]

In units on historical events, such as the Holocaust or Little Rock, teachers use texts, eyewitness testimonials, videos, and images to develop lessons around these themes. In one related to identity, for instance, students are asked to reflect on a text, such as Chimamanda Adichie's TED talk,[10] "The Danger of a Single Story," and on their own identities in visual and writing activities. One is an "identity chart," in which they write their name in a box and then draw lines from the box to words that describe how they see their own identity. Another is an "identity box":

> One way to help students think about their identity is by asking them to create an identity box. To model the process, create your [the teacher] own identity box (or paper bag). It might focus on who you are today or who you were as a teen. On the outside of a cardboard box or brown paper bag write words that others might use to describe you now or then. Inside the box or bag place pictures of people important in your life and brief descriptions of events that have shaped who you are or mementos of those experiences. Share one or two items from inside and outside of the box with the class. Be sure to explain the significance of each item by telling how it helped to influence your identity.
>
> Ask students to use a paper bag or a cardboard box to create their own identity box. On the outside, ask them to write the words others might use to describe them. On the inside, ask them to place pictures, brief descriptions, or mementoes of individuals or experiences that are important to their identity. When the boxes are complete, invite students to share one or two items from the inside or outside of their box with a partner.[11]

The identity-centered theme is followed by one focused on "We & They":

> Students examine the ways that humans so often create "in" groups and "out" groups and the sometimes profound consequences of creating those groups. In this part of the journey, students explore how and why important ideas about human similarities and differences—such as race, religion, and nation—have greatly influenced the way many societies have defined their membership in the past several centuries.[12]

Subsequent themes have students learn about historical injustices such as the Holocaust. A necessary initial step in helping them grapple with such injustices involves encouraging them to understand their own identities and how different social identities are formed. Facing History and Ourselves' approach to sequencing themes in this manner provides support for the idea that fostering intergroup empathy and concern for social justice begins with having greater clarity about one's own identity.

Dialoguing across Difference: Building Unity without Uniformity

In addition to what youth are learning via academic curricula in school, other approaches aim to provide spaces for young people to process their thoughts, feelings, and experiences related to ethnicity and race with *each other*. Intergroup dialogue is a strategy in which members of different ethnic-racial groups are asked to engage in conversations about their own in-group identities and to learn more about the identities and experiences of people who are different from them.

A considerable barrier to these types of dialogues in colleges and universities across the United States is the common practice in many of our institutions of expending considerable resources to recruit student bodies that are in theory diverse but providing considerably fewer resources to support the integration of students from diverse walks of life. An excerpt from a *New York Times* article, "The

Lie about College Diversity" aptly describes this problem:http://
www.nytimes.com/2015/12/13/opinion/sunday/the-lie-about
-college-diversity.html?mwrsm=Email

> Have you spent much time on campuses lately? Leafed through
> schools' promotional literature? Listened to their come-ons?
>
> If so, you've probably noticed how often they promise stu-
> dents academic and social experiences customized to their
> already-established preferences, tailor-fitted to their predeter-
> mined interests, contoured to the particular and peculiar niches
> they want to inhabit.
>
> There's a profusion of affinity groups. There are themed liv-
> ing arrangements that allow students with similar backgrounds
> and overlapping hobbies to huddle together. In terms of curric-
> ulum, there's enormous freedom, which can translate into the
> ability to chart and stick to a narrow path with fellow travelers
> whose perspectives are much the same as yours.
>
> So even if a school succeeds in using its admissions process
> to put together a diverse student body, it often fails at the more
> important goal that this diversity ideally serves: meaningful in-
> teractions between people from different backgrounds, with dif-
> ferent scars and different ways of looking at the world.[13]

As noted in chapter 5 of this book and the comments above, being
in a "diverse" space is not sufficient for intergroup empathy to
emerge.[14] Rather, a more proactive, intentional approach is needed
to help youth draw on their understanding of themselves to foster
intergroup empathy, especially in places where they have opportunities to cross ethnic-racial boundaries. The Intergroup Dialogues
(IGD) approach is widely used across college campuses around the
United States and was specifically designed to address the severe
lack of meaningful contact among diverse groups.[15] Patricia Gurin
and her colleagues define IGD as

> a facilitated educational effort that brings an equal number of
> students from two social identity groups ... together in quarter-
> or semester-long, credit-earning courses. Since their inception

in the late 1980s, intergroup dialogues have sought to educate students proactively to understand and work with intergroup conflicts that are not only historical and structural but persistent and present in their daily college lives. IGD aims for students to gain knowledge of intergroup issues, especially group-based social identities and inequalities; to improve and deepen intergroup communication and relationships; and to develop skills in and commitment to intergroup collaboration.[16]

The nuts and bolts of the IGD approach involves implementing a curriculum with "in-class structured activities and opportunities for critical reflection" as well as readings and other assignments to be completed outside of class.[17] Learning and practicing how to engage in discussion, and how to engage in disagreement and conflicts that may arise between the two social identity groups, is an integral part of the IGD approach as well. Facilitators are trained to navigate these discussions and any conflicts that emerge as students discuss social justice issues.

Youth Dialogues on Race and Ethnicity—an Intergroup Dialogues program—has been implemented with high school–aged students in a community setting.[18] It is described in this way:

> In the nation's most segregated metropolitan area, young people are open to discussion of race and ethnicity, but have few opportunities to communicate with people who are different from themselves. Youth Dialogues on Race and Ethnicity in Metropolitan Detroit brings together high school age youth from different racial and ethnic backgrounds and from different neighborhoods and suburbs for intergroup dialogues during the summer.

Youth Dialogues relies on community members as adult allies in the process of having youth explore race and ethnicity with peers who had similar and different backgrounds.[19] Barry Checkoway suggests that the inclusion of such community allies is critical to the success of the program's racial justice goals:

> Young people who live in segregation and participate in intergroup dialogues should not operate in isolation without adult

allies, and some parents, teachers, and agency advisers provided special support before, during, and after the dialogues. As a result, we identified adult allies who seemed sympathetic and brought them together to discuss what adults might do to assist young people working for racial justice and community change.[20]

It's also noteworthy that the program was designed with the premise that it is critical to have "*intra*group dialogue in a homogeneous group ... followed by *inter*group dialogue with a group with whom they have difference."[21] Over the course of ten Saturdays, youth participating in the Youth Dialogues program were convened at a community agency to implement a curriculum based on the Intergroup Relations program at the University of Michigan. One example of what youth do in this program is illustrated by their tour of the metro area. Drawing directly on the complicated, rich history of race relations and segregation in the metro Detroit area, the program "organized a metropolitan tour for participants. We drove down city streets known for segregated facilities and civil rights marches, stopped at cultural institutions and a concrete wall built by real estate developers to separate whites and blacks, and passed new schools and shopping malls in the suburbs."[22] Other key program goals are summarized in the box below.

Adriana Aldana and her colleagues evaluated whether the Youth Dialogues program had an impact on the ethnic-racial identity of participating Black/African American, Asian American, European

---

Youth Dialogues on Race and Ethnicity *Goals*

- Learn and practice dialogue skills
- Tell stories and listen and learn from other group members
- Get to know each other personally
- Strengthen understanding of the relationship of their own personal lives with social group identities and multiple identities
- Identify differences and sources of conflict
- Explore similarities and differences between groups
- Experience conflict as an integral part of the learning process
- Discuss some concrete, contemporary issues involving these groups
- Generate ideas for action projects on which groups might work[23]

American, Middle Eastern American, Latina/o, and Multiracial/ethnic youth who were thirteen to nineteen years old.[24] To do so, they surveyed youth before and after the program. They found that exploration of their ethnic-racial identities—for instance, talking to others or learning more about their group—increased over the course of completing the program, and did so similarly for all ethnic-racial groups.[25] Notably, these authors concluded that:

> In the dialogue program studied, adolescents were first asked to critically examine their own ethnic-racial identity with youth of similar backgrounds. Thus, the structure of *intra*-group dialogue discussions directly prompted students to talk and learn about their identity with others ... The results suggest that intergroup dialogue programs with adolescents have the promise to be a method that facilitates adolescents' exploration of their ethnic-racial identity.[26]

Thus, providing young people from different ethnic-racial groups with opportunities to interact meaningfully with each other is critical, and this can and ought to be done in community settings.

Finally, although this latter discussion has focused on the importance of creating spaces to foster intergroup contact and dialogue, we want to be perfectly clear that we're not suggesting that spaces, organizations, or movements meant to support the unique needs of ethnic or racial groups should be eliminated. These are especially critical for community-building among members of groups historically underrepresented in higher education. Instead, we believe that *in addition to* such spaces, there is a need for these other spaces that are designed to intentionally provide a space for youth to gain a clearer understanding of themselves and others in a manner that helps them to develop intergroup empathy.

Raising Consciousness and Developing a Political Voice

Still other programs focus on supporting youths' sociopolitical development. This involves youth learning about the cultural and political factors that shape an individual's status in society and eventually engaging in actions that work against such forces and interrupt social injustices.[27] The process of sociopolitical development is described as a five-stage process by Roderick Watts and his colleagues, and is outlined in the box below.

Focusing on the programs that deal directly with ethnic-racial issues, as youth are developing their identities and gaining an understanding of how they fit into society, there are things that can be done to support a greater awareness. An important aspect of sociopolitical development, and one on which many researchers and practitioners have focused in their work with young people, is *critical consciousness*.[29] Essentially, critical consciousness reflects a person's capacity to recognize and question unequal resources and attend to how power differences between groups may be leading to those inequalities. Developing critical consciousness not only helps youth gain a more holistic understanding of their identity but also may help youth feel more comfortable crossing group boundaries. That is, if youth have a greater understanding of other groups' experiences with oppression, and have thought about how their own group's experiences are similar to or different from those of other groups, they may be able to navigate such relationships in a more productive way, as we discussed in chapter 5.

Five Stages of Sociopolitical Development

- **Acritical Stage:** Lack of awareness of uneven resources or power between groups. Differences that are recognized are believed to be justified or deserved due to some characteristic of the group with fewer resources.
- **Adaptive Stage:** Differences and injustices are recognized, but the system that leads to the differences is believed to be impossible to change.
- **Pre-Critical Stage:** Critical awareness of inequality and differences in resources across groups begins to emerge. Individuals start to question whether adapting to the status quo is the way forward.
- **Critical Stage:** Individuals want to learn more about injustices, inequality, oppression, and liberation. In this stage, some individuals will come to the conclusion that the inequality is not fair and that some type of social change is necessary.
- **Liberation Stage:** Individuals are clear about oppression and social injustices. They actively work to change the status quo by engaging in social action and participating in activities to rectify injustices.[28]

So, you might be wondering, "What types of programs can help youth develop critical consciousness?" or "How exactly do we help youth develop their sociopolitical understanding?"[30] There are many different models for how programs have engaged youth in this process,[31] but a common ingredient we noticed in the programs we identified was the importance of providing youth with opportunities to engage in a critical dialogue with an experienced facilitator regarding issues of oppression and social injustice.[32] The developers of the Young Warriors program, for instance, explained how they attempted to achieve these goals with African American young men who were freshmen and sophomores in high school:

> The first challenge for our action-research team was developing a training strategy for enhancing critical thinking on social, political, gender and cultural topics while holding the interest of young men. To accomplish this we relied on rap music videos, television shows, and film as the subject matter for the training and as a stimulus for discussion. There were a number of advantages to using this material: it validates an art form the young men valued but adults often despise (so, when adults value it they gain credibility); it is ecologically and culturally relevant to the young men's life experience; and it covered a very wide range of contemporary topics from many different vantage points.[33]
>
> [S]mall group discussions were the heart of the Young Warriors. The trainers primarily used Rap videos and film excerpts followed by questions ... as the strategy for promoting critical consciousness.[34]

Specifically, questions such as "What did you see? What does it mean? What is the person trying to say? Why do you think that? Why do you think that is what it means? Is what you saw and heard good, bad, or neither? What would you do to make it better?" guide the discussion by trained facilitators and help students process the information to which they are exposed.[35] Through this dialogue, Watts and Abdul-Adil explain, students develop critical thinking and critical consciousness skills.[36] We propose that by developing these important skills, youth are then better equipped to successfully engage with peers who are ethnically and racially different from them.

A similar approach, labeled *critically compassionate intellectualism*, was implemented as part of the Mexican American Studies curriculum with low-income Latino students in the Tucson Unified School District in Arizona.[37] This approach had similar goals to those of the Young Warriors program. The program in Tucson required teachers to connect in a meaningful manner with students and their families, help students develop critical consciousness, work with students so that they would view themselves as intellectuals, and promote students' abilities to be agents of change.[38] Most importantly, the program required teachers to recognize that students had considerable knowledge that they gained through their experiences with family and their communities.[39]

A natural parallel can be drawn between this program and the Young Warriors program with respect to the positive impact that adults' validation can have on youths' perceptions of themselves as significant and worthy voices for the social issues affecting their group. This increased self-confidence and efficacy relating specifically to understanding and being able to discuss the circumstances of their ethnic-racial background is necessary for youth to begin to feel a sense of resolution about their ethnic-racial identity.

Moving outside of the school setting, Shawn Ginwright explains that community-based organizations can also provide youth with significant social capital in the form of connections to organizations in Black communities that help build youths' political consciousness and prepare them to be active agents of change in their communities.[40] As part of this process, youth develop a collective racial and cultural identity that gives them a more holistic understanding of their ethnic-racial group in the context of American society. He explains the valuable role of community institutions for Black youth as follows:

> Community institutions such as schools, churches, and youth programs that are located in Black communities are key in developing and sustaining critical social capital for Black youth and

their communities. Rather than view social capital as perfunc-
tory relationships and connections to resources, critical social
capital in Black poor communities must contend with fostering
a critical consciousness, building a strong racial identity, and
developing political optimism and expectations about community change.[41]

In a specific program that Ginwright studied, a community-based
organization in Oakland, California, was able to develop and sustain critical social capital among Black youth by focusing on three
goals: (1) challenge "negative preconceptions of Black youth as civic
problems by conceptualizing them as important political actors in
their communities"; (2) foster "a collective racial and cultural identity"; and (3) help "young people understand the political explana-
tions for their personal challenges."[42]

As an example of how the first goal was accomplished, consider
the following story from Ginwright's work. The executive director
of the community organization had been invited to attend a town
hall meeting called by the chief of police, the mayor, and the local
congresswoman. The purpose of the meeting was to discuss the
community's experience with police misconduct. When the executive director arrived at the meeting, she learned that no youth had
been invited. She quickly called several youth members of the organization and invited them not only to attend the meeting but to get
on the open mic and share their perspective. The benefits of this
were clearly evident in one young man's statement when he was
reflecting on the experience:

> [LE adults] see stuff that you don't see in yourself, and they try
> to bring it out of you. They see me as an activist or something,
> and I'm not political like that. But when [the current LE execu-
> tive director] lets me speak my mind to folks like the mayor and
> political people, it makes you want to live up to that image, you
> know.[43]

Importantly, the executive director's actions not only created a
space for the young people's voices to be heard but recast the Black

youth in the community as influential political actors. This recasting is important for youths' identity formation as well, given that youth are defining themselves, in part, based on how they think that others perceive them. Furthermore, Ginwright explained that this experience and others like it were key ingredients for helping build mutual trust and respect between the adults in the organization and the youth that they served.

It is important to recognize that sometimes these goals have to be achieved by engaging youth with community connections that are somewhat less conventional, such as dance crews and networks of hip-hop artists and producers.[44] Ginwright explains that this is because community or school connections that are more common avenues for building youth social capital (such as student council or community-based recreation centers) may not be available due to the lack of state investment in education and basic social services for some low-income Black communities. Nevertheless, as noted by Ginwright, connections can be established and youth can get the support they need when adults in their communities are committed to helping youth reach their potential.

You might be wondering if this is only important for youth from marginalized backgrounds. Although the idea of sociopolitical development was originally conceived of as an important process for oppressed people—to help those who are oppressed to be aware of unjust social processes and develop skills that would lead to social change[45]—more recently it has been recognized as an important process for members of nonmarginalized, privileged groups, particularly so that those who are in positions of power can develop the ability to work toward reducing social injustices and serve as allies.[46]

In fact, some programs have been developed specifically to prepare educators (who tend to be members of the majority White population) to meet the needs of students who come from traditionally marginalized communities.[47]For example, Shelley Zion, Ben Kirshner, and Christina Jean developed a two-semester course for teachers in which they reflected on their privileged or oppressed identity groups, learned how to facilitate critical conversations about educational equity with students, and learned how to conduct an action research project that focused on oppression in the educational setting.[48] The development of the course was driven largely by the belief that, in order to adequately serve students from diverse backgrounds, and who have traditionally been underserved, educators must have the knowledge and skills to deliver a curriculum that is culturally responsive and inclusive; this can only be achieved by giving teachers opportunities to "learn [about] and practice acting as agents of change against oppression in the educational system."[49]

Strengthening Youth's Ethnic-Racial Identity

The programs we have discussed up to this point clearly increase youths' awareness and understanding of issues of inequality, prejudice, and racism, as well as provide spaces in which youth can discuss these issues with diverse peers and adult allies. Many of these approaches require young people to carefully consider their own ethnic-racial identities as a step toward having conscious engagement with ethnic-racial issues more broadly. Indeed, as we explained at length in chapter 3, ethnic-racial identity is an important lens through which individuals interpret their world, as it relates to race and ethnicity. Next, we consider a program that is designed specifically to facilitate healthy ethnic-racial identity development in youth.

THE IDENTITY PROJECT INTERVENTION: HELPING YOUTH EXPLORE AND GAIN CLARITY IN SCHOOL

One approach that has demonstrated promising results for fostering youths' ethnic-racial identity development is the Identity Project intervention program.[50] The Identity Project was developed specifically to provide adolescents with tools and strategies that would help them learn more about their ethnic-racial background via an eight-week program in which students meet once a week for about an hour. Because developing a clear sense of who one is with re-

Primary Objectives of the Identity Project Intervention Program

- Help students understand that their identities are made up of many different factors and their ethnic-racial background is one of these.
- Expose students to different strategies that they can use to learn about their background.
- Increase students' understanding of the existence of stereotypes and discrimination for members of different groups in the US across history.
- Expose students to the idea that diversity exists both within groups and between groups.
- Increase students' awareness and understanding of ethnic-racial identity development as a journey that does not have a "right" or "wrong" course and that does not unfold in the same manner for everyone.

spect to race and ethnicity is an important part of development for all youth,[51] the intervention was developed to be relevant to youth from any ethnic-racial background—not specific to any one group. This aspect of the program also makes it easier to use in a variety of settings. Although at this point the program has only been carried out in the school setting, it was developed in a way to make it easily adaptable to any group setting in which youth regularly meet with an adult facilitator at least once a week for eight consecutive weeks.

The primary objectives of the Identity Project are achieved via a series of eight lessons that include brief lectures, classroom activities, and large-group discussion of homework assignments. During each session, students are introduced to basic concepts, such as stereotypes and discrimination, and they actively participate in activities that help them learn about their own ethnic-racial heritage. For example, students create a family tree that describes the heritage of their parents, grandparents, and great-grandparents. They complete this activity partly in class and partly as a homework assignment. This is because students have to talk to their parents and other extended family to find out things, such as where their maternal and paternal grandparents were born and the ethnic identification of those family members.

Via this process, students not only learn about their family history, but they have an opportunity to engage their family members in discussions about their heritage. In a sense, this activity can ignite and facilitate teachable moments with family members regarding ethnic-racial identity. Back in the classroom setting, students use the information they gathered from their families to create a poster board that depicts their family's heritage. Students then work in pairs with their peers to share their family history and discuss how their own ethnic-racial self-identification is similar to and different from the self-identification of other members of their family. By engaging in these activities, students are actively exploring their background while also thinking about how they self-identify and why.

In another homework assignment, students interview a person—a grandparent or neighbor, for instance—who shares their ethnic-racial heritage. During the interview, students gather information about the person's background and traditions and, in a subsequent classroom-based activity, students connect the experiences of the person they interviewed to their own experiences and attitudes. Examining their own identity in relation to another person's helps students think more deeply about why they identify the way that they do. Back in the classroom setting, students engage in a large-group discussion in which they reflect on their interviews with one another. A common theme of this discussion is the many different ways that individuals identify, and different reasons for how they choose to identify themselves in terms of their ethnic-racial background.

Another homework assignment involves sharing an important symbol, tradition, or practice from one's heritage with the class. In one classroom, an Apache student brought a jug of tea to share with the class. He wrote the following description on a notecard, which he placed next to the tea, for his peers to learn about the symbolic nature of this tea for the Apache people—*his* people:

> "Izeh tsuseh," also known as wild tea, has been used by the Apache for centuries. Izeh means "medicine" and "tsuseh" means "long and thin," to describe the plant itself. It is found in higher elevations, especially after a rainy season at the end of the summer. The plant is harvested in a special way; it is important not to pull the plant up by the root to ensure that it continues to

grow. The stalks of the tea are steeped in boiling water until it gets to a deep orange color. The tea is [*sic*] can be used to treat the cold and flu. It is usually not sweetened but to complement it today I provided a natural sweetener which comes from the agave plant. The agave was also harvested by the Apache and the "sugar cane like" stalk was baked underground for days before it could be eaten.[52]

Students' engagement in activities such as the one described above helps them not only to actively learn more about their background but to present the material they are learning in a way that clearly communicates the ideas to others. This process of *teaching others* about one's background is likely an important aspect of why the intervention has been successful in promoting adolescents' ethnic-racial identity development, as described below.

The initial test of the Identity Project intervention program was carried out in a large ethnically and racially diverse high school in the Southwest United States.[53] To test the program, we randomly selected four classrooms in the school to receive the Identity Project curriculum (i.e., the *intervention*) and four classrooms to receive a different curriculum (the *nonintervention control* group) that had nothing to do with identity.[54] Before the program began, students in all eight classrooms completed surveys in which they answered questions about how much they had previously explored aspects of their ethnic-racial background and whether they felt that they had a good sense of what this aspect of their identity meant to them.[55]

Exactly twelve weeks after the initial survey (and after experiencing the intervention or the control curriculum), students once again filled out surveys.[56] We found that students in the Identity Project classrooms had increased their exploration of their ethnic-racial background—such as by reading books or searching the Internet to learn more about their heritage. By contrast, the exploration behaviors of students in the nonintervention classrooms had not changed at all.[57] Six weeks after that, we surveyed students once again and found that those in the Identity Project classrooms now had a greater sense of clarity and understanding of their ethnic-racial background. Again, these changes did not happen for students in the nonintervention classrooms. It is also important to note that these findings were similar for adolescents who were members of ethnic-racial minority groups (such as Asian, Latino, Black, and American Indian adolescents), and the ethnic-racial majority (i.e., White).[58]

As with many of these structured programs,[59] the Identity Project provides students with an opportunity to spend time learning more about their background in a setting that is facilitated by a knowledgeable adult, and the lessons (which are delivered during the regular school day) provide youth with a dedicated time and space where they can discuss potentially sensitive topics. These elements of the program enable youth to engage in the important, though sometimes challenging, work of figuring out their identities and answering the important "Who am I?" question that is so central to the developmental period of adolescence.

ILLUSTRATIONS FROM FAMILY INTERVENTIONS

In considering how to strengthen young people's ethnic-racial identity, it is also important to consider how families can play an important role, because decades of research have now demonstrated that family is perhaps the most important social influence on ethnic-racial identity in youth.[60] The family-oriented programs we consider here focus less directly on youth but nevertheless contribute to young people's healthy ethnic-racial identity development.[61] In particular, we highlight examples of activities that have been aimed at parents to support and strengthen their efforts to teach youth about ethnicity and race, and you will note that each is geared toward a specific ethnic-racial group.[62] The larger programs in which these activities are embedded were not designed to focus solely on the ethnic-racial aspects of parenting but rather to support positive parenting practices among members of the group they target. So it's enlightening that, in each one, spending time talking with youth about ethnic-racial issues was viewed as a critical piece of positive parenting practices for the ethnic-racial groups they targeted because it was thought to be a key way to strengthen either the parent's or the child's sense of connection with, and understanding of, their ethnic-racial group. We'll discuss each one in turn.

Strong African American Families.[63] The Strong African American Families program is a seven-week intervention designed by Velma Murry and her colleagues for rural African American families with eleven-year-old children.[64] Parents attend the weekly sessions at local community centers, and material is taught through interactive games, discussions, and role plays, among other activities, as follows:

> Families met for seven weekly sessions at local community centers. During each meeting, youth and caregivers attended separate 1-hour sessions, followed by a 1-hour joint session in which families practiced the skills they had learned in their respective sessions through discussions and games. African American facilitators with previous experience in teaching or working with families led all sessions.[65]

Although issues germane to parenting African American children may arise during any of the weeks, Week 6 is dedicated specifically to the topic "Encouraging Racial Pride," which addresses not only building racial pride but also ways of handling discrimination. In doing so, the facilitators work with parents to learn how to handle difficult situations, identify strengths of African American families, and build strong racial pride in the family.[66] Their rationale for supporting racial socialization reflected the particular relevance of race to the experiences of African American parents and their children:

> Unlike racial majority parents, African American parents have the added responsibility of teaching their children how to cope with experiences in a society in which their group is often devalued.... Optimally, African American parents' messages about race prepare their children for encounters with discrimination while emphasizing pride in being African American ... many African American parents emphasize self-acceptance and racial pride with their children by transmitting messages that African

Americans are "strong, beautiful people with a rich history." These messages appear to enhance youth development and increase the likelihood that adolescents will reject stereotypic images about their group. Adaptive racial socialization is associated with high self-esteem and positive racial identity during adolescence.[67]

A randomized control trial of this program showed that participating in the Strong African American Families intervention enhanced racial pride—along with other aspects of positive self-concept—in the children of parents who participated, as compared to those whose parents were in the control (nonintervention) group.[68] In this way, this program can contribute to youth developing a more positive sense of their identity as it relates to their ethnic-racial background.

Parenting in 2 Worlds. A final example of parent-oriented activities in community-based programs can be seen in the Parenting in 2 Worlds (P2W) program, which was designed for urban American Indian parents/guardians of an American Indian child ages ten to seventeen. The program is described as such:

> Designed to be flexible, the P2W curriculum allows all families to relate their own tribal and cultural practices and beliefs to the curriculum content. Curriculum lessons invite the participants to engage with and share their experiences of Native cultural values relating to parenting and healthy family functioning, rather than specify what those values are or should be.
>
> The P2W pilot followed a 10-workshop, 5-week manualized curriculum that included workshops on (1) identifying your family's traditions, norms, and values; (2) communicating with your child; and (3) guiding your child's behavior effectively. Trained community-based urban AI [American Indian] facilitators delivered the curriculum, leading two workshops per week, using various facilitation strategies: informational discussions, individual and small group activities, videos, role-plays, games, scenarios, group presentations, activity sheets, and home activities.[69]

In a preliminary study, parents were surveyed before and after the program about a range of issues, including their own ethnic-racial identity. Parents reported a significant increase in their sense of commitment and how much they explored their ethnic-racial identity, and they also reported a stronger sense of identification with an American Indian way of life after completing the P2W program. Although the P2W program does not directly target youths' ethnic-racial identity, by impacting parents' ethnic-racial identity, it can play an indirect role in youths' identity processes as well.

Considerations for Practitioners

STAFF PROFICIENCY WITH ETHNIC AND RACIAL IDENTITY ISSUES: AN ESSENTIAL INGREDIENT

The skills of program facilitators and educators are certainly an essential ingredient for a community-based program or school-based curriculum to succeed in helping youth navigate ethnic-racial issues and questions. Having facilitators explore and engage with one another around issues of race is key in being able to provide spaces in which youth can do the same. For example, facilitators of the Intergroup Dialogues program discussed earlier are asked to think deeply about identity issues in order to be able to understand what they "bring" to the facilitation dynamic. As Kelly Maxwell, Mark Chesler, and Biren Nagda explain:

> Social group identity is relevant not only to the conduct of intergroup dialogues but to the training and practice of facilitation. The training and supervision we provide facilitators is experienced and interpreted through the lens of their locations in the society's structures of race, gender, socioeconomic class, sexual orientation, religion, and other social categories. These identities, locations, and associated experiences provide and reinforce sets of values, talents/skills, and expectations facilitators bring to the dialogic encounter and to their leadership role. Moreover, the responses of students in the dialogue, as well as facilitators'

expectations or assessments of these responses, also play a role in their approaches and actions. We can expect, then, that IGD facilitators' social group identities play a role in how they think about acting, plan to act, and do act as they relate with participants and their co-facilitators.[70]

In one such implementation of the IGD program, one of the ways they do this is to ask trainees to reflect on the role of their social identities in their perceptions of the group dynamics and in their own facilitation practices. Ximena Zúñiga and her colleagues explain:

> One of the hardest challenges intergroup dialogue facilitators face is learning to notice, describe, and examine the gaps or tensions that often exist between their intentions in making a facilitation move (or abstaining from making one) and the impact of what actually happens in the "here and now." A critical reflective stance can help practitioners gain insight into self and others' intentions (e.g., assumptions and motivations) during a difficult or confusing moment. It can also help facilitators identify what may have led to "what happened," including the extent to which social identity–based processes may have influenced what happened, and help them explore what they could have done differently and why.[71]

In one Massachusetts school, the principal has initiated cultural proficiency seminars to help his staff be able to support the positive identity and academic development of their very diverse student body:

> One way [Cambridge Street Upper School principal] Fernandez is trying to give the students the support and confidence [they need] ... is by tackling the charged topic of race head on. He is starting with his teachers—as in many schools, mostly white, mostly female—by having every one of them talk about race every week ...
>
> Fernandez launched weekly cultural proficiency seminars for his entire staff, focusing on race. Fifty minutes, four times a week, every week, the teachers get together in groups to read about and explore issues of race in professional development seminars—

one each for the sixth-, seventh- and eighth-grade staff and another for the specialists ...

Being able to lead his staff "to help them embrace a culturally proficient environment" was an important factor in taking the principal job, and he said he's grateful he found "a school in a progressive community and the support of my superordinates, [in a district] that says it celebrates social justice" and lets him do something about it.

The seminars are built around weekly readings, initially "Culturally Proficient Instruction" by Kikanza Nuri-Robins and Delores Lindsey and other contemporary articles, that help prime the pump for the staff members. Conversations often connect to classroom experiences, though, with teachers sometimes bringing in an incident or discussion from class to bounce off ideas and get feedback ...

And the seminars clearly are about the "me" in the teaching. "This issue is one around identity," Fernandez said. "Who am I? What do I bring to the table? The identity that you and I carry isn't just the one that our parents taught us about, but it is also about what other people think we have when we walk down the street. Other people place identities on us whether we want them or not."[72]

The reflection about what practitioners bring to the table—such as those given above—mirrors, in important ways, the kind of thoughtfulness about race and ethnicity that we are encouraging in youth.

Principal Fernandez's approach also underscores the particular relevance of such reflection in the school setting. Embracing a "culturally proficient environment," however, also entails supporting teachers in delivering antibias curricula. Ruchi Agarwal and her colleagues, for instance, note that teaching for social justice can mean different things to different people, and it is therefore important to be clear about the key markers of teaching for social justice when training educators:

Educators who teach for social justice (a) enact curricula that integrate multiple perspectives, question dominant Western narratives, and are inclusive of the racial, ethnic, and linguistic diversity in North America; (b) support students to develop a critical consciousness of the injustices that characterize our society; and (c) scaffold opportunities for students to be active participants in a democracy, skilled in forms of civic engagement and deliberative discussion.[73]

In an effort to understand whether beginning teachers were successfully integrating social justice instruction into their pedagogical approaches after a preservice teacher education training program, Agarwal and her colleagues followed the case studies of three beginning teachers.[74] Based on their observations, they made three recommendations targeted toward those who are training educators committed to creating a classroom environment that challenges racist, sexist, classist, ableist, and heterosexist norms. First, teacher education programs should facilitate discussions that communicate to teachers that teaching for social justice is a journey and will not be something that will come easily or quickly. Too often, teachers can get frustrated or discouraged because their efforts seem to be falling short of the goals they had for the classroom. This is common, and Agarwal and colleagues emphasize the need to support teachers who are embarking on this journey and encouraging them to keep at it.

Second, teacher education programs should not focus exclusively on presenting beginning teachers with exemplar models for social justice teaching.[75] Instead, programs will be more effective if they present cases that demonstrate the challenges of incorporating social justice curricula in combination with success stories. The more realistic approach helps new teachers recognize the potential constraints and consider different ways to overcome and cope with them in their work with students.

Finally, a practice that is common in teacher education programs, but that Agarwal and her colleagues believe to be especially important for learning to enact social justice curricula, involves practicing reflective-thinking skills.[76] They explain that for social justice curricula, in particular, it is critical for teacher education programs to reconsider how they are teaching the process of reflection to teachers, because reflection needs to focus more on what students learned and accomplished rather than on how the teacher fell short of his or her own vision. Agarwal and her colleagues note that this approach helps teachers focus more on their successes and skill in teaching for social justice.

Psychologist Howard Stevenson offers another approach to helping practitioners build what he calls "racial literacy" by building skills to appraise and proactively cope with the stress or anxiety brought about in racial situations.[77] Racial literacy is the ability to understand, assess, cope with, and resolve stressful racial encounters. In his approach, individuals engage in *recasting*: "an activity of repeated and guided self-reflection that increases awareness of 'in-the-moment' ... [racial] encounters" and its related stress, which hinders intergroup relations.[78] The primary goals and corresponding strategies of recasting are summarized in the box below. Stevenson further explains that recasting is *not* a substitute for eradicating racism and, we would add, xenophobia:

> Anxiety is not the only way to characterize racial conflict or racism, but it is more likely to explain the persistence of avoidance and denial behaviors when individuals undergo uncomfortable racial interactions. This theory in no way exonerates intentional racial hatred, bigotry, and violence ... It promotes the reappraisal and stress reduction of racial interactions and portends hopeful outcomes for those who can reduce this stress.[79]

Recasting Goals and Strategies

- Use stories and storytelling to demonstrate awareness of stress and other characteristics associated with racial encounters.
- Use journaling to write about experiences of and assess stress caused by racial encounters.
- Relax to be able to reappraise and reduce stress linked to racial encounters.
- Debate with others in order to engage with racial conflicts, rather than avoid them.
- Use role-plays to resolve racial conflicts.

Two examples of the kinds of questions used to elicit stories and journal entries from practitioners include, "When did I experience a racial encounter and what did I do?" and "What is my current knowledge of and emotional attachment to the history of my racial group?" Other skills—breathing and exhaling (relaxation), debating about racial stereotypes, and role-playing responses and rebuttals to racism—are developed over time. Thus, Stevenson developed this approach to equip practitioners, for instance, with tools to help them navigate the emotionally threatening aspects of negotiating racial inequality or conflict on a daily basis that, for many, get in the way of working toward racial justice.

A final thought about staff proficiency and racial literacy, to borrow Stevenson's term, concerns White practitioners working with youth of color. Indeed, this is the case in many schools across the United States, where we know that the youth of color, who comprise a majority of the K–12 population, will encounter a White teacher in their classrooms.[80] But it's not only relevant in schools. Those who aim to be allies to communities and youth of color—in *and* out of school—have additional issues to consider during such intergroup exchanges. On the website Medium, Christopher Keelty reflects on the importance of leaning in to possible discomfort in the process of becoming an ally:

> Here's something I can promise, if you take my advice ... and start paying attention to more marginalized voices: You are going to encounter some opinions that will upset you. Some that might make you feel discriminated against, some that might even make you feel victimized by racism.
>
> Don't stop listening. Don't tune out. Lean into your discomfort. Force yourself to consider other opinions, and understand why people might say something you find offensive. I'm not saying you can't still disagree—in fact, the ability to respectfully disagree is itself a skill many Americans, especially White Americans, are not great at. So learn.
>
> You'll learn a lot of terms you might not have encountered before, among them "White Fragility." This is a reference to the

tendency among White people to take offense when they are called out for saying or doing something discriminatory or even racist. It's that thing you may have noticed where some White people think "racist" is itself a discriminatory slur, and instead of listening and examining what about their behavior might be problematic they get offended and even demand an apology from the person they have offended.[81]

Although challenging oneself in these ways is not easy, it is well worth the effort. Put simply, it is a critical aspect of being able to support youth as they negotiate ethnic-racial issues, interactions, and anxieties in their lives. And considering that families are the most influential context in which youth are growing up, the idea of challenging oneself is particularly relevant to parents, a group to which we now turn.

What Can Parents Do?

As of this writing, a quick search of the phrase "how parents talk to their kids about race" on the Internet returned 76,600,000 hits.[82] Focusing more specifically on White parents, with the search "how White parents talk to their kids about race," narrows the search only slightly—returning 49,300,000 hits.[83] So, there is a lot of information on this topic on the Internet, yet many parents are not having these conversations. We know that talking about race and ethnicity is no less challenging for parents than it is for practitioners working with youth. But it's precisely because of the central role of parents in adolescents' ethnic-racial identity development across childhood and adolescence that we dedicate a section exclusively to this group of readers.[84]

Writing to parents, Stevenson encourages us to draw on our own racial literacy—as defined earlier in this chapter—to help youth accurately assess the threat posed by racial conflicts, more effectively reduce such threat in racial encounters, and more assertively challenge racial injustices and advocate for racial equity. It's not surprising, then, that he encourages parents to cultivate and improve our *own* racial literacy first. As we noted above, there are many programs that have been developed that provide strategies for consciously engaging with ethnic-racial issues in structured settings such as schools or community organizations—some of these are even geared to parents. Below, we highlight some of the strategies that parents have turned to in one-on-one interactions with their children.

"THE TALK"

Perhaps no conversation is as difficult as the one that involves telling your child that he or she may be targeted someday simply because of the color of their skin. "The talk" typically refers to the conversation—or series of conversations—African American parents have about the racism that their children are likely to be exposed to in the United States. Often it's done in the context of their potential interactions with law enforcement and includes advice about the strategies youth can use to, essentially, survive these situations. One author describes it as such:

> For me, it went like this: If you are pulled over in your car, keep your hands on the steering wheel. Give the officer your license. If your registration is in your glove box, tell the officer that you're going to retrieve it from there, and move slowly.
>
> If you are stopped by an officer while you are on the street, keep your hands visible.
>
> Don't say anything besides "yes" and "no." Be compliant. Be polite.[85]

The children's book *Momma, Did You Hear the News?* was written to help parents navigate these challenging conversations about the racialized nature of racial profiling and police brutality.[86] Among African American youth, the talk can serve an important role in the process of ethnic-racial identity formation, because it illuminates the role of race and racism in their lives.[87] However, having discussions about the talk with youth from all ethnic and racial backgrounds can also serve as an opportunity to raise awareness of and unpack racial injustices.

THINKING ABOUT "THE TALK" IN THE CONTEXT
OF OTHER ETHNIC-RACIAL GROUPS

There is an increasing awareness by members of *other* groups of the talk and its significance among African American communities. So, what about these other groups? Are they having a talk about racism as well, and if not, should they be? One Mexican American mother's experience highlights how she learned about the talk and its new meaning in the context of her racially diverse family and with her Multiracial children:

> Before the election, my husband told me he would need to have "the talk" with the kids about racial issues he wanted them to be prepared for. My husband wanted to have the talk as soon as possible, even though our kids are eight, six, and four. In his mind, it is important for our children to know that it is different growing up black in America at the earliest possible time so they can understand and be prepared for the first time they hear the N-word. He was only in third grade when a white schoolmate first used the N-word to bully him. He wanted them to know how they should act when they are stopped by the police for "driving while black," which has happened to him.
>
> I thought it was too early for our kids. But I probably should have listened, since right after the election, our five-year-old daughter was told by a classmate that she would have to go on the other side of the wall once it was built. She came home from school that day and asked, "Mommy, when do I need to go on the other side of the wall?"
>
> I felt powerless. I wanted to rage at the other child who had said that to her. But then I remembered, *She is watching me always.* So instead, we had a conversation about why people say things like this. I explained it can be out of fear, misinformation, or sadly in some cases to bully others.
>
> So now I know that it's time for my kids to have the talk, and I need to add to my husband's list of things to be prepared for: how to react when someone tells them to go back to Mexico, or

to help build the wall, or asks them if they are legal or to stop speaking Mexican. It's Spanish, I know, but a lot of people don't.[88]

In the following story, one White mother describes her experience grappling with racism targeted at African Americans in a way that would be intuitive for her young White daughter. Her strategy involved attending an antibias day camp on Martin Luther King Jr. Day with her daughter. At the event, she led a group of activists, educators, parents, and children in singing "I Can't Breathe" in honor of Eric Garner. She recalls her motivations:

> I thought of his family, of all the families of color who face police harassment, violence, and murder, and how not talking about this ugly truth doesn't protect them. I thought about the African American mothers who have to talk to their young sons and daughters about how to act in front of the police so they aren't shot. I thought of a Black friend whose young son broke the toy gun from his Halloween army guy costume so he wouldn't be shot like Tamir Rice. I thought about the way my daughter was learning about Martin Luther King Jr. at school as someone who just "wanted everyone to get along."[89]

After explaining to the children in the audience who he was, she told them about the significance of the words "I can't breathe." Hearing about racial profiling and police brutality understandably impacted the children emotionally. She writes:

> That night my White daughter had nightmares of the police coming and taking her dad and I away. And I know she wasn't the only child in that room who became upset as they processed this racist violence. Racism really sucks. Introducing our children to the pain of White supremacy makes me really sad. It made me wonder if I had really screwed up. And I might have.
>
> But here's what I know.
>
> The pain, fear, anger, and confusion that my daughter felt was absolutely how she should feel, how we should all feel, when we

are confronted with the injustice and violence of White supremacy and police brutality. It should rock our worlds. It is important to give our children, and ourselves, space to feel those emotions and work through them towards actions that affirm Black Lives Matter. If we are committed to supporting our children to recognize unfairness and teaching them to act for justice, we can't be afraid of their deep and real emotions. In fact, the United States needs more people to feel just how wrong White supremacy is in order to end it.

Echoing the need to move beyond feelings of guilt, she concludes:

As a White woman and mother, I came to recognize my White privilege in my 20's, and I had a lot of feelings about it, namely shame and guilt. Many of us White folks get stuck in those emotions which are ultimately not helpful, though they are understandable, and if we can't move past them into action for racial justice, valuable allies are lost.

NO PAIN, NO GAIN?

I think talking about race might be a "no pain, no gain" thing. If you come out of that conversation and you're not feeling any discomfort or worry or guilt there, it probably wasn't deep enough, or honest enough, or complex enough.[90]

As the stories above illustrate, there is no single road map for the often unplanned opportunities for conscious engagement regarding the ethnic-racial dilemmas that arise in the course of raising one's children. What their stories do share is a sense that some level of pain and fear—which must be recognized and dealt with—compels them to make the most of teachable moments anyway. Rebecca Bigler, a renowned expert on child development, described how an experience she had with her young daughter provided a challenging, but important, teachable moment when her daughter was working on a school assignment.[91] Her daughter had spent hours creating a picture of a fish made up of hundreds of faces—all of the faces were of White children. Bigler explained,

> She was so proud of it, and I knew if I said anything that her face would fall, and I tried to be so careful—it's wonderful, I said, but there's one way [it] could be improved. I only see white faces, and I think brown faces and darker faces are all beautiful, and when you take that to school, your friends who don't have white faces might feel sad or left out.

She then explained that her daughter's face did fall, but they worked together to revise the collage. In the end, she believed that her daughter felt even happier knowing that all of her classmates were now represented in her work. Bigler then went on to explain that it was a commitment to "grab those teachable moments even when it won't be easy." Thus, although there is no one way to take hold of these one-on-one opportunities to consciously engage with youth, they are greatly facilitated by having reflected on one's own beliefs, thoughts, feelings, and biases.

DEVELOPING CULTURAL COMPETENCY

In order to have these conversations with our children, it's necessary for us to develop *cultural competency*. This term is one that is used often and has different meanings for different people. In this book, we draw on the following definition offered by social work scholar Shirley Better:

> [Cultural competency is a] set of congruent attitudes, practices, policies, and structures that come together in a person's interactions, systems, and organizations to allow for positive relationships and outcomes in cross-cultural situations. It is a developmental process based upon the belief that all individuals can learn to embrace differences.[92]

With cultural competency, individuals can recognize and appreciate the values of a culture different from their own.[93] However, as Better explains in her book on strategies for social change, a key ingredient for becoming culturally competent is knowing your own culture and understanding that everyone has a culture that informs one's values, beliefs, and ways of interpreting the world. She notes that before we can begin to learn about others, we must learn about ourselves. In addition, Better explains that becoming culturally competent is not a simple task to be taken lightly and, in fact, requires quite a bit of practice of specific behaviors while examining one's personal values and attitudes. The box below outlines some of the essential behaviors to practice.

Better suggests that culturally competent individuals should have four principles that ultimately guide their behavior as it relates to interacting with others. First, we must recognize that culture has a major influence on behaviors, values, organizations, and social institutions. Also, we must remember that people of color must not only master their own culture but also that of the dominant culture, which is typically not based on their group's values and experiences. European Americans, in contrast, rarely experience this process of having to "learn" a second culture. Second, it is necessary to understand that all minorities are not treated similarly by the dominant

---

Behaviors to Practice for Developing Personal and Interpersonal Cultural Competence

1. **Be nonjudgmental**—putting aside preconceived notions and accepting others on their own terms.
2. **Be flexible**—readjust as needed to work toward positive relationships.
3. **Personalize the interaction**—express personal feelings appropriately in a warm and open manner.
4. **Get in touch with your feelings**—be aware of your initial reactions as you interact with those who are different from you; accept that uneasy feelings may arise and don't let those feelings get in the way of engaging across difference.
5. **Listen carefully**—ask for clarification and be aware that words/phrases have different values across groups.
6. **Observe attentively**—don't assume a similar worldview.
7. **Keep a sense of humor**.
8. **Be respectful**—mutually fulfilling relationships must have a foundation of respect; although cultures differ, each person's culture should be respected.
9. **Show empathy**—consider the situation or issue from the other person's point of view whenever possible.

group in US society. If we are not aware of this, we can fall into the trap of trying to identify the deficiencies in a group (or a person) because we erroneously believe that other minority groups have successfully "made it," so there must be something deficient about those who haven't found success (rather than an acknowledgment of a flawed system that privileges certain groups over others). Third, culturally competent individuals should acknowledge the group identity of individuals rather than singling them out as an exception to what may be considered "typical" for members of their group. For example, telling a Latino individual, "You speak English so well!" is not a compliment. Although the person saying this comment may have had the best intentions, when you unpack this statement, it means: (a) you didn't expect the person to speak English well, and (b) you didn't expect this because you believe that all Latinos are deficient in English proficiency. Therefore, this "compliment" is unintentionally insulting and demeaning the person's group. This is important for cultural competency because, as stated by Better, "the dignity of a person is not guaranteed unless the dignity of his or her people is also preserved."[94] The fourth guiding principle for culturally competent individuals is to be aware that diversity exists within cultures. Generally, it is important to recognize that ethnic-racial groups are not monolithic entities, and to value both individual and group differences when engaging with people from other groups.

Part 2—The Future of Research on Conscious Engagement
In this book we have presented the findings from many studies from social, cultural, and developmental psychology, education, sociology, human development, and the like. We've covered a lot of terrain, and the current state of the research has been helpful for getting us to this point. Yet important gaps remain in our collective knowledge. Indeed, as researchers who are actively engaged in this field, we recognize that there is still much to learn. In the last part of this chapter, we focus directly on a way forward for researchers interested in advancing our understanding of how youth navigate

race and ethnicity in their lives and the programs that may be most effective at helping them do so in a productive manner.

Four key issues come to mind. First, more research is needed to help us gain a clearer understanding of how different contexts can support youths' ethnic-racial identity development and their capacity to engage in positive intergroup contact. Second, more research is needed to determine whether programs focused on ethnic-racial identity and fostering positive intergroup relations are more effective when they are delivered to groups of youth who share an ethnic-racial background or to groups that are more diverse with respect to ethnicity and race. Third, for researchers to develop highly effective programs with youth, there needs to be a greater understanding of when and for whom they work, and whether a program developed in one context is transferrable to another context. Finally, the work that needs to be done can most efficiently and effectively be accomplished by implementing the principles of scientific collaboration, or a "team science" approach. We elaborate on each of these recommendations in the sections that follow.

Issue 1: Advancing Our Understanding of Social Influences on Ethnic-Racial Identity and Intergroup Relations

In chapter 4, we discussed the numerous settings—such as families, schools, and communities—in which youth develop an understanding of themselves in terms of race and ethnicity, yet there are several significant gaps in this research base. One critical gap is that few studies examine ethnic-racial socialization in community-based organizations in which youth spend their after-school hours. One reason for this gap is that, although there are many culturally grounded, community-based activities and programs, very little of the research associated with them reports on youths' ethnic-racial experiences per se. Notable exceptions are found in research on out-of-school activities, which includes extracurricular activities and programs at church or community centers like the YMCA.[95] For example, Alex Lin, Sandra Simpkins, Cecilia Menjívar, and their colleagues found that parents of Mexican descent in Arizona perceived that enhanced cultural knowledge, awareness, and pride, as well as maintenance of cultural heritage, were among the benefits of their adolescents' participation in organized activities.[96] Yet social influences on identity can be positive and negative—the latter includes messages conveying social exclusion or marginalization of one's group. Indeed, this same research group has found that youth participating in organized activities report encountering ethnic teasing by other youth and implicit stereotyping by adults in such settings. Because ethnic-racial socialization is among the most significant predictors of youths' ethnic-racial identity development, more studies in out-of-school settings would provide a potentially rich avenue for further research to build on what we know about ethnic-racial identity development and youths' intergroup relations.

Another significant gap pertains to our limited understanding of how the specific contexts of family and school can facilitate the positive connection between ethnic-racial identity and positive intergroup relations. Although there has been a good deal of research conducted in the context of families and schools, we need more insights into the conditions in each of these contexts that can best promote ethnic-racial identity development in youth and, *simultaneously*, cultivate more positive intergroup relations. In families, we need to better understand how parents navigate ethnic-racial boundaries and pass on their ideologies to their children. We also have an extremely limited understanding of how White parents are navigating these topics with their children and, relatedly, we know little about which strategies are most effective for promoting ethnic-racial competencies in their children. Our research has been limited to understanding how to effectively socialize ethnic-racial minority youth to have a clear understanding of their background and to be prepared for experiences with ethnic-racial discrimination. Yet we know little about how to prepare White youth to be allies for youth of color. All youth need support in developing the skills to be able to engage in positive intergroup relations.

In schools, there are many layers of influence that can be studied and questions that remain open for exploration. As an example, in thinking about how schools serve as a holistic context for the development of youths' understanding of themselves and others as members of ethnic-racial groups, we have recently begun considering school-based social emotional learning (SEL) approaches. SEL refers to "the process through which children and adults acquire and effectively apply the knowledge, attitudes, and skills necessary to understand and manage emotions, set and achieve positive goals, feel and show empathy for others, establish and maintain positive relationships, and make responsible decisions."[97] These types of programs often seek to improve the quality of interactions and relationships among students and between students and teachers— ultimately, the culture and climate of the entire school. Given that the aim of such programs is to support a positive social-emotional atmosphere within a school, we explored the intergroup contact attitudes and friendships among students in a school implementing a SEL program. We found that in this context, those students who had more positive intergroup attitudes didn't just "talk the talk," they were actually more likely to befriend more students from other ethnic-racial groups. In addition, students' intergroup attitudes are "contagious," meaning that their intergroup contact attitudes become more like those of their friends over time.[98] An important next question is, do SEL programs *themselves* facilitate both healthy ethnic-racial identity development and cross-group interactions, and if so, *how*?[99] Equally important, a SEL program that seeks to cultivate a positive, mutually trusting atmosphere among a diverse student body and between students and teachers will not succeed (or its success will be limited) if the practitioners tasked with carrying out the program do not have the support of their administrators for the initial implementation and continued professional development necessary to sustain it.

Another significant gap in this area pertains to our limited understanding of how different social influences may intersect. Although there is a fair amount of research across many disciplines and fields that unpacks how ethnic-racial socialization occurs within a given context (e.g., schools, families), we know less about how these socialization experiences *across* these settings mutually inform one another. For instance, how do youth reconcile ethnic-racial experiences in community-based settings that potentially conflict with those at home or school? Or how do messages about ethnicity or race at home shape youths' friendships at school? In this line of inquiry, it would be important to articulate what youths' capacity to reconcile such experiences might mean for ethnic-racial identity development. Furthermore, we need a better understanding of whether interventions promoting positive intergroup relations with youth are more effective if they target youth in school settings (where peer relations are highly salient), in family settings (where they also have access to parents, which could make the program more effective because of parents' paramount role in child socialization), or in both.

A related point is that programs don't have to be limited to the setting in which they've been developed and in which we've presented them in previous sections. As an example, the Identity Project was developed for a school setting, but it can be delivered in after-school settings as well. Implementing the Identity Project as a school-based program that is part of the general academic curriculum is ideal, because all students (regardless of their interest in or openness to issues of diversity) experience the program. If the program is optional or offered as an after-school or weekend extracurricular activity, it is highly likely that only the youth and parents who are interested in the topic would enroll. Certainly, research on the effectiveness of implementing this type of program across these multiple contexts would help us understand the role of each in facilitating or hindering the goals of the program.

Issue 2: Should Programs Be Carried Out in Homogeneous or Heterogeneous Settings?

The current state of the research base in this area really doesn't provide a definitive answer to this question, as the existing programs that focus on intergroup contact, critical consciousness, or ethnic-racial identity have not been tested in studies that take into account the diversity of youth participants. It is possible that a program may be equally effective in either type of setting. For example, there may be important benefits to being in an ethnically and racially homogenous group when discussing sensitive topics such as racism. If so, then being in a more homogeneous setting may make the program particularly effective with respect to that content. However, for this and other content, there also may be benefits to being in a heterogeneous setting in that such settings provide youth with opportunities to engage in perspective-taking and learn from others who are different from them. For instance, if the program content and focus is such that youth would benefit most from being in ethnic and racially diverse groups—as may be the case when trying to help youth develop skills to engage productively across difference—then such a program may be more effective in the diverse context. Although our understanding of these important nuances is limited by the lack of research, the many open questions make this a fruitful area for future research.

Issue 3: Clarify the "Real-World" Conditions Needed for Successful Programs

Going forward, we need to have greater confidence that research findings "from the lab" can withstand "real-world" conditions. To elaborate on this point, it's useful to consider Elizabeth Paluck and Donald Green's exhaustive review of the literature on interventions in the area of prejudice reduction.[100] They set out to uncover whether there was convincing evidence that certain programs were effective at reducing prejudice. In their review, they noted that the existing interventions had been tested in three different types of settings. First, there were interventions that had been tested in the field but had typically not been led by researchers, and it was very difficult to draw conclusions from these findings because the study did not follow an experimental design. Second, they identified programs that had followed an experimental design and the interventions had been tested in a very structured environment in the research laboratory setting. Paluck and Green explained that here, too, it is difficult to draw conclusions about whether or not these programs will work in more realistic conditions outside laboratories because they have been tested in an artificial setting. Finally, they identified relatively few studies that did follow an experimental design and were also conducted in the field. Ultimately, they explained that their review of hundreds of studies led to the conclusion that there is simply not enough evidence to conclude that any particular intervention will be effective for reducing prejudice—particularly because there is not enough rigorous experimental work in this area that has been conducted in real-world settings. They specifically caution scholars who work in this area to "remain skeptical of the recommendations of laboratory experiments until they are supported by research of the same degree of rigor outside of the laboratory."[101] Thus, it is clear that researchers need practitioners to help them navigate the "real world" in which they must be implementing their programs in order to test their effectiveness, and practitioners need researchers in order to aid in the design and implementation of experimental approaches to test the effectiveness of intervention programs.

Extending this logic a bit further, we also think that researchers and practitioners should work together, as they can help each other think through the complexity of implementing some of the ideas in this book. Such partnerships can be vital for building evidence to support practices geared toward helping youth navigate ethnic-racial issues productively. For example, practitioners can review content and pedagogy of programs that focus on intergroup contact, critical consciousness, or ethnic-racial identity with an eye toward potential barriers in instructors' or facilitators' implementation. Practitioners can also provide critical information about the nature of intergroup relations in the local context that set the stage for the program itself, and can help in interpreting why a program—or any one of its aspects—may be found to be effective or not for the youth population being served. On the other side of the equation, researchers have much to offer practitioners. Perhaps one of the most useful is their capacity to easily provide many different kinds of data that schools and other youth-serving organizations can use to guide their decision making about how to support healthy identity development and intergroup relations among the youth they serve. Practitioners—teachers, principals, community-based staff, and the like—often have a great deal of latitude in how they actually engage with youth regarding issues of race and ethnicity in their day-to-day roles. We can provide an informed perspective with regard to the strategies and tools they decide to implement to support healthy ethnic-racial identity development and race relations in their respective settings.

Issue 4: Team Science

The pressing research questions that are going to move our science forward in the area of youths' ethnic-racial identity and positive intergroup relations will require research teams to work together to answer key questions in the field. One reason for this is that we will need large samples and in multiple places to enable us to test whether approaches are equally effective across different ethnic-racial groups, across settings characterized by different ethnic-racial youth characteristics, and across different regions of the United States. Realistically, these systematic studies can only be carried out by large research teams that span these diverse settings.

A team science approach can also help generate the large studies and diverse samples needed to address another pressing issue, which is the need for more in-depth understanding of how given programs work. For example, how many sessions of the programs described above are necessary for the programs to be effective? This is typically referred to as *dosage* in intervention science, and research designed to identify the lowest necessary dosage is essential to keep program costs low. Furthermore, this information is critical for programs that will be delivered as part of the regular school day, where instruction time for socioemotional curricula is limited. The best way to empirically test what the ideal dosage is for any given intervention program is to randomly assign participants to groups that differ only in the number of intervention sessions that they are receiving. The researcher can then examine at which point there is little value added by including more sessions—for instance, increases in ethnic-racial identity exploration may not be significantly different between a group that receives a six-session program versus a group that receives an eight-session program; but those in the six-session program score significantly higher on exploration than those in a five-session program. These findings can help identify that the ideal number of sessions for that intervention is six. For the issues we are interested in, however, a key aspect of this will also involve understanding whether the answer (in other words, how much dosage is ideal) is the same for youth from different ethnic-racial groups and for youth in different regions of the country. Therefore, the study will require a large sample that spans multiple regions and is diverse with respect to students' ethnic-racial background. This design would be difficult to carry out, logistically, with a single research team.

In addition to enabling the logistics of this complex data collection, a team science approach enables the collaboration of multiple lead investigators who have complementary areas of expertise. Certainly, this approach makes it possible to have diversity in expertise with respect to specific populations, specific age-groups/developmental periods, and historical intergroup contact/conflict in specific regions of the country. As we noted in chapter 5, diversity—including that of perspective and experience—actually promotes greater innovation.[102] Varied expertise in terms of theoretical and methodological tradition—and in terms of practical knowledge in the case of researcher-practitioner partnerships—is essential for developing the programs that will have the most enduring impact in the long run.

———

Conscious engagement with issues of race, ethnicity, and identity begins in youth. We have a significant role to play in this process across myriad social spheres: at home, in school, and in the community. As we've discussed throughout this book, we have come a long way in our understanding of what young people need to be able to navigate their ever-evolving social milieu. Forging our individual paths forward will no doubt involve grappling with our own identities and places in this milieu. These are difficult conversations and challenging topics, but our youth—and ultimately our society—will be much healthier for engaging with them in order to help youth make sense of the complicated and often conflict-ridden world in which they live.

In addition to what we need to do as individual citizens, there is much knowledge to be gained by researchers and practitioners to advance our scientific understanding of the ideal manner in which to intervene with young people. We've presented several directions for future work in this area that will advance the field and ultimately improve our ability to prepare youth to productively navigate the increasingly diverse social milieu that inevitably awaits them in adulthood. There is no question that there is much work yet to be done but, as we've demonstrated throughout this book, we have sufficient scientific evidence to confidently state that all youth—ethnic majority and minority alike—will benefit from engaging in meaningful dialogues about race and ethnicity with caring adults in their lives, which will help them gain a better understanding of their identity and also provide a context from which to engage in more positive relationships with others who are different from them.

Epilogue

> Collaboration is not about gluing together existing egos. It's about the ideas that never existed until after everyone entered the room.
> —AUTHOR UNKNOWN

This book started out as one of the most challenging projects that either of us had ever embarked on. Interestingly, the book also started as one of the most exciting scholarly activities that we had ever pursued—likely a result of our mutual passion for the topic and our strong commitment to finding a way for our research to "matter." Every time we came together to write, we were excited and became even more passionate about the book—something that seemed impossible, given that we had started with an already high level of passion about this activity!

Through this process, which has been a labor of love, we learned about the considerable benefits of true collaboration. We had both collaborated with others in the past, but in the process of writing this book, we came to realize that our best ideas and clearest arguments emerged as a function of side-by-side writing (albeit with the assistance of technological tools that enabled us to simultaneously work in one document while sitting at separate computers).

We discovered that, although we both had access to and knowledge of the same literature, it was the synergy that emerged in our side-by-side writing process that made possible the generation of our most exciting and novel ideas.

We would be remiss to not recognize that the process was also a humbling experience, as we both had to learn to accept constructive criticism of our writing style. In order to write with one voice, we had to slowly adapt to each other's writing intricacies. Furthermore, we found that the emergence of our best ideas, and our writing of the most challenging topics, required a degree of vulnerability on both of our parts. For example, it was only when we allowed ourselves to be vulnerable that we could engage in a frank discussion regarding which topics were critical to include and the most effective way to communicate certain ideas. As academics, we spend our entire careers defending our ideas—against peer reviewers, editors, and funding agencies, for example. Yet this collaborative process reminded us that flexibility, openness to others' perspectives, and compromise lead to better ideas. It also reflects the kind of humility we hope that we and others will practice as we collectively embark on conversations about race with youth, because they certainly have as much to teach us as we do them.

Final Thoughts

As we conclude the writing of this book, the Charlottesville riot is a fresh reminder of the precariousness of race relations in the United States.[1] It seems like a headline pops up on our newsfeeds daily to remind us of the ongoing need for everyday conversations about race, especially the ones that challenge us to be agents of change in our local communities. Ultimately, we hope the ideas we have shared here will be used to nurture young people's capacities for unity in an increasingly diverse society. We realize we're not alone in having this goal—this book represents our modest contribution to that much larger effort.

NOTES

Chapter 1

The subheading in this chapter was taken from C. Turner, "Bias isn't just a police problem, it's a preschool problem," *Morning Edition*, National Public Radio, September 28, 2016, http://www.npr.org/sections/ed/2016/09/28/495488716/bias-isnt-just-a-police-problem-its-a-preschool-problem.

1. Throughout this book we use the term *ethnic-racial* to acknowledge individuals' experiences with ethnicity and race, as these are often difficult to disentangle. We provide a fuller discussion of our reasoning in chapter 3.

2. A. Younes, "Mixed reaction to Trump from prominent Muslim Americans," *Al Jazeera* online, November 10, 2016, http://www.aljazeera.com/indepth/features/2016/11/mixed-reaction-trump-prominent-muslim-americans-161109113236749.html.

3. Bonilla-Silva (2014).

4. Goff et al. (2014).

5. Dore et al. (2014).

6. Trawalter et al. (2012).

7. Pollock (2004).

8. G. Ladson-Billings, "I'm through," Madison 365, http://madison365.com/im-through/.

9. For example, see Chan & Latzman (2015); Flanagan et al. (2009). See also William Cross's description of the five stages of Black identity development in chapter 6 of his seminal book *Shades of Black*.

10. For a comprehensive overview of the history and mission of the Black Lives Matter movement, see https://blacklivesmatter.com/.

11. A. Garza, "Herstory," Black Lives Matter, https://blacklivesmatter.com/about/herstory/.

12. S. M. Meraji & K. Chow, "A letter from young Asian-Americans to their families about Black Lives Matter," *Code Switch*, National Public Radio, July 27, 2016. A transcript of the news story is available at http://www.npr.org/sections/codeswitch/2016/07/27/487375314/a-letter-from-young-asian-americans-to-their-families-about-black-lives-matter.

13. The full letter is available at "Letters for Black lives: An open letter project on anti-Blackness," Medium, July 11, 2016, https://lettersforblacklives.com/dear-mom-dad-uncle-auntie-black-lives-matter-to-us-too-7ca577d59f4c#.b8kbil46n.

14. Elenbaas et al. (2016).

15. For examples, see Killen, Elenbaas, et al. (2015); Killen, Rutland, et al. (2013).

16. Killen, Elenbaas, & Rutland (2015).

17. A. Kaczynski & C. Massie, "White nationalists see advocate in Steve Bannon who will hold Trump to his campaign promises," CNN Politics, November 15, 2016, http://www.cnn.com/2016/11/14/politics/white-nationalists-on-bannon/.

18. M. Pearce, "The 'alt-right' splinters as supporters and critics agree it was white supremacy all along," *LA Times* online, November 29, 2016, http://www.latimes.com/nation/la-na-alt-right-analysis-20161121-story.html.

19. L. Grossman, "ACLU and Planned Parenthood see 'unprecedented' rise in donations after Donald Trump's election," *Time* online, November 14, 2016, http://time.com/4570796/aclu-planned-parenthood-donation-increase-donald-trump/. Also see M. Mark, "The ACLU has received nearly $1 million in donations since Donald Trump's election," *Business Insider* online, November 9, 2016; see full article at http://www.businessinsider.com/aclu-to-donald-trump-see-you-in-court-2016-11.

20. Collins & Williams (1999). Also see the TED talk, "How racism makes us sick," by Dr. David Williams, at https://www.ted.com/talks/david_r_williams_how_racism_makes_us_sick.

21. In an email correspondence regarding this book, she clarified the following: "What was left out of all the articles and blog posts was the research work that I did alongside my research partners ... they were extremely influential in the growth of my craft. Partnering with two women of color was one of the most powerful experiences of my teaching career. Their names are Detra Price-Dennis (assistant professor of Elementary and Inclusive Education at Columbia Teachers College) and Kathlene Holmes ([incoming] dean of the School of Education at the University of St. Thomas). I feel that my partnership with these women is important when fully understanding the context of my acceptance speech."

22. V. Strauss, "Teacher: A student told me I 'couldn't understand because I was a white lady.' Here's what I did then," *Washington Post* online, November 24, 2015, https://www.washingtonpost.com/news/answer-sheet/wp/2015/11/24/teacher-a-student-told-me-i-couldnt-understand-because-i-was-a-white-lady-heres-what-i-did-then/?noredirect=on&utm_term=.00c71179c7dd.

23. D. Black, "Why I left white nationalism," NY Times online, November 26, 2016, http://www.nytimes.com/2016/11/26/opinion/sunday/why-i-left-white-nationalism.html?_r=0. For further reference, see E. Saslow, "The white flight of Derek Black," *Washington Post* online, October 15, 2016, https://www.washingtonpost.com/national/the-white-flight-of-derek-black/2016/10/15/ed5f906a-8f3b-11e6-a6a3-d50061aa9fae_story.html.

24. Sue (2003); Banaji & Greenwald (2013).

25. Phinney, Jacoby, & Silva (2007).

26. Gurin, Nagda, & Zúñiga (2013).

27. Rivas-Drake, Syed, et al. (2014).

28. Rivas-Drake, Umaña-Taylor, et al. (2017).

29. Umaña-Taylor (2017).

30. Gurin, Nagda, & Zúñiga (2013, 43; emphasis added).

31. Vespa, Armstrong, & Medina (2018).

32. Consider the mass shooting at the Emanuel African Methodist Episcopal Church in Charleston, South Carolina, on June 17, 2015. Nine churchgoers were killed by a twenty-one-year-old white male who declared his hatred for black people before shooting the victims. R. Costa et al., "Church shooting suspect Dylann Roof captured amid hate crime investigation," *Washington Post* online, June 18, 2015, https://www.washingtonpost.com/news/morning-mix/wp/2015/06/17/white-gunman-sought-in-shooting-at-historic-charleston-african-ame-church/?utm_term=.d6ebe59844e5. Also consider the experience of two Muslim women who were on a walk with their infants in Brooklyn, New York, when they were physically attacked by a woman who started punching them and yelling, "Get the f—k out of America, b—s." Read the full story, as reported by the *NY Daily News*, at http://www.nydailynews.com/new-york/bigot-ripping-muslim-women-hijabs-hateful-attack-article-1.2785475.

Chapter 2

1. US Census Bureau, "Quick facts," https://www.census.gov/quickfacts/fact/table/US/PST045216.

2. Colby & Ortman (2014).

3. Monte & Ellis (2014).

4. "Modern Immigration Wave," Pew Research Center, September 28, 2015, http://www.pewhispanic.org/files/2015/09/2015-09-28_modern-immigration-wave_REPORT.pdf.

5. J. M. Krogstad & M. H. Lopez, "Hispanic Nativity Shift," Pew Research Center, April 29, 2014, http://www.pewhispanic.org/2014/04/29/hispanic-nativity-shift/.

6. D. Cohn, "It's official: Minority babies are the majority among the nation's infants, but only just," Fact Tank, Pew Research Center, June 23, 2016, http://www.pewresearch.org/fact-tank/2016/06/23/its-official-minority-babies-are-the-majority-among-the-nations-infants-but-only-just/.

7. Orfield, Kucsera, & Siegel-Hawley (2012).

8. Ibid., p. 9.

9. Ibid.

10. Ibid., p. xiii.

11. Ibid.

12. See, for example, Gurin, Dey, et al. (2002).

13. Jayakumar (2008, p. 625).

14. Graham, Munniksma, & Juvonen (2014).

15. Lee, Iceland, & Farrell (2014); Logan (2014); Massey (2008). As Lee, Iceland, & Farrell (2014) note, "Contrary to popular perception, high levels of diversity are not limited to metropolitan America" (431). Indeed, some of the most diverse communities in the United States are located in nonmetropolitan areas, such as Lumberton, North Carolina; Muskogee, Oklahoma; and Kodiak, Alaska. Further, they find that between 1980 and 2010, "virtually all communities [became] more diverse owing to Hispanic and Asian growth" (434).

16. R. Stepler & M. H. Lopez, "U.S. Latino population growth and dispersion has slowed since onset of the great recession," Pew Research Center, September 8, 2016, http://www.pewhispanic.org/2016/09/08/latino-population-growth-and -dispersion-has-slowed-since-the-onset-of-the-great-recession/.

17. Wells et al. (2012).

18. In the article "Georgia wonders: Will newcomers dye the suburbs blue?," about Cobb County outside of Atlanta, Richard Faussett examines what the tremendous increase in its Asian-origin population might mean for its political identity; *NY Times* online, May 3, 2017, https://www.nytimes.com/2017/05/03/us /politics/ossoff-handel-georgia-sixth-district.html.

19. W. H. Frey, "The rise of melting-pot suburbs," Brookings, May 26, 2015, https://www.brookings.edu/blog/the-avenue/2015/05/26/the-rise-of-melting -pot-suburbs/.

20. Xu, Farver, & Pauker (2014).

21. See table 10 in Aud, Fox, & KewalRamani (2010).

22. C. L. Ryan & K. Bauman, "Education attainment in the United States: 2015," US Census Bureau, March 2016, http://www.census.gov/content/dam /Census/library/publications/2016/demo/p20–578.pdf.

23. Olshansky et al. (2012).

24. Zimmerman, Woolf, & Haley (2015).

25. "A First Look," US Department of Education, Office of Civil Rights, revised October 28, 2016, https://www2.ed.gov/about/offices/list/ocr/docs/2013 -14-first-look.pdf.

26. M. Sickmund & C. Puzzanchera (eds.), "Juvenile offenders and victims: 2014 national report," National Center for Juvenile Justice and the Office of Juvenile Justice and Delinquency Prevention, https://www.ojjdp.gov/ojstatbb/nr2014 /downloads/NR2014.pdf.

27. See E. A. Carson & E. Anderson, "Prisoners in 2015," US Department of Justice, Office of Justice Programs, December 2016, https://www.bjs.gov/content /pub/pdf/p15.pdf.

28. "Ending mass incarceration," http://www.sentencingproject.org/wp-con tent/uploads/2015/12/Facts-About-Prisons.pdf.

29. Banaji & Greenwald (2013); Greenwald & Krieger (2006).

30. Project Implicit, https://implicit.harvard.edu/implicit/education.html.

31. Better (2002, p. 99).

32. Massey & Denton (1993, p. 19).

33. National Housing Act of 1934, Public Law 84-345, 48 Stat. 847.

34. Information about the case and the settlement can be found at https://archives.hud.gov/news/2015/pr15–064b.cfm and https://portal.hud.gov/hud portal/documents/huddoc?id=ExecAssBankConAgrmnt.pdf.

35. Hanson & Santas (2014); Ondrich, Stricker, & Yinger (1999).

Chapter 3

1. Bonilla-Silva (1997).

2. Helms (1990).

3. Phinney (1996).

4. Humes, Jones, & Ramirez (2011).

5. Aud, Fox, & KewalRamani (2010).

6. Humes, Jones, & Ramirez (2011, p. 3).

7. See Hayes-Bautista & Chapa (1987) for a detailed overview of the changes in the US Census classification of race and ethnicity from the 1800s to the 1980s.

8. Ibid., p. 64.

9. Helms (1990).

10. Umaña-Taylor, Quintana, et al. (2014).

11. Adriana Umaña-Taylor and Deborah Rivas-Drake co-led the Study Group, and the additional eleven members were (presented in alphabetical order): Bill Cross, Sabine French, George Knight, Rich Lee, Carol Markstrom, Steve Quintana, Seth Schwartz, Eleanor Seaton, Rob Sellers, Moin Syed, and Tiffany Yip.

12. The ERI Study Group developed a fact sheet to provide a clear, concise working definition of the term "ethnic-racial identity" and to answer some basic clarifying questions to help others understand this complex construct. The fact sheet is published on the website of the Society for Research on Adolescence: http://www.s-r-a.org/sites/default/files/ERI21C_FactSheet_FINAL.pdf.

13. The ERI Study Group also published a special section in the journal *Child Development*, which consisted of four articles: Umaña-Taylor, Quintana, et al., "Ethnic and racial identity during adolescence and into young adulthood" (2014); Rivas-Drake, Syed, et al., "Feeling good, happy, and proud" (2014); Schwartz, Syed, et al., "Methodological issues in ethnic and racial identity research with ethnic minority populations" (2014); and Rivas-Drake, Seaton, et al., "Ethnic and racial identity in adolescence" (2014).

14. For an overview of the historical, systemic, and ongoing ethnic-racial discrimination in the United States, see Kaplan (2011).

15. Erikson (1968); Josselson (1980); Marcia (1980).

16. Umaña-Taylor, Quintana, et al. (2014).

17. Aboud (1984 & 1988); Aboud & Doyle (1993).

18. Damon & Hart (1982).

19. Katz (2003); Katz & Kofkin (1997).

20. Aboud (1988).

21. Ibid.; Quintana (1998); Serrano-Villar & Calzada (2016).

22. See chapter 1, "Landmark studies of Negro identity in William E. Cross, Jr." (1991), in *Shades of Black: Diversity in African American identity*, for a critical review of the early research in this area.

23. Clark & Clark (1939a; 1939b; 1940; 1950).

24. Spencer (1982).

25. For Canadian studies by Aboud and others, see Aboud (1984 & 1988), Aboud & Doyle (1993), and Doyle, Beaudet, & Aboud (1988); for English studies by Rutland and others, see Rutland, Cameron, Bennett, et al. (2005) and Rutland, Cameron, Jugert, et al. (2012); and for Australian studies by Nesdale and others, see Nesdale, Durkin, et al. (2005), Nesdale, Griffiths, et al. (2007), and Nesdale, Maass, et al. (2003).

26. Bigler & Liben (2007).

27. Ibid.

28. Umaña-Taylor (2016b).

29. Douglass, Mirpuri, English, et al. (2016).

30. Steele (2010).

31. Cross (1991).

32. Phinney (1990); Umaña-Taylor, Quintana, et al. (2014).

33. Phinney (1990).

34. Umaña-Taylor (2016b).

35. See Elenbaas et al. (2016) and Killen, Elenbaas, & Rutland (2015) for extensive discussions regarding children's strong preferences for equality and fairness.

36. Erikson (1968).

37. Obama (2004).

38. Erikson (1959 & 1968).

39. The ideas in this paragraph were introduced by Erikson in his 1968 publication of *Identity: Youth and crisis*.

40. Sellers, Smith, et al. (1998).

41. Erikson (1968).

42. Umaña-Taylor (2016b).

43. Adichie (2013); Díaz (2007); Irving (2014); Lahiri (2003); Obama (2004); Santiago (1993).

44. Shurer (2016) and E. Brown (2002); Khan, Kasdan, & Mar (2015).

45. Umaña-Taylor (2016b).

46. Phinney (1992).

47. For studies in the Northeast, see French, Seidman, et al. (2006); in the Midwest: Umaña-Taylor, Gonzales-Backen, & Guimond (2009); in the Pacific Northwest: Huang & Stormshak (2011); and in the Southwest: Umaña-Taylor, Updegraff, et al. (2015).

48. Huang & Stormshak (2011). The sample was comprised of youth from the following backgrounds: 18% Latino/Hispanic, 15% African American, 9% Asian/Pacific Islander, 2% American Indian, and 19% Biracial/Mixed ethnicity.

49. Umaña-Taylor, Gonzales-Backen, & Guimond (2009); Umaña-Taylor & Guimond (2010).

50. Umaña-Taylor, Gonzales-Backen, & Guimond (2009).

51. Umaña-Taylor & Guimond (2010).

52. It is important to note that at least one study has not found consistent patterns of increase in ethnic-racial identity. Specifically, Kerstin Pahl and Niobe Way (2006) found no increases in ethnic-racial identity exploration. Their sample, however, was an urban sample in a predominantly minority school setting. It is possible that youth did not demonstrate common patterns of growth in this setting because their ethnicity-race was not particularly salient, given that they were not a significant numerical minority in their school.

53. Helms (1990); Phinney (1989); Phinney & Alipuria (1990); Phinney, DuPont, et al. (1994); Syed & Azmitia (2008).

54. Tatum (2003).

55. Irving (2014, p. xi).

56. Syed & Azmitia (2009).

57. The sample was 37% White, 30% Asian American, 23% Latino, and 10% Black. Students who were Multiracial or Mixed were asked to choose a primary self-designation.

58. Umaña-Taylor, Quintana, et al. (2014).

59. Syed & Azmitia (2008); Umaña-Taylor, Quintana, et al. (2014); Yip (2014).

60. Rivas-Drake, Syed, et al. (2014).

61. See Umaña-Taylor (2011) for a review of these ideas.

62. Sellers, Smith, et al. (1998).

63. Rivas-Drake, Hughes, & Way (2008 & 2009).

64. Douglass & Umaña-Taylor (2017).

65. Sellers, Smith, et al. (1998).

66. Sellers, Morgan, et al. (2001).

67. Ibid.

68. Umaña-Taylor (2011 & 2016b).

69. See Rivas-Drake, Seaton, et al. (2014) for an exhaustive review of literature examining ethnic-racial identity and adjustment among US youth.

70. Miller-Cotto & Brynes (2016); Rivas-Drake, Seaton, et al. (2014); Rivas-Drake, Syed, et al. (2014); Smith & Silva (2011).

71. Rivas-Drake, Syed, et al. (2014).

72. Miller-Cotto & Byrne (2016).

73. Rivas-Drake, Seaton et al. (2014).

74. Umaña-Taylor, Vargas-Chanes, et al. (2008).

75. For reports of this story across the United States, see Fox 40 News [Sacramento, CA], "Petition demands expulsion of 6 Arizona students wearing T-shirt spelling out the 'N' word," January 23, 2016, http://fox40.com/2016/01/23/petition-demands-expulsion-of-6-arizona-students-wearing-t-shirt-spelling-out-the-n-word/; KRQE News [Albuquerque, NM], "Protest outside Phoenix-area school after racial slur photo," January 25, 2016, http://krqe.com/2016/01/25

/protest-outside-phoenix-area-school-after-racial-slur-photo/; ABC News [Phoenix, AZ], "Article over Desert Vista High School racial slur controversy prompts yearbook change," May 7, 2016, https://www.abc15.com/news/region-phoenix -metro/ahwatukee/article-over-desert-vista-high-school-racial-slur-controversy -prompts-yearbook-change; S. DeGrote, "Desert Vista High School vandalized by graffiti containing racial slur," KCTV News [Kansas City, KS], May 12, 2016, http://www.kctv5.com/story/35413884/desert-vista-high-school-vandalized -by-graffiti-containing-racial-slur; and Dan Good, "Teacher who alleged racism at Phoenix school feels vindicated over N-word T-shirts photo: 'These students should be expelled,'" *NY Daily* News online, January 27, 2016, http://www.ny dailynews.com/news/national/teacher-feels-vindicated-n-word-t-shirts-photo -article-1.2510892.

76. Romero & Roberts (2003); Umaña-Taylor, Tynes, et al. (2015); Umaña-Taylor, Updegraff, & Gonzales-Backen (2011).

77. Oyserman (2008); Oyserman & Destin (2010).

78. Umaña-Taylor (2016b).

79. Tynes, Umaña-Taylor, et al. (2012); Umaña-Taylor, Tynes, et al. (2015).

80. G. Rough, "I haven't talked to my kids about race—and maybe that's a problem," All the Moms, USA Today Network, August 14, 2017, http://allthe moms.com/2017/08/14/race-racism-kids-charlottesville-virginia/.

Chapter 4

The epigraph to this chapter is taken from Dalton Conley, *Honky* (Berkeley: University of California Press), pp. 37–54.

1. Umaña-Taylor (2016a; italics in the original).

2. Quote is from K. J. Dell'Antonia, "Talking about racism with white kids," Motherlode, *NY Times* online, November 25, 2014, https://parenting.blogs.ny times.com/2014/11/25/talking-about-racism-with-white-kids/?_r=0.

3. Coates (2015).

4. Katz (2003).

5. Hughes, Bigler, & Levy (2007).

6. Pauker, Apfelbaum, & Spitzer (2015).

7. See an example of a White teenager doing this through the spoken word in this video: S. M. Stewart, "Royce Mann, age 14, 'White Boy Privilege,' slam poem," YouTube, https://www.youtube.com/watch?v=g4QljZ-LOT0.

8. Umaña-Taylor & Bamaca (2004, p. 338).

9. Hughes, Rodriguez, et al. (2006).

10. Umaña-Taylor & Yazedjian (2006).

11. Hughes, Rodriguez, et al. (2006); Juang, Shen, et al. (2016); Nguyen et al. (2015); Supple et al. (2006); Umaña-Taylor & Fine (2004); Umaña-Taylor, O'Donnell, et al. (2014).

12. See Juang & Syed (2010); Brittian, Umaña-Taylor, & Derlan (2013); Rivas-Drake (2011a); Umaña-Taylor, Zeiders, & Updegraff (2013); and Neblett, Banks, et al. (2013).

13. Hughes, Witherspoon, et al. (2009); Umaña-Taylor, O'Donnell, et al. (2014).

14. Umaña-Taylor, O'Donnell, et al. (2014).

15. Douglass & Umaña-Taylor (2017); Fisher, Wallace, & Fenton (2000); Greene, Way, & Pahl (2006); Huynh & Fuligni (2010); Perreira, Fuligni, & Potochnick, (2009); Rivas-Drake, Hughes, & Way (2008); Wong, Eccles, & Sameroff (2003); Umaña-Taylor, Tynes, et al. (2015).

16. Stevenson (1994); Hughes, Rodriguez, et al. (2006).

17. Quintana & Vera (1999).

18. "A conversation on race: A series of short films about identity in America," *NY Times* online, https://www.nytimes.com/interactive/projects/your-stories/conversations-on-race.

19. Armenta et al. (2013).

20. Rivas-Drake (2011a).

21. Quintana, Segura Herrera, & Nelson (2010).

22. Rivas-Drake, Hughes, & Way (2008).

23. Neblett, Rivas-Drake, & Umaña-Taylor (2012).

24. Umaña-Taylor & Yazedjian (2006); Umaña-Taylor, Zeiders, & Updegraff (2013).

25. K. G. Bates, "This week in race: Fox sued, schools resegregate, Shea Moisture gets thirsty," *Code Switch*, National Public Radio, April 28, 2017, http://www.npr.org/sections/codeswitch/2017/04/28/525926179/this-week-in-race-fox-sued-schools-re-segregate-and-shea-moisture-gets-thirsty?utm_source=facebook.com&utm_medium=social&utm_campaign=npr&utm_term=nprnews&utm_content=20170430.

26. Aldana & Byrd (2015).

27. Ramiah et al. (2015).

28. Douglass, Mirpuri, & Yip (2017).

29. Syed & Juan (2012).

30. Rivas-Drake, Umaña-Taylor, et al. (2017); Santos, Kornienko, & Rivas-Drake (2017).

31. Rivas-Drake, Umaña-Taylor, et al. (2017).

32. Carter (2005); Lee (1996); Rosenbloom & Way (2004); Warikoo (2010).

33. Pollock (2004); Douglass, Mirpuri, et al. (2016).

34. Douglass, Mirpuri, English, et al. (2016, p. 73).

35. See, for example, "4 things to tell teens who joke about race," The Root, January 8, 2014, https://www.theroot.com/4-things-to-tell-teens-who-joke-about-race-1790874035; A. Reese, "7 tips on how to deal with racially insensitive friends," Gurl, January 28, 2014, http://www.gurl.com/2014/01/28/tips-on-how-to-deal-with-racist-friends/—1; and Aude-Konan, "I let my white 'friends' get

away with their racism because of 'respectability politics,' " xoJane, June 29, 2015, http://www.xojane.com/issues/i-used-to-let-my-white-friends-get-away-with -their-racism.

36. Fordham & Ogbu (1986). See also Carter's discussion (2005) of the "acting White" hypothesis.

37. Huang (2013, pp. 170–171).

38. Lee (1996).

39. Lee (1996); Valenzuela (1999).

40. Benner & Graham (2011); Carter (2005); Conchas (2001); Delpit (2006); O'Connor et al. (2011); Orfield, Frankenberg, & Siegel-Hawley (2010); Pollock (2004); Rivas-Drake, Hughes, & Way (2008 & 2009); Rosenbloom & Way (2004); Suárez-Orozco, Suárez-Orozco, & Todorova (2008); Valenzuela (1999).

41. Valenzuela (1999, p. 3).

42. Pollock (2004). See also Stevenson's book, *Promoting racial literacy in schools: Differences that make a difference* (2014).

43. Ibid., p. 7.

44. Conchas (2001).

45. Finn & Servoss (2014); Gregory, Skiba, & Noguera (2010); Skiba et al. (2002).

46. A. A. Ferguson, *Bad boys: Public schools in the making of black masculinity* (Ann Arbor: University of Michigan Press).

47. Finn & Servoss (2014); Gregory, Skiba, & Noguera (2010).

48. US Department of Education Office for Civil Rights, "A first look," 2013–2014 Civil Rights Data Collection, June 7, 2016, http://www2.ed.gov/about/offices /list/ocr/docs/2013-14-first-look.pdf.

49. Benner & Graham (2011); Benner & Kim (2008); Douglass & Umaña-Taylor (2017); Fisher, Wallace, & Fenton (2000); Greene, Way, & Pahl (2006); Hughes & Rivas-Drake (2007); Niwa, Way, & Hughes (2014); Rivas-Drake, Hughes, & Way (2008).

50. Hughes & Rivas-Drake (2007). See also Rivas-Drake, Hughes, & Way (2008 & 2009).

51. Sirin & Fine (2007).

52. B. Chappell, "Texas high school student shows off homemade clock, gets handcuffed," *The Two-Way*, National Public Radio, September 16, 2015, http:// www.npr.org/sections/thetwo-way/2015/09/16/440820557/high-school-stu dent-shows-off-homemade-clock-gets-handcuffed.

53. Lee (1996); Qin, Way, & Mukerjee (2008); Thompson, Kiang, & Witkow (2016).

54. Thompson, Kiang, & Witkow (2016, p. 108).

55. Valenzuela (1999).

56. Camacho et al. (2018).

57. Bennett (2006); Rivas-Drake & Witherspoon (2013); Stevenson et al. (2005); Supple et al. (2006); Way et al. (2008); White et al. (2017); Witherspoon, Daniels, et al. (2016).

58. Umaña-Taylor & Yazedjian (2006); Umaña-Taylor & Bámaca (2004); Way et al. (2008).

59. Brietzke & Perreira (2017); Kiang, Perreira, & Fuligni (2011); Kiang, Peterson, & Thompson (2011); Ko & Perreira (2010); Massey (2008).

60. Witherspoon, Daniels, et al. (2016).

61. Rivas-Drake & Witherspoon (2013); Witherspoon, Seaton, & Rivas-Drake (2016).

62. Williams, Steinberg, & Piquero (2010).

63. Prot et al. (2014).

64. See, for example, Tynes, Giang, et al. (2008).

65. Ramasubramanian (2010).

66. Adams-Bass, Bentley-Edwards, & Stevenson (2014).

67. Anderson et al. (2014); Ansari et al. (2015); Khan et al. (2015); Urman et al. (2014).

68. Actors of color have themselves reflected on having to negotiate playing stereotypic roles and lack of representation in media. See, for example, comments by John Leguizamo and Rita Moreno in "Moreno, Leguizamo talk Latin life in 'Hollywouldn't,'" by M. Del Barco, *2 languages, many voices: Latinos in the US* series, National Public Radio, http://www.npr.org/2011/10/24/141594495/moreno-leguizamo-talk-latin-life-in-hollywouldnt; N. Saad, "Aziz Ansari won't do an Indian accent on-screen: Here's why," *LA Times* online, October 26, 2015, http://www.latimes.com/entertainment/tv/showtracker/la-et-st-aziz-ansari-indian-accent-transformers-master-of-none-20151026-story.html); and R. Buxton, "Gina Rodriguez says her mission is 'creating a different perception of minorities in the media,'" Huffpost, April 21, 2014, http://www.huffingtonpost.com/2015/04/21/gina-rodriguez-minorities-in-the-media_n_7109398.html.

69. Weisbuch, Pauker, & Ambady (2009).

70. Prot et al. (2014).

71. Leavitt et al. (2015).

72. Tynes, Reynolds, & Greenfield (2004).

73. Tynes, Umaña-Taylor, et al. (2012); Umaña-Taylor, Tynes, et al. (2015).

74. Tynes, Giang, et al. (2008).

75. Adams-Bass, Stevenson, & Kotzin (2014).

76. Umaña-Taylor, Tynes, et al. (2015).

77. Tynes, Umaña-Taylor, et al. (2012).

Chapter 5

1. Please see C. Fong, "5 realities of being the only Asian in your class," Odyssey, December 8, 2015, https://www.theodysseyonline.com/what-its-like-being-the-only-asian-person-your-class.

2. Shelton & Sellers (2000).

3. Oyserman & Destin (2010).

4. Bornstein & Arterberry (2010); Rakison & Yermolayeva (2010).

5. Pittinsky, Rosenthal, & Montoya (2011).

6. Dunham, Baron, & Carey (2011).

7. Lam & Seaton (2016).

8. Tajfel & Turner (1986).

9. Brewer (1991).

10. Please see A. G. Sulzberger, "Hispanics reviving faded towns on the plains," *NY Times* online, November 13, 2011, http://www.nytimes.com/2011/11/14/us/as-small-towns-wither-on-plains-hispanics-come-to-the-rescue.html.

11. Mallett, Wagner, & Harrison (2011).

12. Hebl, Tickle, & Heatherton (2000).

13. Mallett, Wagner, & Harrison (2011).

14. Allport (1954).

15. Pettigrew & Tropp (2006).

16. Gaertner et al. (1994).

17. Ibid., p. 233.

18. Chavous (2005).

19. Pettigrew & Tropp (2006).

20. Ramiah et al. (2015).

21. Pettigrew and Tropp (2006).

22. Ibid. (2008).

23. More generally, exposure to and participation in diverse settings benefits youth and adults. For example, in an experiment, Anthony Antonio and his colleagues (2004) found that college students in small group discussion that varied in composition exhibited better critical thinking skills and were less prone to "groupthink." For a general overview of the benefits of diversity for innovation, see K. W. Phillips, "How diversity makes us smarter," *Scientific American* online, October 1, 2014, https://www.scientificamerican.com/article/how-diversity-makes-us-smarter.

24. Graham, Munniksma, & Juvonen (2014).

25. Feddes, Noack, & Rutland (2009).

26. Davies et al. (2011).

27. Page-Gould, Mendoza-Denton, & Tropp (2008).

28. González et al. (2017).

29. Jayakumar (2008).

30. Aboud (2005); Katz (2003); see also Apfelbaum et al. (2008).

31. Vittrup (2016); Vittrup & Holden (2011).

32. Van Ausdale & Feagin (1996); Vittrup (2016); see also Katz (2003).

33. Katz (2003). For a recent comprehensive review of the literature on this topic, please see Levy et al. (2016).

34. Personal conversation with the authors.

35. Allport (1954, p. 42).

36. Phinney, Jacoby, & Silva (2007).

37. Rivas-Drake, Umaña-Taylor, et al. (2017).

38. Maramba & Museus (2013).

39. Whitehead et al. (2009).

40. Umaña-Taylor (2017).

41. Cameron, Rutland, & Brown (2007).

42. Gurin et al. (2013).

43. Allport (1954).

44. Erikson (1968).

45. Oyserman (2008); Umaña-Taylor (2016b).

46. Diane Hughes, "Teaching race to children and adolescents," webinar, University-Based Child and Family Policy Consortium, in collaboration with the Society for Research in Child Development, March 13, 2017.

47. Strauss & Cross (2005). The quote is from p. 71.

48. Knifsend & Juvonen (2012).

49. Oyserman & Destin (2010).

50. Oyserman (2008).

51. Watts, Williams, & Jagers (2003, p. 188).

52. Ibid.

53. Lozada et al. (2017).

54. Selvanathan et al. (2017).

55. Quote is from p. 478 in Martínez, Peñaloza, & Valenzuela (2012).

56. Ibid.

57. Umaña-Taylor (2016b).

58. Elenbaas et al. (2016).

59. C. S. Brown (2017); Greene, Way, & Pahl (2006); Hughes, Del Toro, et al. (2016); Niwa, Way, & Hughes (2014).

60. Crystal, Killen, & Ruck (2008).

61. Pettigrew & Tropp (2008).

62. Sierksma, Thijs, & Verkuyten (2015).

63. Gaertner et al. (1994, pp. 225–226).

Chapter 6

1. For example, Dee and Penner (2016) also recently found that ninth graders in the San Francisco Unified School District exposed to an ethnic studies curriculum that "focused on themes of social justice, discrimination, stereotypes, and social movements from U.S. history" exhibited substantial gains in terms of grades, attendance, and credits earned (p. 10).

2. More specifically, as a recent evaluation reports: "Perspectives is an initiative of Teaching Tolerance, a project of the Southern Poverty Law Center. The SPLC is a nonprofit civil rights organization dedicated to fighting hate and bigotry, and to seeking justice for the most vulnerable members of society. Founded by civil rights lawyers Morris Dees and Joseph Levin Jr. in 1971, the SPLC is internationally known for tracking and exposing the activities of hate groups. Since

1991, Teaching Tolerance has produced and distributed free documentary films, books, lesson plans and other materials that promote tolerance and respect in schools. Teaching Tolerance is designed to promote an appreciation for diversity in schools by reducing prejudice, improving intergroup relations and supporting equity for children" (Schuster [2014, p. 7]). See also Teaching Tolerance, http:// perspectives.tolerance.org/.

3. Shuster (2014).

4. See "Introducing the Teaching Tolerance anti-bias framework," Teaching Tolerance, 2014, http://www.tolerance.org/sites/default/files/general/Anti%20 bias%20framework%20pamphlet.pdf. Teaching Tolerance also offers a "Speak Up" pocket guide to interrupting intolerance: https://www.tolerance.org/maga zine/publications/speak-up-at-school.

5. Shuster (2014).

6. Ibid., p. 8.

7. Rubrics, worksheets, graphic organizers, and handouts are also provided. For additional information regarding teachers' reactions to the full suite of curriculum materials, please see https://www.tolerance.org/classroom-resources.

8. See Facing History and Ourselves, https://www.facinghistory.org/. For an evaluation of this program, please see Barr et al. (2015).

9. Facing History and Ourselves (2017, p. 7).

10. As context, the synopsis for this TED talk states, "Our lives, our cultures, are composed of many overlapping stories. Novelist Chimamanda Adichie tells the story of how she found her authentic cultural voice—and warns that if we hear only a single story about another person or country, we risk a critical misunderstanding" (see "The danger of a single story," https://www.ted.com/talks/ chimamanda_adichie_the_danger_of_a_single_story).

11. Facing History and Ourselves (2008). See also "Identity charts," https:// www.facinghistory.org/resource-library/teaching-strategies/identity-charts.

12. Facing History and Ourselves (2017).

13. Bruni (2015).

14. Indeed, some of the most diverse cities are also the most segregated.

15. For an annotated bibliography of other intergroup contact approaches, please see J. Graham, "Interventions to improve intergroup relations: What works, what shows promise, and what this means for civil politics," Civil Politics.org, http://www.civilpolitics.org/content/interventions-to-improve-intergroup-rela tions-what-works-what-shows-promise-and-what-this-means-for-civil-politics/.

16. Gurin, Nagda, & Zúñiga (2013, p. 2).

17. Ibid., p. 3.

18. Chang et al. (2005); Evans et al. (2006); Richards-Shuster & Aldana (2013). For more information on the nature of the University of Michigan Youth Dialogues, please see "Youth dialogues on race and ethnicity," University of Michigan School of Social Work, http://archive.ssw.umich.edu/public/currentProj ects/youthAndCommunity/dialogues.html. For an example of another intergroup dialogue/bridging approach implemented in community settings that is not based

on the IGD Michigan Model, please see Intergroup Resources, http://www.inter groupresources.com/ and "Intergroup resources: Building social justice online and from the ground up," *Neuroanthropology* blog, http://blogs.plos.org/neuro- anthropology/2013/02/13/intergroup-resources-building-social-justice-online -and-from-the-ground-up/.

19. In particular, the program identifies community agencies who "are re- sponsible for selecting youth, providing adult support, securing facilities and transportation for participants, and serving as the fiduciary for youth stipends ... Agency teams were paired with those of different racial/ethnic backgrounds to create six dialogue team pairings. In general, pairings were made between groups that have historic difference with one another. Each team was facilitated by a Uni- versity of Michigan undergraduate of the same race or ethnic background ... The 2006 SYD began with an Orientation program in June. During the orientation, young people, parents, and community allies gathered to celebrate each other, and discuss the roles and activities of the dialogues.... In addition to the dia- logues, the teams also participated in a bus tour of Metropolitan Detroit to high- light the differences amongst groups and discuss the history of segregation in the region; a social activity at Kensington Metro Park; and community service activ- ities" (Evans et al. [2006, pp. 11–13]).

20. Checkoway (2009, p. 44).

21. Ibid., p. 43; emphasis added.

22. Checkoway (2009, pp. 43–44).

23. See page 13 of "Creating change with our own two hands," 2006 Summer Youth Dialogues Evaluation Report, University of Michigan, http://archive.ssw .umich.edu/public/currentProjects/youthAndCommunity/pubs/SYDReport .pdf.

24. Aldana, Rowley, et al. (2012).

25. In Aldana, Rowley, et al. (2012), the increase in ethnic-racial identity ex- ploration was observed for youth whose parents were less highly educated but not among those whose parents were more highly educated.

26. Ibid., pp. 129–131; emphasis added.

27. Watts, Williams, & Jagers (2003).

28. Watts & Abdul-Adil (1998); Watts, Griffith, & Abdul-Adil (1999).

29. Critical consciousness has been described as the "cognitive cornerstone of sociopolitical development." See Diemer et al. (2016) for a brief overview of the construct of critical consciousness and how it can serve as a developmental asset for marginalized youth and communities.

30. Also see Diemer & Li (2011) for a discussion of the role that parents and peers can play in the sociopolitical development of youth.

31. See Morsillo and Prilleltensky (2007) for a description of a school-based and a community-based program that targeted sociopolitical development with youth in Australia.

32. Similar programs also exist for adults. As an example of a program focused on adults who are reentering communities, see Windsor, Jemal, & Benoit (2014)

for a description of Community Wise. Also see Hatcher et al. (2010) for an example of a program developed to promote critical consciousness and social mobilization in the area of HIV/AIDS prevention.

33. Watts and Abdul-Adil (1998, p. 69).

34. Ibid., p. 70.

35. See table 1 in Watts & Abdul-Adil (1998) for a detailed description of the questions used to guide discussion and the elements of critical thinking that they targeted.

36. Because these programs can have a profound impact on the identity development process for youth, it is important to be cautious and intentional in how popular culture is presented and introduced into programs with youth. Watts and Abdul-Adil provide important guidance in this regard: "There are also numerous ways of linking rap to poetry, English, literature appreciation, drama, and other art forms. We urge those who would use rap as a vehicle for youth development to be cautious, however. In unskilled hands, certain types of rap can serve to glamorize misogyny, materialism, gangsta lifestyles and the other sensationalized negative elements of hip-hop culture. This is especially true when adults lend it legitimacy by bringing it into the classroom" (1997, p. 85).

37. In a study of this approach, Cabrera and colleagues (2014) focused more on discussing the positive outcomes that the program had for Latino students' academic achievement, and they did not directly address gains in identity development for the students in their program.

38. Cabrera et al. (2014).

39. Ibid.

40. Ginwright (2007).

41. Ibid., p. 407.

42. Ibid., p. 409.

43. The name of the organization was Leadership Excellence; see ibid., p. 411.

44. Ginwright (2007).

45. Watts & Abdul-Adil (1998).

46. Diemer et al. (2016).

47. According to a 2016 US Department of Education report, "The state of racial diversity in the educator workforce," 82% of public schoolteachers are White. Also see Kumagai and Lypson (2009) for a discussion of specific techniques that can be used to foster critical consciousness in students who are training in the medical profession.

48. Zion, Allen, & Jean (2015).

49. Ibid., p. 915.

50. Umaña-Taylor & Douglass (2016).

51. See our extensive discussion of ethnic-racial identity and its importance for all youths' positive development in chapter 3 of this book.

52. Umaña-Taylor, Douglass, Updegraff, et al. (in press).

53. Ibid.

54. For details regarding the randomized controlled trial, see ibid.

55. Also assessed in the study were students' sense of self-esteem, whether they were experiencing any depressive symptoms, what their grades were, and other indicators of adjustment that are typically assessed in surveys with adolescents.

56. The first post-test took place the week after the program had finished.

57. When we compared the scores of students in the Identity Project classrooms to those of the students in the control classrooms, there were no significant differences between students in the two groups on any of the ethnic-racial identity variables, nor on any of the indicators of adjustment; this meant that we could conclude that any differences that emerged between the groups after the intervention were a result of the different programs that the students in the classrooms received—the Identity Project or the control.

58. A little over a year later (sixty-seven weeks after the initial survey), we conducted our final post-test and found that the increases that we found in ethnic-racial identity exploration and sense of clarity at the twelve- and eighteen-week post-tests led to statistically significant decreases in depressive symptoms, and statistically significant increases in self-esteem, grades, and adolescents' sense of understanding of their overall identity. These findings are consistent with the positive effects that others have found for instruction regarding the history of different ethnic-racial groups on academic outcomes, such as reductions in school dropout rates and increases in grades, as we discussed earlier in this chapter.

59. For an example of a structured course in college designed to promote ethnic-racial identity development among students of color and Multiracial students, please see Ford and Maloney (2012). In their study, they describe a course in which students' completion of "a four-page preliminary paper, and an eight-page final paper, allowed for a nuanced exploration of SOC/multiracial students' articulation of race, racial identity, and racism. Both papers required students to critically reflect on their experiences with and understandings of race by addressing three topical areas: (1) social identities; (2) social structures; and (3) dialogue experiences. The final papers also required students to integrate course readings into their analysis. Specifically, the papers explored questions such as:

Social Identities: "What are some experiences that have made your race/ethnicity visible to you? What and how were you taught, explicitly or implicitly, about what it means to be a person of color/multiracial person, in terms of attitudes, behaviors, your future, the nature of the society, etc.? Broadly speaking, what does it mean to you to be a person of color/multiracial person? What do you know about your ethnic/cultural heritage (i.e., the culture, country or region of the world from which your ancestors came)? And how might this affect your feelings about being considered part of your racial group?"

Social Structures: "Throughout your life, have most of your friends and other people close to you been of the same racial/ethnic background? If so, why do you think this was the case? If not, what do you think led you to cross racial/ethnic lines in these relationships?" (pp. 20–21).

60. Hughes et al. (2007); Priest et al. (2014); Umaña-Taylor, Alfaro, et al. (2009).

61. There are also numerous programs designed to impact parenting in ethnic minority families that have adapted universal programs to be sensitive to cultural issues. See, for example, Domenech Rodríguez and colleagues' (2011) Criando con Amor: Promoviendo Armonía y Superación (CAPAS). In addition, organizations such as Teaching Tolerance have developed tools for parents that address identity issues. See their *Parent guide to preventing and responding to prejudice,* which can be found at http://www.tolerance.org/sites/default/files/general/beyond_golden_rule.pdf.

62. We address the trade-offs of "culturally specific" (aimed at one group) versus "universal" approaches later in this chapter.

63. As another example of a program geared toward African American families, the Fathers and Sons program (Caldwell et al. 2010) has shown promise in supporting father-son discussions of race. Over the course of fifteen sessions, Fathers and Sons provides a culturally specific program to help African American fathers who are not living in the same home be involved in the lives of their eight- to twelve-year-old sons. A defining feature of the program is its emphasis on African American culture and history, and fathers and sons participate in various activities, including community cultural activities and homework assignments. The researchers found that fathers who participated in this program talked to their sons about Black history and pride more than fathers who did not participate in the program.

64. Murry et al. (2007).

65. Ibid., p. 338.

66. See table 1 on p. 336 in Murry et al. (2007).

67. Murry et al. (2007, p. 335).

68. It should also be noted that this positive self-concept was related to a reduced need for peer acceptance and, in turn, less engagement in sexually risky behavior (ibid.).

69. Kulis, Ayers, & Baker (2015, p. 66).

70. Maxwell, Chesler, & Nagda (2011, p. 164).

71. Zúñiga et al. (2011, p. 74).

72. Cummings (2016).

73. Agarwal et al. (2010, p. 328).

74. Ibid.

75. Ibid.

76. Ibid.

77. Stevenson (2014).

78. Ibid., p. 113.

79. Ibid., p. 114.

80. As noted earlier, the most recent estimates are that 82% of public school-teachers are White (Department of Education, 2016).

81. Keelty (2016). For similar commentaries and examples of issues that may arise in learning to be an ally, see Derrick Clifton, "10 simple ways white people can step up to fight everyday racism," *Everyday Feminism,* September 27, 2014,

http://everydayfeminism.com/2014/09/non-racist-white-person/ and "Another day, another hashtag: White people, you gotta get to work NOW," *Awesomely Luvvie*, September 21, 2016, http://www.awesomelyluvvie.com/2016/09/white-people-anti-racism.html.

82. Google, May 22, 2018. The number of hits fluctuated by date; the number reported here was obtained when authors typed "how parents talk to their kids about race" into the search bar in https://www.google.com (using the Firefox browser).

83. Ibid.

84. But, to be clear, though we've geared this section to parents, much of it is also relevant to any adult that has a relationship with youth: youth workers, clergy, family members, and the like.

85. McFarland (2017).

86. Gragg (2017); see also Zahara Hill, "New kids' book helps parents approach 'The Talk' about police brutality," *Black Voices*, Huffpost, April 24, 2017, http://huff.to/2peh9u4.

87. As an example, see Thomas and Blackmon's study (2015) of the role of Trayvon Martin's death on Black parents' racial socialization at home. Among other questions, they asked parents, "Has the death of Trayvon Martin influenced how you prepare your child or children for being African American or Black in our society?" They found that "the shooting spurred fears for parents that children and youth have to face racism and even the possibility of violence and death. Parents reported giving children very specific strategies for dealing with racism, racial profiling, and circumstances in which violence may occur" (p. 84).

88. Collins (2017).

89. Dudley (2015).

90. Dell'Antonia (2014).

91. Ibid.

92. Better (2002, p. 126).

93. Ibid.

94. Ibid., p. 121.

95. Lin, Simpkins, et al. (2016); Lin, Menjívar, et al. (2016); Ngo (2015).

96. Lin, Simpkins, et al. (2016).

97. For more information about social emotional learning, please refer to the Collaborative for Academic, Social, and Emotional (CASEL) website at www.casel.org.

98. Rivas-Drake, Saleem, et al. (in press).

99. For example, we could consider the impact of programs such as Face-to-Face Advisories, which is offered by the Origins Program with the aim of using advisory time to explore one's identity, awareness, and curiosity about cultural differences, recognition of biases, and capacity to advance equity (see L. Crawford, *Face to Face Advisories: Bridging cultural gaps in grades 5–9*, Origins Program, 2013, https://originsonline.org/bookstore/face-face-advisories).

100. Paluck & Green (2009).

101. Ibid., p. 351.
102. See also Page (2007).

Epilogue

1. See one account of this event here: R. Fausset & A. Feuer, "Far-right groups surge into national view in Charlottesville," *NY Times* online, August 13, 2017, https://www.nytimes.com/2017/08/13/us/far-right-groups-blaze-into-national -view-in-charlottesville.html, and one response by the community here: "Organizing for Justice and Mutual Support," Together Cville, https://www.together cville.net/.

REFERENCES

Aboud, F. E. (1984). Social and cognitive bases of ethnic identity constancy. *Journal of Genetic Psychology, 145,* 271–230.

Aboud, F. E. (1988). *Children and prejudice* (pp. 103–127). New York: Basil Blackwell.

Aboud, F. E. (2005). The development of prejudice in childhood and adolescence. In J. F. Dovidio, P. S. Glick, & L. A. Rudman (Eds.), *On the Nature of Prejudice: Fifty Years after Allport* (pp. 310–326). Malden, MA: Blackwell.

Aboud, F. E., & Doyle, A. B. (1993). The early development of ethnic identity and attitudes. In M. E. Bernal & G. P. Knight (Eds.), *Ethnic identity: Formation and transmission among Hispanics and other minorities* (pp. 47–59). Albany: State University of New York Press.

Adams-Bass, V. N., Bentley-Edwards, K. L., & Stevenson, H. C. (2014). That's not me I see on TV: African American youth interpret media images of Black females. *Women, Gender, and Families, 2*(1), 79–100.

Adams-Bass, V. N., Stevenson, H. C., & Kotzin, D. S. (2014). Measuring the meaning of Black media stereotypes and their relationship to the racial identity, Black history knowledge, and racial socialization of African American youth. *Journal of Black Studies, 45*(5), 367–395. Retrieved from doi:10.1177/0021934714530396.

Adichie, C. N. (2013). *Americanah.* New York, NY: Alfred A. Knopf.

Agarwal, R., Epstein, S., Oppenheim, R., Oyler, C., & Sonu, D. (2010). From ideal to practice and back again: Beginning teachers teaching for social justice. *Journal of Teacher Education, 61,* 237–247.

Aldana, A., & Byrd, C. (2015). School ethnic-racial socialization: Learning about race and ethnicity among African American students. *Urban Review, 47*(3), 563–576.

Aldana, A., Rowley, S. J., Checkoway, B., & Richards-Schuster, K. (2012). Raising ethnic-racial consciousness: The relationship between intergroup dialogues and adolescents' ethnic-racial identity and racism awareness. *Equity & Excellence in Education, 45*(1), 120–137.

Allport, G. W. (1954). *The nature of prejudice.* Cambridge, MA: Addison-Wesley.

Anderson, A., Dobbins, B., Sugland, H., Groff, J., Barris, K., Wilmore, L., et al. (Executive Producers). (2014). *Black-ish* [Television series]. New York, NY: American Broadcasting Company.

Ansari, A., Yang, A., Schur, M., Becky, D., & Miner, D. (Executive Producers). (2015). *Master of none* [Television series]. Los Gatos, CA: Netflix.

Antonio, A. L., Chang, M. J., Hakuta, K., Kenny, D. A., Levin, S., & Milem, J. F. (2004). Effects of racial diversity on complex thinking in college students. *Psychological Science, 15*(8), 507–510.

Apfelbaum, E. P., Pauker, K., Ambady, N., Sommers, S. R., & Norton, M. I. (2008). Learning (not) to talk about race: When older children underperform in social categorization. *Developmental Psychology, 44*(5), 1513–1518.

Armenta, B. E., Lee, R. M., Pituc, S. T., Jung, K-R., Park, I.J.K., Soto, J. A., et al. (2013). Where are you from? A validation of the Foreigner Objectification Scale and the psychological correlates of foreigner objectification among Asian Americans and Latinos. *Cultural Diversity and Ethnic Minority Psychology, 19*(2), April 2013, 131–142. Retrieved from http://dx.doi.org/10.1037/a0031547.

Aud, S., Fox, M. A., & KewalRamani, A. (2010). Status and trends in the education of racial and ethnic groups (NCES 2010–015). US Department of Education, National Center for Education Statistics. Washington, DC: US Government Printing Office. Retrieved from https://nces.ed.gov/pubs2010/2010015.pdf.

Banaji, M. R., & Greenwald, A. G. (2013). *Blindspot: Hidden biases of good people.* New York, NY: Random House.

Barr, D. J., Boulay, B., Selman, R. L., McCormick, R., Lowenstein, E., Gamse, B., et al. (2015). A randomized controlled trial of professional development for interdisciplinary civic education: Impacts on humanities teachers and their students. *Teachers College Record, 117*(2), 1–52.

Benner, A., & Graham, S. (2011). Latino adolescents' experiences of discrimination across the first 2 years of high school: Correlates and influences on educational outcomes. *Child Development, 82*(2), 508–519.

Benner, A., & Kim, S. Y. (2008). Experiences of discrimination among Chinese American adolescents and the consequences for socioemotional and academic development. *Developmental Psychology, 45*(6), 1682–1694. Retrieved from http://dx.doi.org/10.1037/a0016119.

Bennett, M. d. (2006) Cultural resources and school engagement among African American youths: The role of racial socialization and ethnic identity *Children & Schools, 28,* 197–206. Retrieved from doi:10.1093/cs/28.4.197.

Better, S. (2002). *Institutional racism: A primer on theory and strategies for social change.* Chicago, IL: Burnham.

Bigler, R. S., & Liben, L. S. (2007). Developmental intergroup theory: Explaining and reducing children's social stereotyping and prejudice. *Current Directions in Psychological Science, 16,* 162–166.

Bohrnstedt, G., Kitmitto, S., Ogut, B., Sherman, D., & Chan, D. (2015). School composition and the Black-White achievement gap (NCES 2015–018). US Department of Education, Washington, DC: National Center for Education Statistics. Retrieved from https://nces.ed.gov/nationsreportcard/pubs/stud ies/2015018.aspx.

Bonilla-Silva, E. (1997). Rethinking racism: Toward a structural interpretation. *American Sociological Review, 62,* 465–480.

Bonilla-Silva, E. (2014). *Racism without racists: Colorblind racism and the persistence of racial inequality in America* (4th ed.). Lanham, MD: Rowman & Littlefield.

Bornstein, M. H., & Arterberry, M. E. (2010). The development of object categorization in young children: Hierarchical inclusiveness, age, perceptual attribute, and group versus individual analyses. *Developmental Psychology, 46*(2), 350–365.

Brewer, M. (1991). The social self: On being the same and different at the same time. *Personality and Social Psychology Bulletin, 17*(5), 475–482.

Brietzke, M., & Perreira, K. (2017). Stress and coping: Latino youth coming of age in a new Latino destination. *Journal of Adolescent Research, 32*(4), 407–432. Retrieved from doi:10.1177/0743558416637915.

Brittian, A. S., Umaña-Taylor, A. J., & Derlan, C. L. (2013). An examination of biracial college youths' family ethnic socialization, ethnic identity, and adjustment: Do self-identification labels and university context matter? *Cultural Diversity and Ethnic Minority Psychology, 19*(2),

Brown, C. S. (2017). *Discrimination in childhood and adolescence: A developmental intergroup approach.* Abingdon, UK: Psychology Press / Taylor & Francis.

Brown, E. (2002). *Real women have curves* [Film]. Los Angeles, CA: Newmarket Films.

Bruni, F. (2015). The lie about college diversity. *NY Times* online. Retrieved from http://www.nytimes.com/2015/12/13/opinion/sunday/the-lie-about-college-diversity.html?mwrsm=Email.

Cabrera, N., Milem, J. F., Jaquette, O., & Marx, R. W. (2014). Missing the (student achievement) forest for all the (political) trees: Empiricism and the Mexican American studies controversy in Tucson. *American Educational Research Journal, 51*, 1084–1118.

Caldwell, C. H., Rafferty, J., Reischl, T. M., De Loney, E. H., & Brooks, C. L. (2010). Enhancing parenting skills among nonresident African American fathers as a strategy for preventing youth risky behaviors. *American Journal of Community Psychology, 45*, 17–35.

Camacho, T., Medina, M., Rivas-Drake, D., & Jagers, R. (2018). School climate and ethnic-racial identity in school: A longitudinal examination of reciprocal associations. *Journal of Community and Applied Social Psychology, 28*(1), 29–41.

Cameron, L., Rutland, A., & Brown, R. (2007). Promoting children's positive intergroup attitudes towards stigmatized groups: Extended contact and multiple classification skills training. *International Journal of Behavioral Development, 31*(5), 454–466.

Carter, P. L. (2005). *Keepin' it real: School success beyond Black and White.* New York, NY: Oxford.

Chan, W. Y., & Latzman, R. D. (2015). Racial discrimination, multiple group identities, and civic beliefs among immigrant adolescents. *Cultural Diversity and Ethnic Minority Psychology, 21*(4), 527–532.

Chang, S., Gunderson, E., Pandit, S., Richards-Schuster, K., & Vails, P. (2005). *Creating a new beginning: Youth speak out on race and ethnicity in metropolitan Detroit; The participatory evaluation of the Youth Dialogues project.* Retrieved from http://archive.ssw.umich.edu/public/currentProjects/youthAndCommunity/pubs/SYD_Report_FINAL_WHOLE_REPORT.pdf.

Chavous, T. M. (2005). An intergroup contact-theory framework for evaluating racial climate on predominantly White college campuses. *American Journal of Community Psychology, 36*(3/4), 239–257.

Checkoway, B. (2009). Youth civic engagement for dialogue and diversity at the metropolitan level. *The Foundation Review, 1*(2). Retrieved from http://scholarworks.gvsu.edu/tfr/vol1/iss2/5.

Clark, K. B., & Clark, M. K. (1939a). The development of consciousness of self and the emergence of racial identification in Negro preschool children. *Journal of Social Psychology, SPSSI Bulletin, 10,* 591–599.

Clark, K. B., & Clark, M. K. (1939b). Segregation as a factor in the racial identification of Negro pre-school children: A preliminary report. *Journal of Experimental Education, 8*(2), 161–163.

Clark, K. B., & Clark, M. K. (1940). Skin color as a factor in racial identification of Negro preschool children. *Journal of Social Psychology, 11(1),* 159–169.

Clark, K. B., & Clark, M. K. (1950). Emotional factors in racial identification and preference in Negro children. *Journal of Negro Education, 19*(3), 341–350.

Coates, T. (2015). *Between the world and me.* New York, NY: Spiegel & Grau.

Colby, S. L., & Ortman, J. M. (2014). Projections of the size and composition of the US Population: 2014 to 2060, current population reports, P25-1143. US Census Bureau. Washington, DC. Retrieved from https://census.gov/content/dam/Census/library/publications/2015/demo/p25-1143.pdf.

Collins, C., & D. R. Williams. (1999). Segregation and mortality: The deadly effects of racism. *Sociological Forum, 14,* 495–523.

Collins, E. (2017). The talk. Retrieved from http://www.lennyletter.com/politics/a758/the-talk/.

Conchas, G. (2001). Structuring failure and success: Understanding the variability in Latino school engagement. *Harvard Educational Review, 71,* 475–504.

Conley, D. (2001). *Honky.* New York, NY: Vintage.

Cross, W. E. (1991). *Shades of Black: Diversity in African American identity.* Philadelphia, PA: Temple University Press.

Cross, W. E., Jr. (1995). The psychology of Nigrescence: Revising the cross model. In J. G. Ponterotto, J. M. Casas, L. A. Suzuki, & C. M. Alexander (Eds.), *Handbook of multicultural counseling* (pp. 93–122). Thousand Oaks, CA: Sage.

Crystal, D., Killen, M., & Ruck, M. (2008). It is who you know that counts: Intergroup contact and judgments about race-based exclusion. *British Journal of Developmental Psychology, 26,* 51–70.

Cummings, J. (2016). Upper school tackles race head on, weekly, with intense cultural proficiency initiative. *Cambridge Day.* Retrieved from http://www

.cambridgeday.com/2016/05/25/upper-school-tackles-race-head-on-weekly-with-intense-cultural-proficiency-initiative/.

Damon, W., & Hart, D. (1982). The development of self-understanding from infancy through adolescence. *Child Development, 53*, 841–864.

Davies, K., Tropp, L. R., Aron, A., Pettigrew, T. F., & Wright, S. C. (2011). Cross-group friendships and intergroup attitudes: A meta-analytic review. *Personality and Social Psychology Review, 15*(4), 332–351.

Dee, T., & Penner, E. (2016). The causal effects of cultural relevance: Evidence from an ethnic studies curriculum. CEPA Working Paper No. 16–01. Stanford Center for Education Policy Analysis: Stanford University. Retrieved from http://cepa.stanford.edu/wp16-01.

Dell'Antonia, K. J. (2014). Talking about racism with White kids. Retrieved from https://parenting.blogs.nytimes.com/2014/11/25/talking-about-racism-with-white-kids/?_r=0.

Delpit, L. (2006). *Other people's children: Cultural conflict in the classroom.* New York, NY: New Press.

Díaz, J. (2007). *The brief wondrous life of Oscar Wao.* New York, NY: Riverhead.

Diemer, M. A., & Li, C. (2011). Critical consciousness development and political participation among marginalized youth. *Child Development, 82*, 1815–1833.

Diemer, M. A., Rapa, L. J., Voight, A. M., & McWhirter, E. H. (2016). Critical consciousness: A developmental approach to addressing marginalization and oppression. *Child Development Perspectives, 10*, 216–221.

Domenech Rodríguez, M. M., Baumann, A. A., & Schwartz, A. L. (2011). Cultural adaptation of an evidence based intervention: From theory to practice in a Latino/a community context. *American Journal of Community Psychology, 47*, 170–186.

Dore, R. A., Hoffman, K. M., Lillard, A. S., & Trawalter, S. (2014). Children's racial bias in perceptions of others' pain. *British Journal of Developmental Psychology, 32*(2), 218–231.

Douglass, S., Mirpuri, S., English, D., & Yip, T. (2016). "They were just making jokes": Ethnic/racial teasing and discrimination among adolescents. *Cultural Diversity and Ethnic Minority Psychology, 22*(1), 69–82. Retrieved from http://dx.doi.org/10.1037/cdp0000041.

Douglass, S., Mirpuri, S. & Yip, T. J. (2017). Considering friends within the context of peers in school for the development of ethnic/racial identity. *Journal of Youth and Adolescence, 46*, 300–316. Retrieved from doi:10.1007/s10964-016-0532-0.

Douglass, S., & Umaña-Taylor, A. J. (2017). Examining discrimination, ethnic-racial identity status, and youth public regard among Black, Latino, and White adolescents. *Journal of Research on Adolescence, 27*(1), 155–172.

Doyle, A. B., Beaudet, J., & Aboud, F. (1988). Developmental patterns in the flexibility of children's ethnic attitudes. *Journal of Cross-cultural Psychology, 19*, 3–18.

Dudley, A. (2015). Talking about Black Lives Matter to White children. Retrieved from http://www.raceconscious.org/2015/06/talking-about-black-lives-matter-to-white-children/.

Dunham, Y., Baron, A., & Carey, S. (2011). Consequences of "minimal" group affiliations in children. *Child Development, 82*(3), 793–811.

Elenbaas, L., Rizzo, M. T., Cooley, S., & Killen, M. (2016). Rectifying social inequalities in a resource allocation task. *Cognition, 155,* 176–187. Retrieved from doi:10.1016/j.cognition.2016.07.002.

Erikson, E. H. (1959). *Identity and the life cycle.* New York: Norton.

Erikson, E. H. (1968). *Identity: Youth and crisis.* New York: Norton.

Evans, N., Gunderson, E., Kaddoura, M., Polk, A., Russell, S., Lederman, R., et al. (2006). *Creating change with our own two hands: 2006 summer Youth Dialogues evaluation report.* Retrieved from http://archive.ssw.umich.edu/public/currentProjects/youthAndCommunity/pubs/SYDReport.pdf.

Facing History and Ourselves. (2008). *Holocaust and human behavior* (Rev. ed.). Brookline, MA: Facing History and Ourselves.

Facing History and Ourselves. (2017). *Holocaust and human behavior* (Rev. ed.). Brookline, MA: Facing History and Ourselves. Retrieved from https://www.facinghistory.org/sites/default/files/publications/Holocaust_Human_Behavior_revised_edition.pdf.

Feddes, A., Noack, P., & Rutland, A. (2009). Direct and extended friendship effects on minority and majority children's interethnic attitudes: A longitudinal study. *Child Development, 80,* 377–390.

Ferguson, A. A. (2000). *Bad boys: Public schools in the making of black masculinity.* Ann Arbor: University of Michigan Press.

Finn, J. D., & Servoss, T. J. (2014). Misbehavior, suspensions, and security measures in high school: Racial/ethnic and gender differences. *Journal of Applied Research on Children: Informing Policy for Children and Risk, 5*(2). Retrieved from http://digitalcommons.library.tmc.edu/cgi/viewcontent.cgi?article=1211&context=childrenatrisk.

Fisher, C. B., Wallace, S. A., & Fenton, R. E. (2000). Discrimination distress during adolescence. *Journal of Youth and Adolescence, 29,* 679–695.

Flanagan, C. A., Syvertsen, A. K., Gill, S., Gallay, L. S., & Cumsille, P. (2009). Ethnic awareness, prejudice, and civic commitments in four ethnic groups of American adolescents. *Journal of Youth and Adolescence, 38,* 500–518.

Ford, K. A., & Maloney, V. K. (2012). "I now harbor more pride in my race": The educational benefits of inter- and intraracial dialogues on the experiences of students of color and multiracial students. *Equity & Excellence in Education, 45*(1), 14–35.

Fordham, S., & Ogbu, J. (1986). Black students' school success: Coping with "the burden of 'acting white.'" *The Urban Review, 18,* 176–206.

French, S., E., Seidman, E., Allen, L., & Aber, J. L. (2006). The development of ethnic identity during adolescence. *Developmental Psychology, 42,* 1–10.

Gaertner, S. L., Rust, M. C., Dovidio, J. F., Bachman, B. A., & Anastasio, P. A. (1994). The contact hypothesis: The role of a common ingroup identity on reducing intergroup bias. *Small Group Research, 25*(2), 224–249.

Ginwright, S. A. (2007). Black youth activism and the role of critical social capital in Black community organizations. *American Behavioral Scientist, 51,* 403–418.

Goff, P. A., Jackson, M. C., Di Leone, B.A.L., Culotta, C. M., & DiTomasso, N. A. (2014). The essence of innocence: Consequences of dehumanizing Black children. *Journal of Personality and Social Psychology, 106*(4), 526–545.

González, R., Lickel, B., Gupta, M., Tropp, L., Luengo Kanacri, B. P., Mora, E., et al. (2017). Ethnic identity development and acculturation preferences among minority and majority youth: Norms and contact. *Child Development, 88*(3), 743–760. Retrieved from https://doi.org/10.1111/cdev.12788.

Gragg, S. W. (2017). *Momma, did you hear the news?* Illustrated by Kim Holt. Amazon Digital Services.

Graham, S., Munniksma, A., & Juvonen, J. (2014). Psychosocial benefits of cross-ethnic friendships in urban middle schools. *Child Development, 85*(2), 469–483.

Greene, M. L., Way, N., & Pahl, K. (2006). Trajectories of perceived adult and peer discrimination among Black, Latino, and Asian American adolescents: Patterns and psychological correlates. *Developmental Psychology, 42,* 218–238.

Greenwald, A. G., & Krieger, L. H. (2006). Implicit bias: Scientific foundations. *California Law Review, 94*(4), 945–967.

Gregory, A., Skiba, R. J., & Noguera, P. A. (2010). The achievement gap and the discipline gap: Two sides of the same coin? *Educational Researcher, 39*(1), 59–68.

Gurin, P., Dey, E. L., Hurtado, S., & Gurin, G. (2002). Diversity and higher education: Theory and impact on educational outcomes. *Harvard Educational Review, 72*(3), 330–366.

Gurin, P., Nagda, B. A., & Zúñiga, X. (2013). *Dialogue across difference: Practice, theory, and research on intergroup dialogue.* New York, NY: Russell Sage Foundation.

Hanson, A., & Santas, M. (2014). Field experiment tests for discrimination against Hispanics in the US rental housing market. *Southern Economic Journal, 81*(1), 135–167.

Hatcher, A., de Wet, J., Bonell, C. P., Strange, V., Phetla, G., Proynk, P. M., & Hargreaves, J. R. (2010). Promoting critical consciousness and social mobilization in HIV/AIDS programmes: Lessons and curricular tools from a South African intervention. *Health Education Research, 26,* 542–555.

Hayes-Bautista, D., & Chapa, J. (1987). Latino terminology: Conceptual bases for standardized terminology. *American Journal of Public Health, 77,* 61–68.

Hebl, M. R., Tickle, J., & Heatherton, T. F. (2000). Awkward moments in interactions between nonstigmatized and stigmatized individuals. In T. F. Heatherton,

R. E. Kleck, M. R. Hebl, & J. G. Hull (Eds.), *The social psychology of stigma* (pp. 275–306). New York: Guilford Press.

Helms, J. E. (1990). *Black and white racial identity: Theory, research, and practice.* Westport, CT: Praeger.

Huang, C., & Stormshak, E. (2011). A longitudinal examination of early adolescence ethnic identity trajectories. *Cultural Diversity and Ethnic Minority Psychology, 17*, 261–270.

Huang, E. (2013). *Fresh off the boat: A memoir.* New York, NY: Spiegel & Grau.

Hughes, D., Del Toro, J., Harding, J. F., Way, N., & Rarick, J. R. (2016). Trajectories of discrimination across adolescence: Associations with academic, psychological, and behavioral outcomes. *Child Development, 87*, 1337–1351.

Hughes, D., Rivas, D., Foust, M., Hagelskamp, C., Gersick, S., & Way, N. (2007). How to catch a moonbeam: A mixed-methods approach to understanding ethnic socialization processes in ethnically diverse families. In S. Quintana and C. McKown (Eds.), *Handbook of race, racism, and the developing child* (pp. 226–277). Hoboken, NJ: Wiley.

Hughes, D., & Rivas-Drake, D. (2007). Children's perceptions of racial discrimination: Developmental correlates and consequences for self-esteem. Biennial meeting of the Society for Research in Child Development, Boston, MA.

Hughes, D., Rodriguez, J., Smith, E. P., Johnson, D. J., Stevenson, H. C., & Spicer, P. (2006). Parents' ethnic-racial socialization practices: A review of research and directions for future study. *Developmental Psychology, 42*(5), 747–770.

Hughes, D., Witherspoon, D., Rivas-Drake, D., & West-Bey, N. (2009). Received ethnic/racial socialization messages and youths' academic and behavioral outcomes: Examining the mediating role of ethnic identity and self-esteem. *Cultural Diversity and Ethnic Minority Psychology, 15*(2), 112–124.

Hughes, J. M., Bigler, R. S., & Levy, S. R. (2007). Consequences of learning about historical racism among European American and African American children. *Child Development, 78*(6), 1689–1705.

Humes, K. R., Jones, N. A., & Ramirez, R. R. (2011). Overview of race and Hispanic origin: 2010. 2010 Census Briefs, C2010BR-02. US Department of Commerce: Economics and Statistics Administration. US Census Bureau.

Huynh, V. W., & Fuligni, A. J. (2010). Discrimination hurts: The academic, psychological, and physical well-being of adolescents. *Journal of Research on Adolescence, 20*, 916–941.

Irving, D. (2014). *Waking up white and finding myself in a story of race.* Cambridge, MA: Elephant Room Press.

Jayakumar, U. M. (2008). Can higher education meet the needs of an increasingly diverse and global society? Campus diversity and cross-cultural workforce competencies. *Harvard Educational Review, 78*(4), 615–651.

Josselson, R. (1980). Ego development in adolescence. In J. Adelson (Ed.), *Handbook of adolescent psychology* (pp. 188–210). New York: Wiley.

Juang, L., & Syed, M. (2010). Family cultural socialization practices and ethnic identity in college-going emerging adults. *Journal of Adolescence, 33*, 347–354.

Juang, L. P., Shen, Y. S., Kim, S. Y., & Wang, Y. J. (2016). Development of an Asian American parental racial-ethnic socialization scale. *Cultural Diversity and Ethnic Minority Psychology, 22*(3), .

Kaplan, H. R. (2011). *The myth of post-racial America: Searching for equality in the age of materialism.* Lanham, MD: Rowman & Littlefield Education.

Katz, P. A. (2003). Racists or tolerant multiculturalists? How do they begin? *American Psychologist, 58,* 897–909.

Katz, P. A., & Kofkin, J. A. (1997). Race, gender, and young children. In S. S. Luthar & J. A. Burack (Eds.), *Developmental psychopathology: Perspectives on adjustment, risk, and disorder* (pp. 51–74). New York, NY: Cambridge University Press.

Keelty, C. (2016). How to easily be a white ally to marginalized communities. Retrieved from https://medium.com/@keeltyc/how-to-easily-be-a-white-ally -to-marginalized-communities-fb0ff326e7ac#.aoepz0uqt.

Khan, N., Kasdan, J., & Mar, M. (Executive Producers); Blomquist, R., Huang, E., & McEwen, J. (Producers). (2015). *Fresh off the boat* [Television series]. Orlando, FL: Fierce Baby Productions; Detective Agency; 20th Century Fox.

Kiang, L., Perreira, K. M., & Fuligni, A. J. (2011). Ethnic label use in adolescents from traditional and non-traditional immigrant receiving sites. *Journal of Youth and Adolescence, 40,* 719–729. Retrieved from doi:10.1007/s10964-010 -9597-3.

Kiang, L., Peterson, J. L., & Thompson, T. L. (2011). Ethnic peer preferences among Asian American adolescents in emerging immigrant communities. *Journal of Research on Adolescence, 21,* 754–761. Retrieved from doi:10.1111 /j.1532–7795.2011.00750.x.

Killen, M., Elenbaas, L., & Rutland, A. (2015). Balancing the fair treatment of others while preserving group identity and autonomy. *Human Development, 58,* 253–272. Retrieved from doi:10.1159/000444151.

Killen, M., Rutland, A., Abrams, D., Mulvey, K. L., & Hitti, A. (2013). Development of intra- and intergroup judgments in the context of moral and social-conventional norms. *Child Development, 84,* 1063–1080. Retrieved from doi:10.1111/cdev.12011.

Knifsend, C., & Juvonen, J. (2012). The role of social identity complexity in inter-group attitudes among young adolescents. *Social Development, 22,* 623–640.

Ko, L. K., & Perreira, K. M. (2010). "It turned my world upside down": Latino youths' perspectives on immigration. *Journal of Adolescent Research, 25,* 465–493. Retrieved from doi:10.1177/0743558410361372.

Kulis, S., Ayers, S. L., & Baker, T. (2015). Parenting in 2 Worlds: Pilot results from a culturally adapted parenting program for urban American Indians. *Journal of Primary Prevention, 36,* 65–70.

Kumagai, A. K., & Lypson, M. L. (2009). Beyond cultural competence: Critical consciousness, social justice, and multicultural education. *Academic Medicine, 84,* 782–787.

Lahiri, J. (2003). *The namesake: A novel.* New York, NY: First Mariner Books.

Lam, V. L., & Seaton, J. (2016). Ingroup/outgroup attitudes and group evaluations: The role of competition in British classroom settings. *Child Development Research.* Retrieved from http://dx.doi.org/10.1155/2016/8649132.

Leavitt, P. A., Covarrubais, R., Perez, Y. A., & Fryberg, S. A. (2015). "Frozen in time": The impact of Native American media representations on identity and self-understanding. *Journal of Social Issues, 71,* 39–53.

Lee, B. A., Iceland, J., & Farrell, J. (2014). Is ethnoracial residential integration on the rise? Evidence from metropolitan and micropolitan America since 1980. In J. Logan (Ed.), *Diversity and disparities: America enters a new century* (pp. 415–456). New York, NY: Russell Sage Foundation.

Lee, S. J. (1996). *Unraveling the "model minority" stereotype: Listening to Asian American youth.* New York, NY: Teachers College Press.

Levy, S. R., Lytle, A., Shin, J. E., & Hughes, J. M. (2016). Understanding and reducing racial and ethnic prejudice among children and adolescents. In T. D. Nelson (Ed.), *Handbook of prejudice, stereotyping, and discrimination* (2nd ed.). New York, NY: Psychology Press / Taylor & Francis.

Lin, A. R., Menjívar, C., Ettekal, A. V., Simpkins, S. D., Gaskin, E. R., & Pesch, A. (2016). "They will post a law about playing soccer" and other ethnic/racial microaggressions in organized activities experienced by Mexican-origin families. *Journal of Adolescent Research, 31*(5), 557–581.

Lin, A. R., Simpkins, S. D., Gaskin, E. R., & Menjívar, C. (2016). Cultural values and other perceived benefits of organized activities: A qualitative analysis of Mexican-origin parents' perspectives in Arizona. *Applied Developmental Science.* Retrieved from http://dx.doi.org/10.1080/10888691.2016.1224669.

Logan, J. (2014). *Diversity and disparities: America enters a new century.* New York, NY: Russell Sage Foundation.

Lozada, F., Jagers, R. J., Smith, C. D., Bañales, J., & Hope, E. C. (2017). Prosocial behaviors of Black adolescent boys: An application of a sociopolitical development theory. *Journal of Black Psychology, 43*(5) 493–516.

Mallett, R. K., Wagner, D. E., & Harrison, P. R. (2011). Understanding the intergroup forecasting error. In L. R. Tropp & R. K. Mallett (Eds.), *Moving beyond prejudice reduction: Pathways to positive intergroup relations* (pp. 63–80). Washington, DC: American Psychological Association.

Maramba, D. C., & Museus, S. D. (2013). Examining the effects of campus climate, ethnic group cohesion, and cross-cultural interaction on Filipino American students' sense of belonging in college. *Journal of College Student Retention: Research, Theory & Practice, 14,* 495–522.

Marcia, J. E. (1980). Identity in adolescence. In J. Adelson (Ed.), *Handbook of adolescent psychology* (pp. 159–187). New York: Wiley.

Martínez, M. L., Peñaloza, P., & Valenzuela, C. (2012). Civic commitment in young activists: Emergent processes in the development of personal and collective identity. *Journal of Adolescence, 35,* 474–484.

Massey, D. (2008). *New faces in new places: The changing geography of American immigration.* New York, NY: Russell Sage.

Massey, D. S., & N. Denton. (1993). *American Apartheid: Segregation and the making of the underclass.* Cambridge: Harvard University Press.

Maxwell, K. E., Chesler, M., and Nagda, B. A. (2011). Identity matters: Facilitators' struggles and empowered use of social identities in intergroup dialogue. In K. E. Maxwell, B. A. Nagda, & M. C. Thompson (Eds.), *Facilitating intergroup dialogues: Bridging differences, catalyzing change* (pp. 163–178). Sterling, VA: Stylus.

McFarland, M. (2017). A matter of survival: "The talk" is a conversation about parents, kids and police. Retrieved from http://www.salon.com/2017/02/20/a-matter-of-survival-the-talk-is-a-conversation-about-parents-kids-and-police/.

Miller-Cotto, D., & Byrnes, J. P. (2016). Ethnic/racial identity and academic achievement: A meta-analytic review. *Developmental Review, 41*, 51–70.

Monte, L. M., & Ellis, R. R. (2014). Fertility of women in the United States: 2012; Population characteristics. Census Bureau: Washington, DC. Retrieved from https://www.census.gov/content/dam/Census/library/publications/2014/demo/p20-575.pdf.

Morsillo, J., & Prilleltensky, I. (2007). Social action with youth: Interventions, evaluation, and psychopolitical validity. *Journal of Community Psychology, 35,* 725–740.

Murry, V. M., Berkel, C., Brody, G. H., Gerrard, M., & Gibbons, F. X. (2007). The Strong African American Families program: Longitudinal pathways to sexual risk reduction. *The Journal of Adolescent Health, 41,* 333–342.

Neblett, E. W., Jr., Banks, K. H., Cooper, S. M., & Smalls-Glover, C. (2013). Racial identity mediates the association between ethnic-racial socialization and depressive symptoms. *Cultural Diversity and Ethnic Minority Psychology, 19*(2), 200–207.

Neblett, E. W., Rivas-Drake, D., & Umaña-Taylor, A. (2012). The promise of racial and ethnic protective factors in promoting ethnic minority youth development. *Child Development Perspectives, 6*(3), 295–303. Retrieved from doi: 10.1111/j.1750-8606.2012.00239.x.

Nesdale, D., Durkin, K., Maass, A., & Griffiths, J. A. (2005). Threat, group identification, and children's ethnic prejudice. *Social Development, 14*(2), 189–205.

Nesdale, D., Griffiths, J. A., Durkin, K., & Maass, A. (2007). Effects of group membership, intergroup competition, and out-group ethnicity on children's rating of in-group and out-group similarity and positivity. *British Journal of Developmental Psychology, 25,* 359–373.

Nesdale, D., Maass, A., Griffiths, J. A., & Durkin, K. (2003). Effects of in-group and out-group ethnicity on children's attitudes toward members of the in-group and out-group. *British Journal of Developmental Psychology, 21,* 177–192.

Ngo, B. (2015). Hmong culture club as a place of belonging: The cultivation of Hmong students' cultural and political identities. *Journal of Southeast Asian American Education and Advancement, 10*(2), 1–20.

Nguyen, C. P., Wong, Y. J., Juang, L. P., & Park, I.J.K. (2015). Pathways among Asian Americans' family ethnic socialization, ethnic identity, and psychological well-being: A multigroup mediation model. *Asian American Journal of Psychology, 6*(3), 273–280.

Niwa, E. Y., Way, N., & Hughes, D. L. (2014). Trajectories of ethnic-racial discrimination among ethnically diverse early adolescents: Associations with psychological and social adjustment. *Child Development, 85*(6), 2339–2354. Retrieved from doi:10.1111/cdev.12310.

Obama, B. H. (2004). *Dreams from my father: A story of race and inheritance.* New York, NY: Three Rivers Press.

O'Connor, C., Mueller, J., Lewis, R. L., Rivas-Drake, D., & Rosenberg, S. (2011). Being Black and strategizing for academic excellence in a racially stratified academic hierarchy. *American Educational Research Journal, 48*, 1232–1257.

Olshansky, S. J., Atonucci, T., Berkman, L., Binstock, L. H., Boersch-Supan, A., Cacioppo, J. T., et al. (2012). Differences in life expectancy due to race and educational differences are widening, and many may not catch up. *Health Affairs, 31*, 1803–1813.

Ondrich, J., Stricker, A., & Yinger, Y. (1999). Do landlords discriminate? The incidence and causes of racial discrimination in rental housing markets. *Journal of Housing Economics, 8*(3), 185–204.

Orfield, G., Frankenberg, E., & Siegel-Hawley, G. (2010). Integrated schools: Finding a new path. *Educational Leadership, 68*(3), 22–27.

Orfield, G., Kucsera, J., & Siegel-Hawley, G. (2012). *E pluribus … segregation: Deepening double segregation for more students.* Retrieved from http://civil rightsproject.ucla.edu/research/k-12-education/integration-and-diversity /mlk-national/e-pluribus...separation-deepening-double-segregation-for -more-students/orfield_epluribus_revised_omplete_2012.pdf.

Oyserman, D. (2008). Racial-ethnic self-schemas: Multidimensional identity-based motivation. *Journal of Personality, 42*(5), 1186–1198.

Oyserman, D., & Destin, M. (2010). Identity-based motivation: Implications for intervention. *Counseling Psychologist, 38*(7), 1001–1043.

Page, S. (2007). *The difference: How the power of diversity creates better groups, firms, schools, and societies.* Princeton, NJ: Princeton University Press.

Page-Gould, E., Mendoza-Denton, R., & Tropp, L. R. (2008). With a little help from my cross-group friend: Reducing anxiety in intergroup contexts through cross-group friendship. *Journal of Personality and Social Psychology, 95*(5), 1080–1094.

Pahl, K., & Way, N. (2006). Longitudinal trajectories of ethnic identity among urban Black and Latino adolescents. *Child Development, 77*, 1403–1415.

Paluck, E. L., & Green, D. P. (2009). Prejudice reduction: What works? A review and assessment of research and practice. *Annual Review of Psychology, 60*, 339–367.

Pauker, K., Apfelbaum, E. P., & Spitzer, B. (2015). When societal norms and social identity collide: The race talk dilemma for racial minority children. *Social Psychological and Personality Science, 6*(8), 887–895. Retrieved from doi:10 .1177/1948550615598379.

Perreira, K., Fuligni, A. J., & Potochnick, S. (2009). Fitting in: The roles of social acceptance and discrimination in shaping the academic motivations of Latino youth in the US southeast. *Journal of Social Issues, 66*(1), 131–153. Retrieved from doi:10.1111/j.1540–4560.2009.01637.x.

Pettigrew, T. F., & Tropp, L. R. (2006). A meta-analytic test of intergroup contact theory. *Journal of Personality and Social Psychology, 90*(5), 751–783.

Pettigrew, T. F., & Tropp, L. R. (2008). How does intergroup contact reduce prejudice? Meta-analytic tests of three mediators. *European Journal of Social Psychology, 38*(6), 922–934.

Phinney, J. S. (1989). Stages of ethnic identity development in minority adolescents. *Journal of Early Adolescence, 9,* 34–49.

Phinney, J. S. (1990). Ethnic identity in adolescents and adults: Review of research. *Psychological Bulletin, 108,* 499–514. Retrieved from doi:10.1037/0033 –2909.108.3.499.

Phinney, J. S. (1992). The Multigroup Ethnic Identity Measure: A new scale for use with diverse groups. *Journal of Adolescent Research, 7,* 156–176.

Phinney, J. S. (1996). When we talk about American ethnic groups, what do we mean? *American Psychologist, 51,* 918–927.

Phinney, J. S., & Alipuria, L. L. (1990). Ethnic identity in college students from four ethnic groups. *Journal of Adolescence, 13,* 171–183.

Phinney, J. S., DuPont, S., Espinosa, C., Revill, J., & Sanders, K. (1994). Ethnic identity and American identification among ethnic minority youths. In A. Bouvy, F.J.R. van de Vijver, P. Boxki, & P. Schmitz (Eds.), *Journeys into cross-cultural psychology* (pp. 167–183). Amsterdam, Netherlands: Swets & Zeitlinger B. V.

Phinney, J. S., Jacoby, B., & Silva, C. (2007). Positive intergroup attitudes: The role of ethnic identity. *International Journal of Behavioral Development, 31,* 478–490.

Pittinsky, T. L., Rosenthal, S. A., & Montoya, R. M. (2011). Measuring positive attitudes toward outgroups: Development and validation of the Allophilia Scale. In L. R. Tropp & R. K. Mallett (Eds.), *Moving beyond prejudice reduction: Pathways to positive intergroup relations* (pp. 41–60). Washington, DC: American Psychological Association.

Pollock, M. (2004). *Colormute: Race talk dilemmas in an American school.* Princeton, NJ: Princeton.

Priest, N., Walton, W. J., White, F., Kowal, E., Baker, A., & Paradies, Y. (2014). Understanding the complexities of ethnic-racial socialization processes for both minority and majority groups: A 30-year systematic review. *International Journal of Intercultural Relations, 43,* Part B, 139–155.

Prot, S., Anderson, C. A., Gentile, D. A., Warburton, W., Saleem, M., Groves, C. L., et al. (2014). Media as agents of socialization. In J. E. Grusec & P. D. Hastings (Eds.), *Handbook of socialization: Theory and research* (2nd ed.) (pp. 276–300). New York, NY: Guilford Press.

Qin, D., Way, N., & Mukerjee, P. (2008). The other side of the model minority story: The familial and peer challenges faced by Chinese American adolescents.

Youth & Society, 39(4), 480–506. Retrieved from doi:10.1177/0044118X083 14233.

Quintana, S. M. (1998). Children's developmental understanding of ethnicity and race. *Applied and Preventive Psychology, 7,* 27–45.

Quintana, S. M., Segura Herrera, T. A., & Nelson, M. L. (2010). Mexican American high school students' ethnic self-concepts and identity. *Journal of Social Issues, 66*(1), 11–28.

Quintana, S. M., & Vera, E. M. (1999). Mexican American children's ethnic identity, understanding of ethnic prejudice, and parental ethnic socialization. *Hispanic Journal of Behavioral Sciences, 21*(4), 387–404.

Rakison, D. H., & Yermolayeva, Y. (2010). Infant categorization. *WIREs Cognitive Science, 1*(6), 894–905.

Ramasubramanian, S. (2010). Television viewing, racial attitudes, and policy preferences: Exploring the role of social identity and intergroup emotions in influencing support for affirmative action. *Communication Monographs, 77*(1), 102–120. Retrieved from doi:10.1080/03637750903514300.

Ramiah, A. A., Schmid, K., Hewstone, M., & Floe, C. (2015). Why are all the White (Asian) kids sitting together in the cafeteria? Resegregation and the role of intergroup attributions and norms. *British Journal of Social Psychology, 54*(1), 100–124.

Richards-Schuster, K., & Aldana, A. (2013). Learning to speak out about racism: Youths' insights on participation in an intergroup dialogues program. *Social Work with Groups, 36*(4), 332–348.

Rivas-Drake, D. (2011a). Ethnic-racial socialization and adjustment among Latino college students: The mediating roles of ethnic centrality, public regard, and perceived barriers to opportunity. *Journal of Youth and Adolescence, 40*(5), 609–619.

Rivas-Drake, D. (2011b). Public ethnic regard and academic adjustment among Latino adolescents. *Journal of Research on Adolescence, 21*(3), 537–544.

Rivas-Drake, D., Hughes, D., & Way, N. (2008). A closer look at peer discrimination, ethnic identity, and psychological well-being among urban Chinese American sixth graders. *Journal of Youth and Adolescence, 37*(1), 12–21.

Rivas-Drake, D., Hughes, D., & Way, N. (2009). Public ethnic regard and perceived socioeconomic stratification: Associations with well-being among Dominican and Black American youth. *Journal of Early Adolescence, 29*(1), 122–141.

Rivas-Drake, D., Saleem, M., Schaefer, D., Medina, M., & Jagers, R. J. (2018). Intergroup contact attitudes across peer networks in school: Selection, influence, and implications for cross-group friendships. *Child Development.*

Rivas-Drake, D., Seaton, E. K., Markstrom, C., Quintana, S., Syed, M., Lee, R., et al. & Study Group on Ethnic and Racial Identity in the 21st Century (2014). Ethnic and racial identity in adolescence: Implications for psychosocial, academic, and health outcomes. *Child Development, 85,* 40–57. Retrieved from doi:10.1111/cdev.12200.

Rivas-Drake, D., Syed, M., Umaña-Taylor, A. J., Markstrom, C., French, S., Schwartz, S. J., et al. & Study Group on Ethnic and Racial Identity in the 21st Century (2014). Feeling good, happy, and proud: A meta-analysis of positive ethnic-racial affect and adjustment. *Child Development, 85*, 77–102. Retrieved from doi:10.1111/cdev.12175.

Rivas-Drake, D., Umaña-Taylor, A., Schaefer, D., & Medina, M. (2017). Ethnic-racial identity and friendships in early adolescence. *Child Development, 88*(3), 710–724. Retrieved from doi:10.1111/cdev.12790.

Rivas-Drake, D., & Witherspoon, D. (2013). Racial identity from adolescence to young adulthood: Does prior neighborhood experience matter? *Child Development, 84*(6), 1918–1932. Retrieved from doi:10.1111/cdev.12095.

Romero, A. J., & Roberts, R. E. (2003). The impact of multiple dimensions of ethnic identity on discrimination and adolescents' self-esteem. *Journal of Applied Social Psychology, 33*, 2288–2305.

Rosenbloom, S. R., & Way, N. (2004). Experiences of discrimination among African American, Asian American, and Latino adolescents in an urban high school. *Youth and Society, 35*, 420–451.

Rutland, A., Cameron, L., Bennett, L., & Ferrell, J. (2005). Interracial contact and racial constancy: A multi-site study of racial intergroup bias in 3–5 year old Anglo-British children. *Applied Developmental Psychology, 26*, 699–713.

Rutland, A., Cameron, L., Jugert, P., Nigbur, D., Brown, R., Watters, C., et al. (2012). Group identity and peer relations: A longitudinal study of group identity, perceived peer acceptance, and friendships amongst ethnic minority English children. *British Journal of Developmental Psychology, 30*, 283–302.

Santiago, E. (1993). *When I was Puerto Rican: A memoir*. New York, NY: Da Capo Press.

Santos, C., Kornienko, C., & Rivas-Drake, D. (2017). Peer network influence on ethnic-racial identity development: A multi-site investigation. *Child Development, 88*(3), 725–742. Retrieved from doi:10.1111/cdev.12789.

Sellers, R. M., Morgan, L. M., & Brown, T. N. (2001). A multidimensional approach to racial identity: Implications for African American children. In A. Neal-Barnett (Ed.), *Forging links: Clinical-developmental perspectives on African American children* (pp. 23–56). Westport, CT: Praeger.

Sellers, R. M., Smith, M. A., Shelton, J. N., Rowley, S.A.J., & Chavous, T. M. (1998). Multidimensional model of racial identity: A reconceptualization of African American racial identity. *Personality and Social Psychology Review, 2*, 18–39.

Selvanathan, H. P., Techakesari, P., Tropp, L. R., & Barlow, F. K. (2017). Whites for racial justice: How contact with Black Americans predicts support for collective action among White Americans. *Group Processes & Intergroup Relations*. Retrieved from doi:https://doi.org/10.1177/1368430217690908.

Serrano-Villar, M., & Calzada, E. J. (2016). Ethnic identity: Evidence of protective effects for young, Latino children. *Journal of Applied Developmental Psychology, 42*, 21–30.

Shelton, J. N., & Sellers, R. M. (2000). Situational stability and variability in African American racial identity. *Journal of Black Psychology, 26*(1), 27–50.

Shurer O. (2016). *Moana* [Film]. Burbank, CA: Walt Disney Studios Motion Pictures.

Shuster, K. (2014). *A formative evaluation of Perspectives for a Diverse America: Final report 2013–2014.* Retrieved from http://www.tolerance.org/sites/default/files/general/PDA%20Pilot%20Study.pdf.

Sierksma, J., Thijs, J., & Verkuyten, M. (2015). In-group bias in children's intention to help can be overpowered by inducing empathy. *British Journal of Developmental Psychology, 33,* 45–56.

Sirin, S. R., & Fine. M. (2007). Hyphenated selves: Muslim American youth negotiating identities on the fault lines of global conflict. *Applied Development Science, 11*(3), 151–163.

Skiba, R. J., Michael, R. S., Nardo, A. C., & Peterson, R. L. (2002). The color of discipline: Sources of racial and gender disproportionality in school punishment. *Urban Review, 34,* 317–342.

Smith, T. B., & Silva, L. (2011). Ethnic identity and personal well-being of people of color: A meta-analysis. *Journal of Counseling Psychology, 58,* 42–60.

Spencer, M. B. (1982). Preschool children's social cognition and cultural cognition: A cognitive developmental interpretation of race dissonance findings. *Journal of Psychology, 112,* 275–286.

Steele, C. M. (2010) *Whistling Vivaldi: How stereotypes affect us and what we can do.* New York: W. W. Norton.

Stevenson, H. C. (1994). Racial socialization in African American families: The art of balancing intolerance and survival. *The Family Journal, 2*(3), 190–198.

Stevenson, H. C. (2014). *Promoting racial literacy in schools: Differences that make a difference.* New York, NY: Teachers College Press.

Stevenson, H. C., McNeil, J. D., Herrero-Taylor, T., & Davis, G. Y. (2005). Influence of perceived neighborhood diversity and racism experience on the racial socialization of Black youth. *Journal of Black Psychology, 31,* 273–290. Retrieved from http://dx.doi.org/10.1177/0095798405278453.

Strauss, L. C., & Cross, W. E. (2005). Transacting Black identity: A two-week daily-diary study. In J. Eccles & C. Chatman (Eds.), *Navigating the future: Social identity, coping, and life tasks.* New York, NY: Russell Sage.

Suárez-Orozco, C., Suárez-Orozco, M., & Todorova, I. (2008). *Learning a new land: Immigrant students in American society.* Cambridge, MA: Harvard University Press.

Sue, D. W. (2003). *Overcoming our racism: The journey to liberation.* San Francisco, CA: Jossey-Bass.

Supple, A. J., Ghazarian, S. R., Frabutt, J. M., Plunkett, S. W., & Sands, T. (2006). Contextual influences on Latino adolescent ethnic identity and academic outcomes. *Child Development, 77,* 1427–1433. Retrieved from doi:10.1111/j.1467-8624.2006.00945.x.

Syed, M., & Azmitia, M. (2008). A narrative approach to ethnic identity in emerging adulthood: Bringing life to the identity status model. *Developmental Psychology, 44*, 1012–1027.

Syed, M., & Azmitia, M. (2009). Longitudinal trajectories of ethnic identity during the college years. *Journal of Research on Adolescence, 19*, 601–624.

Syed, M., & Juan, M.J.D. (2012). Birds of an ethnic feather? Ethnic identity homophily among college-age friends. *Journal of Adolescence, 35*, 1505–1514. Retrieved from doi:10.1016/j.adolescence.2011.10.012.

Tajfel, H. (1981). *Human groups and social categories: Studies in social psychology.* New York: Cambridge University Press.

Tajfel, H., & Turner, J. (1986). The social identity theory of intergroup behavior. In W. Austin & S. Worchel (Eds.), *Psychology of intergroup relations* (2nd ed., pp. 7–24). Chicago: Nelson-Hall.

Tatum, B. (2003). *Why are all the Black kids sitting together in the cafeteria? And other conversations about race.* New York: Basic Books.

Thomas, A. J., & Blackmon, A. (2015). The influence of the Trayvon Martin shooting on racial socialization practices of African American parents. *Journal of Black Psychology, 41*(1), 75–89.

Thompson, T. L., Kiang, L., & Witkow, M. (2016). "You're Asian; you're supposed to be smart": Adolescents' experiences with the model minority stereotype and longitudinal links with identity. *Asian American Journal of Psychology, 7*(2), 108–119.

Trawalter, S., Hoffman, K. M., & Waytz, A. (2012). Racial bias in perceptions of others' pain. *PLOSOne, 7*(11), 1–8.

Tynes, B. M., Giang, M. T., Williams, D. R., & Thompson, G. N. (2008). Online racial discrimination and psychological adjustment among adolescents. *Journal of Adolescent Health, 43*, 565–569. Retrieved from doi:10.1016/j.jadohealth.2008.08.021.

Tynes, B., Reynolds, L., & Greenfield, P. M. (2004). Adolescence, race, and ethnicity on the Internet: A comparison of discourse in monitored vs. unmonitored chat rooms. *Applied Developmental Psychology, 25*, 667–684.

Tynes, B. M., Umaña-Taylor, A. J., Rose, C. A., Lin, J., & Anderson, C. J. (2012). Online racial discrimination and the protective function of ethnic identity and self-esteem for African American adolescents. *Developmental Psychology, 48*, 343–355. Retrieved from doi:10.1037/a0027032.

US Department of Education. (2016). *The state of racial diversity in the educator workforce.* Retrieved from https://www2.ed.gov/rschstat/eval/highered/racial-diversity/state-racial-diversity-workforce.pdf.

Umaña-Taylor, A. J. (2011). Ethnic identity. In S. J. Schwartz, K. Luyckx, & V. L. Vignoles (Eds.), *Handbook of identity theory and research* (pp. 791–809). New York: Springer.

Umaña-Taylor, A. J. (2016a). A post-racial society in which ethnic-racial discrimination still exists and has significant consequences for youths' adjustment.

Current Directions in Psychological Science, 25(2), 111–118. Retrieved from doi:10.1177/0963721415627858.

Umaña-Taylor, A. J. (2016b). Ethnic-racial identity: Conceptualization, development, and associations with youth adjustment. In L. Balter & C. S. Tamis-LeMonda (Eds.), *Child psychology: A handbook of contemporary issues* (3rd ed.) (pp. 305–327). New York: Psychology Press / Taylor & Francis.

Umaña-Taylor, A. J. (2017). Youths' perceptions of factors that facilitate and hinder ethnic-racial identity development. Unpublished manuscript.

Umaña-Taylor, A. J., Alfaro, E. C., Bámaca, M. Y., & Guimond, A. B. (2009). The central role of familial ethnic socialization in Latino adolescents' cultural orientation. *Journal of Marriage and Family, 71*, 46–60.

Umaña-Taylor, A. J., & Bámaca, M. (2004). Immigrant mothers' experiences with ethnic socialization of adolescents growing up in the United States: An examination of Colombian, Guatemalan, Mexican, and Puerto Rican mothers. *Sociological Focus, 37*(4), 329–348.

Umaña-Taylor, A. J., & Douglass, S. (2016). Developing an ethnic-racial identity intervention from a developmental perspective: Process, content, and implementation. In N. J. Cabrera & B. Leyendecker (Eds.), *Handbook of positive development of minority children and youth* (pp. 437–453). Cham, Switzerland: Springer.

Umaña-Taylor, A. J., Douglass, S., Updegraff, K. A., & Marsiglia, F. (In press). A small-scale randomized efficacy trial of the Identity Project: Promoting adolescents' ethnic-racial identity exploration and resolution. *Child Development*.

Umaña-Taylor, A. J., & Fine, M. A. (2004). Examining a model of ethnic identity development among Mexican-origin adolescents living in the U.S. *Hispanic Journal of Behavioral Sciences, 26*, 36–59. Retrieved from doi:10.1177/0739986303262143.

Umaña-Taylor, A. J., Gonzales-Backen, M. A., & Guimond, A. B. (2009). Latino adolescents' ethnic identity: Is there a developmental progression and does growth in ethnic identity predict growth in self-esteem? *Child Development, 80*, 391–405. Retrieved from doi:10.1111/j.1467-8624.2009.01267.x.

Umaña-Taylor, A. J., & Guimond, A. B. (2010). A longitudinal examination of parenting behaviors and perceived discrimination predicting Latino adolescents' ethnic identity. *Developmental Psychology, 46*, 636–650.

Umaña-Taylor, A. J., O'Donnell, M., Knight, G. P., Roosa, M. W., Berkel, C., & Nair, R. (2014). Ethnic socialization, ethnic identity, and Mexican-origin adolescents' psychosocial functioning: Examining the moderating role of school ethnic composition. *Counseling Psychologist, 42*, 170–200.

Umaña-Taylor, A. J., Quintana, S. M., Lee, R. M., Cross, W. E., Rivas-Drake, D., Schwartz, S., et al. & Study Group on Ethnic and Racial Identity in the 21st Century (2014). Ethnic and racial identity during adolescence and into young adulthood: An integrated conceptualization. *Child Development, 85*, 21–39. Retrieved from doi:10.1111/cdev.12196.

Umaña-Taylor, A. J., Tynes, B., Toomey, R. B., Williams, D., & Mitchell, K. (2015). Latino adolescents' perceived discrimination in online and off-line settings: An examination of cultural risk and protective factors. *Developmental Psychology, 51,* 87–100. Retrieved from doi:10.1037/a0038432.

Umaña-Taylor, A. J., Updegraff, K. A., & Gonzales-Backen, M. A. (2011). Mexican-origin adolescent mothers' stressors and psychosocial functioning: Examining ethnic identity affirmation and familism as moderators. *Journal of Youth and Adolescence, 40,* 140–157. Retrieved from doi:10.1007/s10964-010 -9511-z.

Umaña-Taylor, A. J., Updegraff, K. A., Jahromi, L. B., & Zeiders, K. H. (2015). Trajectories of ethnic-racial identity and autonomy among Mexican-origin adolescent mothers in the United States. *Child Development, 86,* 2034–2050. Retrieved from doi:10.1111/cdev.12444.

Umaña-Taylor, A. J., Vargas-Chanes, D., Garcia, C. D., & Gonzales-Backen, M. A. (2008). An examination of Latino adolescents' ethnic identity, coping with discrimination, and self-esteem. *Journal of Early Adolescence, 28,* 16–50. Retrieved from doi:10.1177/0272431607308666.

Umaña-Taylor, A. J., & Yazedjian, A. (2006). Generational differences and similarities among Puerto Rican and Mexican mothers' experiences with familial ethnic socialization. *Journal of Social and Personal Relationships, 23*(3), 445–464.

Umaña-Taylor, A. J., Zeiders, K. H., & Updegraff, K. A. (2013). Family ethnic socialization and ethnic identity: A family-driven, youth-driven, or reciprocal process? *Journal of Family Psychology, 27*(1), 137–146.

Urman, J. S., Silverman, B., Pearl, G., Granier, J., & Silberling, B. (Executive Producers). (2014). *Jane the virgin* [Television series]. Burbank, CA: CW Network.

Valenzuela, A. (1999). *Subtractive schooling: U.S.-Mexican youth and the politics of caring.* Albany, NY: SUNY Press.

Van Ausdale, D., & Feagin, J. R. (1996). *The first R: How children learn race and racism.* New York, NY: Rowman & Littlefield.

Vespa, J., Armstrong, D. M., & Medina, L. (2018). Demographic turning points for the United States: Population Projections for 2020 to 2060. *Population Estimates and Projections Current Population Reports, P25-1144.* Washington DC: US Census Bureau.

Vittrup, B. (2016). Color blind or color conscious? White American mothers' approaches to racial socialization. *Journal of Family Issues, 39,* 668–692.

Vittrup, B., & Holden, G. (2011). Exploring the impact of educational television and parent-child discussions on children's racial attitudes. *Analyses of Social Issues and Public Policy, 11,* 82–104.

Warikoo, N. K. (2010). Symbolic boundaries and school structure in New York and London schools. *American Journal of Education, 116*(3), 423–451. Retrieved from doi:10.1086/651415.

Watts, R. J., & Abdul-Adil, J. K. (1998). Promoting critical consciousness in young, African-American men. *Journal of Prevention & Intervention in the Community, 16*(1–2), 63–86.

Watts, R. J., Griffith, D. M., & Abdul-Adil, J. K. (1999). Sociopolitical development as an antidote for oppression—theory and action. *American Journal of Community Psychology, 27*, 255–271.

Watts, R. J., Williams, N. C., & Jagers, R. J. (2003). Sociopolitical development. *American Journal of Community Psychology, 31*, 185–194.

Way, N., Santos, C., Niwa, E. Y., & Kim-Gervey, C. (2008). To be or not to be: An exploration of ethnic identity development in context. *New Directions for Child and Adolescent Development, 120*, 61–79. Retrieved from doi:10.1002/cd.216.

Weisbuch, M., Pauker, K., & Ambady, N. (2009). The subtle transmission of race bias via televised nonverbal behavior. *Science, 326*(5960), 1711–1714.

Wells, A. S., Ready, D., Duran, J., Grzesikowski, C., Hill, K., Roda, A., et al. (2012). Still separate, still unequal, but not always so "suburban": The changing nature of suburban school districts in the New York Metropolitan area. Chapter 7 in W. F. Tate, IV (Ed.), *Research on schools, neighborhoods and communities: Toward civic responsibility* (pp. 125–150). AERA Presidential Volume. Washington, DC: American Educational Research Association.

White, R.M.B., Knight, G. P., Jensen, M., & Gonzales, N. A. (2017). Ethnic socialization in neighborhood contexts: Implications for ethnic attitude and identity development among Mexican-origin adolescents. *Child Development*. Retrieved from doi:10.1111/cdev.12772.

Whitehead, K. A., Ainsworth, A. T., Wittig, M. A., & Gadino, B. (2009). Implications of ethnic identity exploration and ethnic identity affirmation and belonging for intergroup attitudes among adolescents. *Journal of Research on Adolescence, 19*(1), 123–135.

Williams, J. L., Steinberg, L., & Piquero, A. R. (2010). Ethnic identity and attitudes toward the police among African American juvenile offenders. *Journal of Criminal Justice, 38*, 781–789.

Windsor, L. C., Jemal, A., & Benoit, E. (2014). Community Wise: Paving the way for empowerment in community reentry. *International Journal of Law and Psychiatry, 37*, 501–511.

Witherspoon, D. P., Daniels, L. L., Mason, A. E., & Smith, E. P. (2016). Racial-ethnic identity in context: Examining mediation of neighborhood factors on children's academic adjustment. *American Journal of Community Psychology, 57*(1–2), 87–101. Retrieved from doi:10.1002/ajcp.12019.

Witherspoon, D. P., Seaton, E., & Rivas-Drake, D. (2016). Neighborhood characteristics and expectations of racially discriminatory experiences among African American adolescents. *Child Development, 87*(5), 1367–1378. Retrieved from doi:10.1111/cdev.12595.

Wong, C. A., Eccles, J. S., & Sameroff, A. (2003). The influence of ethnic discrimination and ethnic identification on African American adolescents' school and socio-emotional adjustment. *Journal of Personality, 71*, 1197–1232.

Xu, Y. Farver, J. M., & Pauker, K. (2014). Ethnic identity and self-esteem among Asian and European Americans: When a minority is the majority and the majority is a minority. *European Journal of Social Psychology, 45*(1), 62–76.

Yip, T. (2014). Ethnic identity in everyday life: The influence of identity development status. *Child Development, 85,* 205–219.

Zimmerman, E. B., Woolf, S. H., & Haley, A. (2015). Understanding the relationship between education and health: A review of the evidence and an examination of community perspectives. Agency for Healthcare Research and Quality, Rockville, MD. Retrieved from http://www.ahrq.gov/professionals/education/curriculum-tools/population-health/zimmerman.html.

Zion, S., Allen, C. D., & Jean, C. (2015). Enacting a critical pedagogy, influencing teachers' sociopolitical development. *Urban Review, 47,* 914–933.

Zúñiga X., Kachwaha, T., DeJong, K., & Pacheco, R. (2011). Preparing critically reflective intergroup dialogue facilitators: A pedagogical model and illustrative example. In K. E. Maxwell, B. A. Nagda, & M. C. Thompson (Eds.), *Facilitating intergroup dialogues: Bridging differences, catalyzing change* (pp. 71–84). Sterling, VA: Stylus.

INDEX

Abdul-Adil, J., 136–37

Aboud, Frances, 50

academic success: and cultural socialization, 77–78; cultural symbols and celebration of, 82; degree attainment, high school diploma, 32; diversity and, 27; outcomes or proficiencies and racial/ethnic disparity, 31–32; preferential treatment of White students, 80; and pride in ethnic-racial identity, 60, 64, 67

Adams-Bass, Valerie, 96, 97

adolescence: and abstract thinking, 8; and authenticity, 86–87; cognitive development during, 8, 52–53; and exploration of identity, 54–57; and identity development, 8, 48–49, 51–52, 58–59; as opportunity for intervention, 120–22; and others' perceptions, 54–55; and social exposure, 52; and teaching about race, 81

adults: and "authentic caring," 92–93; communications of beliefs, norms, and values by, 111; and conversations about race and racism, 68–70, 98; intervention by, 93–94; and support of multiculturalism, 92; and validation of cross-group friendships, 107–8. *See also* parents; teachers, staff, or other practitioners

African Americans: communities and development of sociopolitical consciousness, 137–38; community social dynamics and, 93–94; and educational disadvantages, 31–33; health and life expectancy of, 32–33; and police as antagonists, 94, 154–55; and punishment in schools, 33; stereotypes and self-esteem of, 50; Strong African American Families program, 145–46; and "the talk" as part of childhood, 154–55; youth on stereotypes, 94–95

after-school programs, 161–62, 164

Agarwal, Ruchi, 149–51

Aldana, Adriana, 82, 133–34

alienation, 93

Allport, Gordon, 16, 102, 106, 111, 112, 114–16

"alt-right" movement, 9–10

Ambady, Nalini, 96

American Apartheid (Massey and Denton), 38–39

"American" identity, 21

American Indians, 82, 142–43; cultural survival issues, 1; demographic statistics, 21, 22; identity and prosocial relationships, 14; institutionalized discrimination against, 1; Parenting in 2 Worlds program, 146–47; representation of, 97

anti-bias approaches, 125–30; teacher training and support for, 149–50

antisocial behaviors, 78

anxiety. *See* fear or anxiety

appropriation, cultural, 86

Armenta, Brian, 79

Asian Americans: and educational attainment, 31–32; institutionalized discrimination against, 1; and "model minority" stereotype, 91; population demographics, 21–24; and support for BlackLivesMatter, 6; youth on identity, 72, 81–82, 103–4

Asian Indian Americans: youth on identity, 15, 67, 72, 84–85

"authentic caring," 91–92

awareness of racial difference, 100–101, 109; and cognitive development, 8, 49–51; color-blind or postracial approach to, 100–101; White Americans and awareness of racism, 10–11, 156–57

awareness of racism or prejudice: adults and, 36–38; and identity exploration, 16–17, 54–55, 100–101; and perception of social expectations, 79, 118; and social

A NOTE ON THE TYPE

This book has been composed in Adobe Text and Gotham. Adobe Text, designed by Robert Slimbach for Adobe, bridges the gap between fifteenth- and sixteenth-century calligraphic and eighteenth-century Modern styles. Gotham, inspired by New York street signs, was designed by Tobias Frere-Jones for Hoefler & Co.